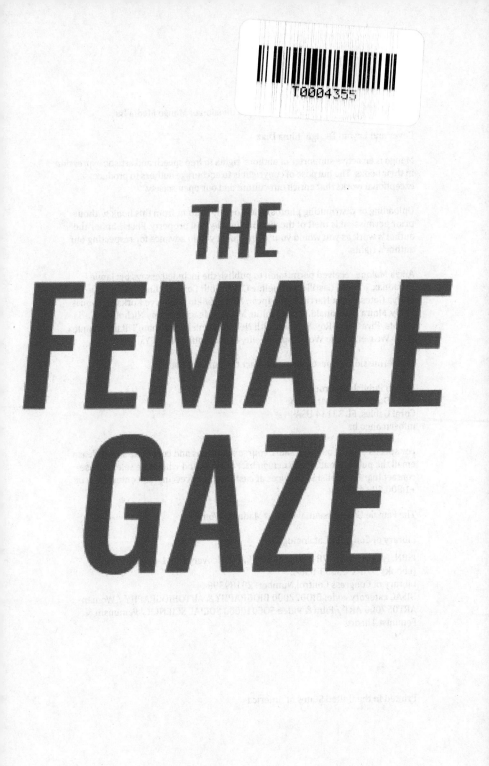

THE
FEMALE
GAZE

Mango Publishing Group
2850 Douglas Road, 4th Floor
Coral Gables, FL 33134 USA
info@mango.bz

For special orders, quantity sales, course adoptions and corporate sales, please email the publisher at sales@mango.bz. For trade and wholesale sales, please contact Ingram Publisher Services at customer.service@ingramcontent.com or +1.800.509.4887.

The Female Gaze: Essential Movies Made by Women

Library of Congress Cataloging

ISBN: (paperback) 978-1-64250-804-8, (hardcover) 978-1-63353-837-5, (ebook) 978-1-63353-838-2
Library of Congress Control Number: 2018959944
BISAC category code: BIO022000 BIOGRAPHY & AUTOBIOGRAPHY / Women
ART057000 ART / Film & Video SOC010000 SOCIAL SCIENCE / Feminism & Feminist Theory

Printed in the United States of America

THE
FEMALE
GAZE

ESSENTIAL MOVIES MADE BY WOMEN

ALICIA MALONE

mango

CORAL GABLES

Dedicated to all the film lovers, supporters of women in film,
and aspiring filmmakers out there...

Contents

Introduction

*"One might simplify this by saying: men act and women appear.
Men look at women. Women watch themselves being looked at. This
determines not only most relations between men and women but also
the relation of women to themselves. The surveyor of woman in herself
is male: the surveyed female. Thus she turns herself into an object—and
most particularly an object of vision: a sight."*

—John Berger, *Ways of Seeing*

In 1973, film critic Laura Mulvey wrote an explosive essay called
"Visual Pleasure and Narrative Cinema." In it, she used examples
from Hollywood films to explore how the perspective of the
camera lens (the types of angles, editing, and lighting used) is
masculine, with the women onscreen looked at as passive sexual
objects. There are many examples of this throughout film history,
from the way Lana Turner's character is introduced legs first in
The Postman Always Rings Twice to Megan Fox leaning over a car
engine in *Transformers*. These two movies are very different, but
in both cases the camera directly mirrors the hungry gaze of the
male characters.

Mulvey's piece quickly became famous—and contentious—and
her ideas continue to be dissected today. To put it simply, Mulvey
was interested in what happens to us when the majority of the
films we watch are made by men and seen through this "male
gaze." This gaze places the male characters in a position of power.
In film, men are almost always doing the *looking*, with women left
in the weaker position of being *looked at*. This not only contributes
to the slew of passive female characters we see onscreen, but

also affects how each of us view women—and how women view themselves.

There is a very good argument to be made that an equivalent "female gaze" simply cannot exist, because society is not set up that way. The male gaze is a byproduct of our imbalanced world, one where men hold the majority of the power. While the term "the female gaze" is used throughout this book (and as its title), this is not intended to imply a narrow view of gender or an ignorance of the structure of our world. It is a phrase used here to open up a conversation about the experience of seeing film and being seen in film for those who don't identify with being white, cis, or male.

What happens, for example, when we look at the world from a female point of view? How do women see themselves? How do women see other women? What makes a movie essentially feminine? What can audiences of any gender identification gain by looking at film through a female lens? These and other questions are at the heart of this book.

With conversations about women's experiences in Hollywood currently at fever pitch, I am often asked how to best support women in film. The answer? Watch movies made by women. Every click, download, or DVD purchase helps to send a message that we want more. That is why I wanted to write the book you now hold in your hands: to provide an easy, accessible list of some of my favorite movies made by women—many of whom have been overlooked or forgotten, despite their important contributions to the history of cinema.

Each of the fifty-two films in this book is made by a woman and features stories about women. Though the focus is mainly on narrative and drama in films, each of the movies you will discover here is unique in tone and genre, and they are drawn from across very different time periods and locations. Some of my criteria in choosing the films was intended to ensure that there was a representation of diversity of era, country, race, and sexual orientation; and that each film is readily available to watch on streaming services or DVD.

As a way to include voices other than my own, I asked a group of established and aspiring female film critics to write short odes to movies they love made by women. This book represents a wealth of perspectives—and while at times their choices mirrored my own, at other times they helped to introduce even more films to this packed little guidebook. From dreamlike portrayals of turn-of-the-century matriarchal families to unapologetic explorations of sex work and complex female friendships, there is something here for everyone.

For each film chosen here, you will find the production details, a short synopsis, and some interesting backstory about the film and its filmmaker, along with what the uniquely feminine perspective does for the story. The idea is to give you the flavor of what each film offers and why I feel it is worth rediscovering.

As you move through these chapters, there are several things to note; first, the sparseness of female-directed films at the beginning of the twentieth century and how that changed starting in the 1970s. You'll also note how it's not until the 1990s that I include a female director of color, and how many of these filmmakers only made one feature film. There are also quite a few directors who eschew the modifier of "female" or who have rejected the notion of their films being called "feminist." And the quotes used from critics and authors mainly come from white men. All of this demonstrates how female filmmakers (and our experiences of film as a whole, including who has historically written about film) have been limited by the barriers of gender, race, and sexual orientation.

It can be frustrating to wonder what kinds of stories we might have experienced if a wider variety of people had been allowed to tell them. But it's important to celebrate what we do have, because despite the odds, women have been making movies from the beginning of cinema itself. And there is much more to discover than what I have included. My selection here represents only a small sample of the many wonderful movies that have been directed by female filmmakers. I capped the list at fifty-two in case you wanted to watch a film a week for a year and use this book as part of the #52FilmsByWomen challenge started by the Women in Film organization. But of course, you can simply dip in and out of this collection at your own pace and use this guide to explore those titles that most take your fancy.

Above all, my wish is that this book provides you with a valuable starting point: a concise and engaging list of my favorite films made by women. From here, I hope you take it upon yourself to explore these and other filmmaking gems more deeply. Enjoy!

The Consequences of Feminism

(Les Résultants du Féminisme)

Gaumont Studio, 1906, France | Black & White, 7 minutes, Comedy

A gender role reversal comedy set in a fictional world where men are the ones being objectified.

The Consequences of Feminism

Director: Alice Guy
Producer: Gaumont Studios
Cinematography: Unknown
Screenplay: Alice Guy
Starring: Unknown

"There is nothing connected with the staging of a motion picture that a woman cannot do as easily as a man."

—Alice Guy-Blaché

It is difficult to believe that a film called *The Consequences of Feminism* was made back in 1906. This is a title which might even be controversial if it were used today. And yet, it exists—a black-and-white silent movie made by the first female director in movie history, set in a world where gender roles have been reversed.

This is apparent from the very first scene in *The Consequences of Feminism*. The film opens inside a shop where a group of men are occupied with making hats. Suddenly, a woman strides through the door, pointing with her cane at the hat she wants. While waiting, she looks appreciatively at the working men, reaching out to touch the chin of one, who immediately shies away from her hand. After she leaves, another man is tasked with delivering the hat, and he pauses in front of the mirror to apply his makeup. Outside, he is immediately pounced on by a woman who places her hands all over him. He is saved by another woman, who seems kind and gentle as she leads him to a park bench. But before long, she too is forcing herself on him. A couple of women walking by see what is happening and quickly scurry away.

The film continues in this manner for the rest of its seven-minute duration, with later scenes set inside a house and at a women-only establishment. In all cases, the women are clearly in charge, with the men relegated to the positions of workers, housemaids, and caretakers for the children. All the women in this film are pushy, and they objectify, sexually harass, and abuse the men. The men resist as best they can, but eventually give in.

Finally, the men have had enough of their treatment, and they band together to take back their dominant position in society and reestablish the "correct" social order. This is where the true brilliance of this little satire lies. To accept the ending is to admit that half of the world's population is currently subject to a raw deal.

"She is doing successfully what men are trying to do. She is succeeding in a line of work in which hundreds of men have failed."

Photoplay magazine, 1912

Nothing has been changed about the appearance of the characters: all the women in the film wear dresses of the period, while the men are in suits. It is only the behavior that is different. Guy has swapped both the power structure of society and the general traits of the genders for comedic effect. The film does not imagine what exactly might happen if we lived in a matriarchal society—that women would sexually harass men—but it shows quite plainly what it is like to live in a patriarchal one.

Of course, we can't know for sure what statement Guy wanted to make with this film or if her intention was simply to entertain the audience by showing men acting like women. But the title suggests there is more to her vision, that perhaps it is a parody of what people feared would happen if women were to gain more rights. And by showing the men fighting together at the film's conclusion, Guy seems to be stating why feminism is necessary.

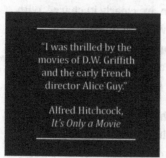

The Consequences of Feminism was made during what we now call the "first wave" of feminism. At the time the use of that word was quite new—"feminism" was only coined in the late 1800s in France, as "*féminisme*." Of course, women had been speaking up for themselves long before then, but it was in the 1860s that a more formal movement started to take shape focused on winning the right to vote. By 1906, many filmgoers would have indeed been thinking about the consequences of this new movement.

The premise of the film plays comedically into the fears some people still nurse about feminism—that its true goal is not equality of the sexes (as is the very definition of the term) but that it is instead about waging war on men. This is an irrational fear which supposes that women want to take power away from men to the point where men become the oppressed and women the oppressors.

All of this is the baggage modern audiences inevitably bring to watching *The Consequences of Feminism*. Viewing this short silent film, it is almost impossible not to think about current conversations about gender and assault. So much is said here without a single piece of dialogue or even a title card being used. It is a movie that was well ahead of its time—and that is ahead of our time, too.

This was also true of the director. Alice Guy was arguably one of the most important figures in the history of cinema. Not only was she the very first female filmmaker, but she was one of the first film directors in the world, whether male or female. And yet few in the industry know her name. Her story is rarely taught in film classes or mentioned in books. And for many decades her work was lost, or incorrectly attributed to male colleagues.

Alice Guy was born in 1873 and started her film career in the late 1800s while working as a secretary at a photography company in Paris, France. Her boss, Léon Gaumont, had been developing a 60mm motion picture camera. He allowed Guy to borrow it on the agreed-upon condition that it wouldn't interfere with her other work. The first film she made was in 1896, when she was just twenty-three years old. It was a short called *The Cabbage Fairy*, and was one of the first narrative movies in the world.

"She was more than just a talented businesswoman. She was a filmmaker of rare sensitivity with a remarkable poetic eye and an extraordinary feel for locations."

Martin Scorsese, presenting a posthumous tribute in 2011

From there, her list of achievements is remarkable. She was the first person to direct a movie with synchronized sound, using a Léon Gaumont invention called the Chronophone decades before the mainstream sound revolution would come to pass. She cofounded and ran her own studio, which she called Solax. She made over 1,000 movies over the course of her career while also being a wife and a mother. Her comedies are particularly impressive, with inventive ideas neatly packaged into short-form satire, like very early sketch comedy. Guy also filmed dance sequences, dramas, and even a religious epic called *The Life of Christ* in 1906. This was one of the most ambitious productions in cinema at the time, involving a staggering 300 extras.

With all her experimentation, Alice Guy helped to form the basis of film grammar and structure. She encouraged her actors toward a more modern style, asking them to "be natural" instead of posing and posturing to the camera.

In 1912, using her married name of Alice Guy-Blaché, she made another comedy where the gender roles were reversed. *In the Year 2000* feels like a remake of *The Consequences of Feminism*, with the difference that this time it is the women who win in the end. On its release in 1912, the magazine *Moving Picture World* wrote about *In the Year 2000*, saying:

> "A great number of prognostications often terrify us with visions [of] what will be when women shall rule the earth and the time when men shall be subordinates and adjuncts. It is rather a fine question to decide—for chivalrous men, anyway. Today with the multiplicity of feminine activities and the constant broadening of feminine spheres, it's difficult to predict what heights women will achieve... Women in this film are supreme, and man's destiny is presided over by woman. No attempt is made at burlesque—but the very seriousness of the purpose makes the situations ludicrous."

Alice Guy-Blaché was awarded the Legion of Honor in 1953 and died in 1968 at the age of ninety-four. Around 130 of her 1,000 films remain, with much work being done to restore and preserve her important place in history.

🎥 THE FEMALE GAZE

Alice Guy uses the device of gender role reversal to make her audience think about how women are treated in the real world and how ludicrous it is to believe that women would act exactly like men if they were given more power.

≡ FAST FACTS

* ★ Alice Guy played a vital role in the development of cinema and worked in both France and the US during the birth of the film industry.

* ★ Guy married fellow Gaumont Studios employee Herbert Blaché in 1907. Shortly after their wedding, the two moved to the US, where Guy set up Solax Studios.

★ After her divorce, Guy returned to France in the 1920s, but she found it impossible to get work as a film director.

★ In the early 1900s, film wasn't thought to be an important art form. Many silent films were destroyed and accurate archives weren't kept. The achievements of early filmmakers such as Alice Guy remained largely hidden until the work of film historians such as Anthony Slide. He wrote about Guy in his book *Early Women Directors*, published in 1977, and edited *The Memoirs of Alice Guy-Blaché* in 1986.

Holly Weaver on *La Souriante Madame Beudet* (1922)

Six years prior to the release of her riot-inducing surrealist film *La Coquille et le Clergyman*, Germaine Dulac was exercising her female gaze in what would later become a feminist classic: *La Souriante Madame Beudet*. The film's eponymous hero (Germaine Dermoz) is an intelligent woman who, when she's not seeking solace in books or playing piano, sits at the receiving end of the selfishness and "suicide jokes" of her buffoonish husband (Alexandre Arquillière), whom she despises.

Although at first her subtle expressions portray a sense of apathy toward him, her thoughts and dreams tell us otherwise. Through the use of close-ups, mental images, and superimposition, Dulac allows us to delve into the psyche of her protagonist as she fantasizes about other men and being rid of her husband. However, as her feeling of imprisonment intensifies, these fantasies turn into nightmares since she cannot shake the image of Monsieur Beudet appearing around every corner, trapping her in an endless cycle of torment.

The motif of the "façade" is central to the film: the opening exterior shots of the tranquil village are betrayed by the gradual discovery of what is occurring behind closed doors, just as Madame Beudet's "smiling" façade is belied by insight into her mind. Dulac's commitment to the dichotomy between interiority and exteriority is further enforced through her use of light and shadow, creating a perpetual chiaroscuro. Nowhere is this contrast more striking than on the face of Madame Beudet herself, particularly while she sits at the window staring out with a deep *tristesse*, the presence of light and dark expressing both her fear of leaving and her reluctance to stay. Dermoz's ability to covertly portray Madame Beudet's inner torment is astonishing—whether it's a look of disgust as she watches her husband sloppily eating dinner or a look of bitter hatred as the sheer mental image of him breaks her blissful reverie. Although Madame Beudet's gestures become more erratic as she reaches a breaking point, her facial expressions retain a sense of impenetrability, unlike those of her husband, whose wide eyes and wicked grin give him the appearance of a maniacal clown from start to finish.

The film's climax sees Monsieur Beudet playing his "suicide joke" once more by holding a revolver, which Madame has preemptively loaded, to his head. However, this time he turns it on her and fires a shot—but misses, and immediately runs over to comfort her. Thinking she intended to kill herself and not him, he begins smothering her with affection and ponders aloud, "How would I have lived without you?" Monsieur Beudet's false assumption about Madame's mentality shows the importance of the female gaze in film: a woman-led exploration of a woman's psyche can provide an intimate portrayal of how the struggles we face run much deeper than what appears on the surface, as Dulac demonstrates so perfectly in her masterpiece.

Holly Weaver is a fourth-year BA French and Spanish student at the University of Leeds. After graduation, she hopes to earn a master's degree in film studies.

Dance, Girl, Dance

RKO Radio Pictures, 1940, USA | Black & White, 90 minutes, Drama

*A complex female friendship/rivalry between two dancers
of opposite styles.*

Director: Dorothy Arzner

Producer: Erich Pommer

Cinematography: Russell Metty

Screenplay: Tess Slesinger, Frank Davis, based on a story by Vicki Baum

Starring: Maureen O'Hara ("Judy O'Brien"), Louis Hayward ("Jimmy Harris"), Lucille Ball ("Bubbles"), Ralph Bellamy ("Steve Adams"), Virginia Field ("Elinor Harris")

"I was averse to having any comment made about being a woman director... because I wanted to stand up as a director and not have people make allowances that it was a woman."

—Dorothy Arzner

There's a moment in *Dance, Girl, Dance* which may elicit spontaneous applause. The scene comes toward the end of the movie and features a scathing speech about the objectification of women for entertainment purposes. And this impassioned speech may also make the audience think about how they too have unfairly judged these characters.

Dance, Girl, Dance follows a female dance troupe trying to make a living. At the center of the group is Judy O'Brien (Maureen O'Hara), a shy brunette who hopes to elevate the art form using her ballet routine. This places her in direct opposition to another dancer in the group, Bubbles (Lucille Ball), a feisty blonde who sees nothing wrong with using her sexuality to earn money. While performing together in Ohio, the two ladies meet and each fall for the same young man, Jimmy Harris (Louis Hayward), who is going through a messy divorce. Their fight for his affection continues in New York, where the troupe moves in search of work.

In the big city, Judy aspires to join the American Ballet Company. Her efforts are encouraged by the leader of the troupe, Madame Basilova (Maria Ouspenskaya). But when Bubbles finds fame in a burlesque show performing under the name Tiger Lily White, she hires Judy to get the crowd excited before the main performance. When Judy performs her ballet routine, she gets only jeers from the audience, who have after all come to see women strip.

"She was the only American woman director to make the transition from the silent era to sound, and she became a symbol for what women could accomplish in the new medium."

Anthony Slide, *The Silent Feminists*

The female friendship at the center of *Dance, Girl, Dance* is quite complex. Bubbles and Judy view each other as rivals, because that is what society has led them to believe. At the same time, the two women do help each other out; and it's clear that underneath it all, they care for one another. In this way they're like an odd couple or two characters in a buddy movie.

Both women are also trying to move out of the social class they were born into—Bubbles through money and fame, Judy through art and respect. Here, dance is not only a form of self-expression, but a way for both women to become financially independent. And the contrast between Judy's elegant ballet and Bubbles' sexy burlesque numbers reflect the divide between what was considered "low" or "high" theater at the time.

These characters are not one-dimensional. Bubbles is not simply a "bad girl." Her insecure pursuit of fame is actually a little tragic, while at the same time, it feels empowering to watch her embrace her sexuality. She feels no shame, and the movie does not shame her. Bubbles just has that extra "oomph" that everyone is searching for. Similarly, Judy is not just the "good girl." She is innocent but not naive, with a lot of burning ambition inside her. And if pushed too far, she snaps.

This brings me back to that pivotal scene. Without spoiling the moment too much, there's a point where Judy has had enough of the crowd. She is trying to perform her ballet routine, but they only yell at her to take her clothes off. Judy stops dancing and walks to the front of the stage, where she crosses her arms and stares at the audience. "Go on. Laugh!" she says. "Get your money's worth. Nobody's going to hurt you. I know you want me to tear my clothes off so you can look your fifty cents' worth. Fifty cents for the privilege of staring at a girl the way your wives won't let you. What do you suppose we think of you up here—with your silly smirks your mothers would be ashamed of? We'd laugh right back at the lot of you, only we're paid to let you sit there and roll your eyes and make screaming clever remarks. What's it for? So you can go home and strut before your wives and sweethearts and play at being the stronger sex for a minute? I'm sure they see through you just like we do!"

> "Arzner was a filmmaking phenomenon in those days. She was the only serious female director of her time and the first woman member of the Directors Guild of America. She fascinated both Lucille and me."
>
> Maureen O'Hara, 'Tis Herself: A Memoir

It is a searing, powerful moment—and one which is as much about movie audiences in general as it is about the jeering audience in that particular theater. It's as if Judy (or perhaps Dorothy Arzner) is confronting all of us, about how we have been looking at and judging the women in the film. It is a comment on how women are seen simply as objects to look at, expected to strip for our viewing pleasure. And it's important to note that the crowd in the movie are not all men. There are women there too, who squirm uncomfortably during Judy's speech, also guilty of imposing the "male gaze." But crucially, it is a woman who is the first to stand up and applaud Judy's speech.

The film does not, however, make things so simple for its protagonists. Judy has reclaimed her power and is about to leave the stage when Bubbles slaps her. This starts a vicious fight which spills out onstage in front of the crowd. So in the end, the women denigrate themselves for entertainment, just as the audience wanted.

Dance, Girl, Dance is a "backstage" musical that was created almost entirely by women. The original story was written by Vicki Baum, author of *Grand Hotel*, which was released as a film in 1932. Like that of *Grand Hotel*, Baum's concept for *Dance, Girl, Dance* also features complex women with dreams and higher aspirations. This story was turned into an original script by Tess Slesinger with additional work by Frank Davis. Slesinger was a novelist as well as a screenwriter, and one of her short stories was the first be published in America that featured an abortion. And of course, the director of *Dance, Girl, Dance* was Dorothy Arzner, the only female filmmaker working in the studio system in the 1930s. She continued to direct until the early '40s, and *Dance, Girl, Dance* was her penultimate (but most famous) film.

"She was a very important Hollywood director...She was a wonderful woman, and she was very encouraging to me. I think what meant so much, as I always had self-doubt, was that she would say: you are going to do fine. She was very famous. I just had the good luck that I was her student."

Francis Ford Coppola

This is all the more interesting given that Dorothy Arzner was never supposed to be its director. Roy Del Ruth had been hired by RKO producer Erich Pommer because of his experience in the world of musicals, having directed three such films for MGM, all starring Eleanor Powell. But with *Dance, Girl, Dance*, he struggled to find a clear vision for the story. Soon after filming commenced, he was fired by Pommer and replaced by Dorothy Arzner. Arzner had only limited musical experience, having codirected *Paramount on Parade* in 1930, but brought with her a talent for crafting feminist films featuring complex women.

Once hired, she significantly reworked the script and reshot every scene that Del Ruth had completed.

Arzner made two important changes to the story. First, she enhanced the central conflict by focusing on the difference between the two dancers. "I decided the theme should be *The Art Spirit* versus the commercial *Go-Getter*," Arzner later said. Then she also changed the character of the male head of the dance troupe to a woman—from "Basiloff" to "Basilova." This added another interesting female relationship to the story, that of student and teacher, which was given further complexity thanks to a few lingering looks Madame Basilova directs at Judy. And with Basilova's slicked back hair and necktie, the new dance troupe head looked a little like Dorothy Arzner herself.

Arzner was an outlier in Hollywood. The only female director who made the transition from silent film to sound, she dressed in suits and was an outspoken feminist and lesbian at a time when nobody was "out." She claimed to have been born in 1900, though all her records had been lost in the San Francisco earthquake in 1906. After the earthquake, her family moved to Los Angeles, where her father ran the Hoffman Cafe. The café became a favorite hangout for movie stars, and it was there that she met William C. DeMille, brother of Cecil B. DeMille. William gave Arzner her first job in Hollywood, where she started out as a script typist and later as an editor. But she knew from the beginning where she wanted to end up. "I remember making the observation, 'If one was going to be in this movie business, one should be a director because he was the one who told everyone else what to do.' "

As a film director, Arzner was commercially successful, making movies featuring female protagonists across many different genres. Her movie *Christopher Strong* in 1933 gave Katharine Hepburn her first starring role, as a female aviator.

The reaction to *Dance, Girl, Dance* when it was released in 1940 was lukewarm. The film was buried and forgotten, receiving only poor box office results. Reviews were fairly positive, but most of the praise went to Lucille Ball. This was one of her first starring roles, and it was obvious she was something special. "If RKO accomplishes nothing else with the venture," one reviewer wrote, "it has informed itself that it has a very important player on the lot in the person of Miss Ball, who may require special writing. But whatever the requirements, she has the makings of a star."

After *Dance, Girl, Dance*, Dorothy Arzner made just one more film, *First Comes Courage*, released in 1943. During production, she contracted pneumonia and was so sick that director Charles Vidor had to come on board to finish the movie. Arzner recovered from that illness but retired from making movies. She continued to direct, making fifty Pepsi-Cola commercials for her good friend Joan Crawford. In the 1960s, Arzner began teaching at UCLA, where her students included a young filmmaker by the name of Frances Ford Coppola. In 1975, she was given a tribute by the Directors Guild of America. Four years later, Dorothy Arzner passed away at her home near Palm Springs.

It was only in the 1970s, thirty years after its release, that *Dance, Girl, Dance* finally found a receptive audience. Thanks to essays by writers such as Pam Cook, Claire Johnston, and Judith Mayne, the movie was rediscovered and reevaluated and became something of a feminist cult classic. During this time, analysis of the "male gaze" in classic cinema was gaining traction. As many of these writers noted, though *Dance, Girl, Dance* scorned the objectification of women, it was also itself guilty of it— demonstrating the limitations of classical Hollywood, even with a female director behind the lens. Other film critics were simply excited to discover the story of Dorothy Arzner. She was a rare woman in film history who achieved success within an extremely male-dominated industry.

⚜ THE FEMALE GAZE

The scene with Judy's speech to the audience is a scathing commentary on the way women are used in entertainment. Dorothy Arzner's camera makes it seem as if Judy is talking straight to us, and in a way, she is; she invites the audience to consider how they have been treating the female characters in the movie so far.

⚏ FAST FACTS

★ Dorothy Arzner directed four silent films and thirteen talking pictures between 1927 and 1943. She is also the inventor of the boom microphone. On the set of *The Wild Party*, released in 1929, Arzner placed a microphone on the end of a fishing rod to give her actors more room to move.

★ The working title for *Dance, Girl, Dance* was *Have It Your Own Way*.

★ Similar to the characters they played, Lucille Ball and Maureen O'Hara had a competitive relationship, though it remained friendly. In her memoir, O'Hara wrote that they "enjoyed a competitive rivalry on petty and harmless things, like fighting over which of us would get the dance stockings without the ladders or runs."

★ Following the filming of their big fight scene, O'Hara and Ball went to the studio cafeteria for lunch. It was at that moment, with her clothes torn and her hair a mess, that Lucille Ball first laid eyes on Desi Arnaz. It was love at first sight—for Ball, at least.

Sumeyye Korkaya on *Meshes of the Afternoon* (1943)

Maya Deren's *Meshes of the Afternoon* is a critically acclaimed work in American experimental cinema. After watching it, one might have the urge to spew a number of quizzical expletives. This is not uncommon, given Deren's incredible usage of the surrealist form to create a dreamlike experience. The intense cut sequences only heighten the audience's anxiety, and by consequence, portray the distortion of reality. The film is indeed a mesh of the afternoons experienced by a woman played by Maya Deren. The repetition in each scene is unmistakable due to the continuously reappearing objects.

After processing Deren's frighteningly authentic vision into the female psyche, one can't help but parallel this experience to that of gaslighting. Gaslighting is a form of manipulation within intimate relationships that causes the victim to forget their very self. The abuser holds power by contorting reality to his liking and distorting memories for his benefit. In *Meshes of the Afternoon*, the central figure desperately attempts to piece together her memories with three main objects: the flower, the key, and the knife. These are symbolic objects alluding to romance, privacy, and violence respectively.

Rather than display the timeline of events, Deren sequences the film in a way that permits the audience to experience the emotional turmoil behind gaslighting. This act of prioritizing emotion over rigid time structures dismisses the gendered division between emotion and logic. While mainstream film productions are subjected to the male gaze, the abstract and independent nature of avant-garde films allows for some escape. *Meshes of the Afternoon* explores the volatility of gaslighting through surrealism and the rejection of the male gaze.

Sumeyye Korkaya graduated from the University of Michigan with a Women's Studies degree. She loves cultivating relationships with her sister-friends by dissecting romantic comedies, planning exclusive soirees, and blueprinting a future women's resort.

The Hitch-Hiker

RKO Radio Pictures, 1953, USA | Black & White, 71 minutes, Thriller
Two men are held hostage by a dangerous serial killer.

Director: Ida Lupino

Producer: Collier Young

Cinematography: Nicholas Musuraca

Screenplay: Collier Young, Ida Lupino, Robert L. Joseph

Starring: Edmond O'Brien ("Roy Collins"), Frank Lovejoy ("Gil Bowen"), William Talman ("Emmett Myers")

"Often I pretended to a cameraman to know less than I did. That way I got more cooperation."

—Ida Lupino

At the very beginning of *The Hitch-Hiker*, a short piece of text appears. Over footage indicating the murder of two newlyweds, it reads, "This is the true story of a man and a gun and a car. The gun belonged to the man. The car might have been yours—or that young couple across the aisle. What you will see in the next seventy minutes could have happened to you. For the facts are actual."

The plot of this suspense thriller is indeed based on a true story: that of hitch-hiker William Cook, who went on a killing spree and murdered six people. It tells the story of Roy Collins (Edmond O'Brien) and Gil Bowen (Frank Lovejoy), two friends driving to Mexico for a weekend fishing trip. They hope to escape their home lives, their children, and their wives, but on the way there they make the mistake of picking up a hitch-hiker. This turns out to be Emmett Myers (William Talman), a serial killer wanted for the murder of several other people who had unknowingly picked him up. He is now attempting to flee to Mexico. With his gun pointed at them, Roy and Gil are forced to do what Myers wants. Along the way the killer abuses his power in a sadistic cat-and-mouse game.

The director responsible for *The Hitch-Hiker* was Ida Lupino. Shot with an all-male crew, there are virtually no female characters, no love interests, and no typically "feminine" situations in this story. The film noir genre is one that is especially associated with masculinity, typically providing a commentary on the place of men in postwar America: their losses, their sense of passivity, their distrust of authority, and how their identities are challenged on their return home. They may have escaped the trauma of war, but they now face uncertainty about what lies ahead.

The Hitch-Hiker plays with these themes of escape, passivity, identity, and uncertainty. The two friends had been planning an escape from their own lives, but now experience the uncertainty of not knowing if they will survive. They are too paralyzed by fear to react, trapped by their identities as "unheroic" men. The character of Myers represents a certain form of masculinity, relying on a gun to feel powerful. As Roy says to Myers at one point in the film, "You haven't got a thing without a gun. Without it, you're nothing."

It is an incredibly tense movie, with the question of what Myers might do to these men left hanging over the entire run time. Will he kill them? Will they escape? At seventy-one minutes, *The Hitch-Hiker* is a taut, economical film, sparse in dialogue and completely without subplots. It features only a handful of characters and just a few locations. This ramps up the tension, keeping the focus on the three men inside the car, all driving toward an inevitable end—one way or the other.

The constant threat of violence is heightened by the enclosed space of the car, a tension Lupino maintains by using a series of tight shots centered on the faces of the men. Outside the car lies the vast, desolate landscape of the Mexican desert, but even these wide-angle shots feel constricted. She uses white-hot lighting to demonstrate just how inhospitable the terrain is, making any escape impossible. Lupino has explained her thinking in the book, *The Making of The Hitch-Hiker*, saying, "To heighten the film's suspense, I shot scenes in the claustrophobic confines of the car, and to intensify the grit outside, on hot, barren expanses of the desert."

"She was a woman of extraordinary talents, and one of those talents was directing. Her tough, glowingly emotional work as an actress is well remembered, but her considerable accomplishments as a filmmaker are largely forgotten—and they shouldn't be. The five films she directed between 1949 and 1953 are remarkable chamber pieces that deal with challenging subjects in a clear, almost documentary fashion, and they represent a singular achievement in American cinema."

Martin Scorsese, *New York Times*, 1995

In those rare moments when the three men stop and get out of the car, Lupino offers tantalizing glimpses of a possible escape. But as each of those ideas are thwarted, the tight close-ups return, echoing the constriction felt inside the car...until soon that is where they are, once again.

It is also a beautifully atmospheric film, shot in exquisite black-and-white by cinematographer Nicholas Musuraca. Musuraca was especially gifted at stark chiaroscuro camerawork, as demonstrated by his work on *Out of the Past* and *The Spiral Staircase*. His style involved highly contrasting the light and shadows—a signature of the film noir genre.

Notably absent from this example of film noir is the femme fatale. The villain here is Myers, portrayed in a chilling performance by William Talman. Like the real killer, William Cook, Emmett Myers has one paralyzed eye that always remains open. Roy and Gil never know when he's asleep or awake. And the way he toys with them is disturbing—there is a scene where Myers forces Gil to shoot a can out of Roy's hand. "It's just a game," he says; "What's the matter? You scared?"

At the time *The Hitch-Hiker* was made, Ida Lupino was the only female director working in Hollywood. She was born into a family of entertainers in England in 1918. When she arrived in Hollywood in the early 1930s, Lupino was initially styled as a Jean Harlow-esque teenage sexpot, and she fought for years to win more substantial acting roles. But by the 1940s, with films like *High Sierra* with Humphrey Bogart behind her, Ida Lupino had become one of the most successful actresses around. She studied the work of the directors with whom she was paired and had her first chance to step behind the lens by accident. In the late 1940s, Lupino and her husband Collier Young had decided to set up their own production company called, "The Filmmakers." Their goal was to make realistic movies based around social issues. The first film they produced was *Not Wanted*, which looked at the stigma surrounding unwed mothers. Lupino and Young had hired veteran Hollywood director Elmer Clifton to helm the picture, but when he suffered heart problems during preproduction, Ida Lupino stepped in to finish it.

From there, her directing career took off. And after making four films focused on women's issues, she transitioned into hard-hitting, fast-paced thrillers with *The Hitch-Hiker*. Lupino wrote the screenplay alongside Collier Young, who by that stage had become her ex-husband, with writer Robert Joseph also doing some work on the script. For research, Lupino interviewed the real-life hostages of William Cook and was able to get permission to make the film from both the victims and from Cook himself. This allowed her to sprinkle in true facts among the fiction—though in order to appease the censors, Lupino had to cut down the body count from six to three.

The Hitch-Hiker ended up being one of her most successful films. Made on a budget of just $100,000, the movie earned large profits at the box office. It also garnered great reviews, with *TIME* magazine calling it "a crisp little thriller." But ironically, this success ended up contributing to the demise of Lupino's production company. Collier Young was unhappy that RKO Pictures were walking away with the bulk of the film's profits, so he decided that he would start to distribute their films himself. But without the experience necessary to pull this off, the company's finances crumbled.

Despite making a hit, after *The Hitch-Hiker*, Ida Lupino was only given the opportunity to direct two more features. She later transitioned into directing television and continued to act until 1978, before passing away in 1995.

Included in the official press notes for *The Hitch-Hiker* was an interview with Lupino called "Ida Lupino Retains Her Femininity as Director." Speaking about her style as a filmmaker on set, Lupino was quoted as saying: "I retain every feminine trait. Men prefer it that way. They're more cooperative if they see that fundamentally you are of the weaker sex even though [you are] in a position to give orders, which normally is the male prerogative, or so he likes to think, anyway. While I've encountered no resentment from the male of the species for intruding into their world, I give them no opportunity to think I've strayed where I don't belong. I assume no masculine characteristics, which can often be a fault of career women rubbing shoulders with their male counterparts, who become merely arrogant or authoritative."

Considering the time in which she lived, it's remarkable that Ida Lupino had the type of career that she did at all. She was an actress who made the decision to step away from her successful and promising career to go behind the camera, as well as a filmmaker who made bold movies looking at gender roles at a time when there were no other women doing anything similar in Hollywood. To survive, Ida Lupino knew she had to be strong-willed, ambitious, and cunning. She wasn't taught how to direct, she simply did it instinctively. And as *The Hitch-Hiker* shows, she could do it just as well as any man.

🎥 THE FEMALE GAZE

With *The Hitch-Hiker*, Ida Lupino was a rare woman director who explored masculinity and identity within the genre of film noir. Gone are the femme fatales and damsels in distress; here Lupino focuses solely on male characters. Her protagonists must decide if they are heroes (i.e., "real men") or not. She uses simple camera techniques to enhance and hold the tension throughout the entire story. By making this film, Lupino proved that women could be just as adept at directing suspense thrillers as their male counterparts.

≡ FAST FACTS

★ Ida Lupino is credited with directing six feature films on subjects ranging from rape to kidnapping. She was the first woman to helm a film noir and the first since Dorothy Arzner to consistently work in Hollywood.

★ Lupino's director's chair bore her nickname: "Mother of All of Us."

★ The tagline for *The Hitch-Hiker* read "There's Death in His Upraised Thumb!"

★ As part of her research, Ida Lupino visited the real serial killer, William Cook, at San Quentin prison. She later called the experience "very scary."

★ Though he portrayed a dangerous killer here, actor William Talman went on to find fame playing Raymond Burr's nemesis, LA District Attorney Hamilton Burger, in the TV show *Perry Mason*.

★ Lupino often appeared in her own movies, making cameo appearances—just like Alfred Hitchcock.

Cleo from 5 to 7

(Cléo de 5 à 7)

Rome Paris Films, 1962, France | Black & White and Color, 90 minutes

A real-time drama following a singer waiting for the results of a medical test.

Director: Agnès Varda

Producers: Georges de Beauregard, Carlo Ponti

Cinematography: Paul Bonis, Alain Levent, Jean Rabier

Screenplay: Agnès Varda

Starring: Corinne Marchand ("Florence 'Cléo' Victoire"), Dominque Davray ("Angèle"), Antoine Bourseiller ("Antoine"), Dorothée Blanck ("Dorothée")

"In my films I always wanted to make people see deeply. I don't want to show things, but to give people the desire to see."

—Agnès Varda

Throughout cinema history, there have been several films made in "real-time," meaning that the events shown are allowed to unfold at the same pace that the characters experience them. This is a useful device for ramping up suspense in stories about people under pressure—with the minutes ticking down toward the possible discovery of a murder (*Rope*), a jury's decision (*12 Angry Men*), a bank robbery (*Victoria*), or even the oxygen levels inside a coffin (*Buried*). In *Cleo from 5 to 7*, Agnès Varda uses this anxiety-infused technique to add drama to her gentle film about a woman walking through the streets of Paris.

The title is in fact a little misleading, as the film actually follows Florence "Cléo" Victoire (Corinne Marchand) for an hour and a half as she waits for the results of a medical diagnosis. It begins at 5:00 p.m. with Cléo having her tarot cards read, and finishes at 6:30 p.m. as her test results are received. In between, Cléo wanders through 1960s Paris, visiting friends, drinking in cafés, walking through a park, traveling in cabs and trams, rehearsing her act, and finally, meeting a lovely soldier. She covers much ground in just ninety minutes, and we learn a lot about her in the process. Cléo is a pop singer with three minor hits to her name. She is impulsive, volatile, and given to quick changes in emotion and adding as much drama as her friends will put up with. She's also superficial and vain, admiring herself in every reflective surface. In this way, Agnès Varda avoids sentimentality. The audience feels for Cléo's impending medical diagnosis, but she's not always likable.

> "Varda is sometimes referred to as the godmother of the French New Wave. I have been guilty of that myself. Nothing could be more unfair. Varda is its very soul, and only the fact that she is a woman, I fear, prevented her from being routinely included with Godard, Truffaut, Resnais, Chabrol, Rivette, Rohmer and...Jacques Demy. The passage of time has been kinder to her films than some of theirs, and *Cleo from 5 to 7* plays today as startlingly modern."
>
> Roger Ebert

Instead of the single-take concept that many of these real-time movies employ, Agnès Varda uses jump cuts, handheld cameras, transitions from color to black-and-white film, and unconventional framing to give the film a sense of playful freedom. She utilizes some of the same techniques as the burgeoning cinema verité ("real cinema") genre to add a feeling of immediacy. And so, by placing Cléo's story in real-time and using a documentary style, this everyday story becomes highly dramatic onscreen. It's also something of a time capsule of 1960s Paris, incorporating real footage of the bustling city streets. There is also a fun silent film inserted into the middle of the story, starring Jean-Luc Godard, Anna Karina, and Jean-Claude Brialy.

The major theme in *Cleo from 5 to 7* is time. This refers to both objective time (the actual minutes) and subjective time (how time can seem to contract or expand depending on your situation). The other theme is about women being "seen"—how Cléo sees herself, how she is seen by others, and how much (or little) she sees others—all told through the perceptive eyes of Agnès Varda.

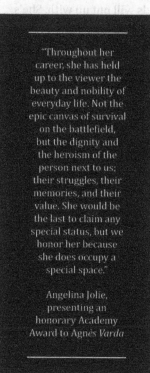

The experimental nature of *Cleo from 5 to 7* is reminiscent of other films from the French New Wave such as Jean-Luc Godard's *Breathless* and *The 400 Blows* by François Truffaut. But although the latter film is often credited with starting this cinematic movement, Agnès Varda's *La Pointe Courte* (named after the small fishing village where it was filmed) was released five years earlier and is now regarded as the first film of the French New Wave. This movement contained two distinct camps of filmmakers, each with their own style. The "Right Bank" used handheld cameras, jump cuts, and fast switches of tone. Many of these directors were movie lovers who came from film criticism and wrote for the influential magazine *Cahiers du Cinéma*, including directors such as Godard, Truffaut, and Claude Chabrol. The "Left Bank" used a less erratic style and were more concerned with politics. They saw film not so much as merely a form of entertainment but rather as being on the same level with literature and art. Filmmakers in this group included Alain Resnais, Chris Marker, and Jacques Demy.

Agnès Varda's style may seem at first glance to be more Right Bank, but she associated herself with the Left. She didn't come from a film criticism background, instead studying literature, psychology, art history, and photography before moving into film. Born in Brussels in 1928, she changed her name from Arlette to Agnès at eighteen. Her family moved from Belgium to France to escape German bombing at the start of World War II, and she spent her teenage years living in the port city of Sète. Varda then moved to Paris to study and afterwards found work as a photographer for the Théâtre National Populaire (TNP), taking photos of stage productions. There Varda met two actors, Philippe Noiret and Silvia Monfort, who agreed to star in her debut film, *La Pointe Courte*. In between making *La Pointe Courte* and *Cleo from 5 to 7*, Varda met Jacques Demy, whose debut *Lola* was released in 1961 to rave reviews. They fell in love, marrying in 1962 and remaining together until his death in 1990.

Throughout the 1960s, Agnès Varda was an important voice in the French New Wave. She was the only female filmmaker working in France at that time and was actively engaged with social issues. Varda made narrative dramas and documentaries, often with female protagonists, and her films commented on current issues, such as *Le Bonheur* (*Happiness*) released in 1965, which looked at the sexual revolution. Her work is varied, but each of her films contain striking visuals owing to her background as a photographer.

When Jacques Demy passed away in 1990, Agnès Varda made a trio of personal films as a tribute to him. *Jacquot de Nantes* was a dramatized version of his childhood. For *Les Demoiselles ont eu 25 ans* (*The Young Girls Turn 25*), Varda traveled to the town of Rochefort to celebrate the twenty-fifth anniversary of Demy's *The Young Girls of Rochefort*. And *L'univers de Jacques Demy* (*The World of Jacques Demy*) delved into his body of work and legacy.

In the 2000s, Agnès Varda continued to make documentaries, each demonstrating a wonderfully inventive and lyrical style. Most recently, she teamed up with visual artist JR to make *Faces Places*, released in 2017, where they traveled around the French countryside in a photo booth van taking photos of everyday people and pasting them onto the sides of buildings. Eyes are a strong motif throughout the film—evoking both a celebration of the art that Varda's unique perspective has given the world and her need to see the world before she lost her eyesight completely.

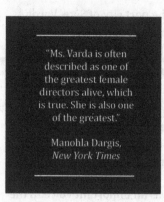

> "Ms. Varda is often described as one of the greatest female directors alive, which is true. She is also one of the greatest."
>
> Manohla Dargis,
> *New York Times*

When *Faces Places* was nominated for Best Documentary by the Motion Picture Academy of 2018, Agnès Varda became the oldest Oscar nominee in history. She was also awarded a special lifetime achievement Oscar in 2017 after receiving an honorary Palme d'Or at the 2015 Cannes Film Festival in recognition of her remarkable contributions to cinema. Now ninety years old, Agnès Varda shows no sign of slowing down—either in work or in activism. At the 2018 Cannes Film Festival, she walked the steps of the Palais des Festivals with eighty-one other women in a protest against gender inequality. Throughout the history of the Cannes Film Festival, only eighty-two female directors have ever been accepted into the official competition, and only two have won the Palme d'Or: Jane Campion and Agnès Varda.

As she stood at the stop of the stairs, actor Cate Blanchett and Varda read out a speech in English and French which included this rousing call to action:

> *"Women are not a minority in the world, yet the current state of our industry says otherwise. As women, we all face our own unique challenges, but we stand together on these stairs today as a symbol of our determination and commitment to progress...The stairs of our industry MUST be accessible to all. Let's climb."*

Just like her character Cléo, Agnès Varda has been on quite a journey.

☞ THE FEMALE GAZE

The ending of *Cleo from 5 to 7* has been the cause of some debate. Some see it as a cop-out, a woman being saved by a man. Others say it's a beautiful commentary on finding love in the face of possible death by cancer and war. Regardless, the film has been celebrated as a feminist work both for the way that it features a complex and sometimes unlikable female character (instead of an idealized stereotype) and for its commentaries on how women see themselves and are seen by others.

☰ FAST FACTS

- ★ Agnès Varda was the only woman working in the French New Wave, and made her first film, *La Pointe Courte*, at just twenty-seven years old.

- ★ She was dubbed "the grandmother of the French New Wave" when she was just thirty years old.

- ★ The budget of *Cleo from 5 to 7* was $64,000, and it took five weeks to film.

- ★ Her film *Vagabond*, released in 1985, won the Golden Lion at the Venice Film Festival.

- ★ Throughout her career, Varda has more than fifty credits as a director to her name as well as more than forty as a writer.

- ★ In 2009, Varda was made a Commander of the Legion of Honour—an award of merit in France—for her achievements in cinema.

- ★ When the Academy of Motion Pictures, Arts and Sciences conferred the Honorary Award on Varda in 2017, she became the first female director to ever receive that honor.

Daisies

(Sedmikrásky)

Filmové Studio Barrandov, 1966, Czechoslovakia | Black & White and Color, 72 minutes, Comedy/Drama

This experimental film follows two young women causing chaos.

Director: Věra Chytilová

Producers: Ladislav Fikar, Bohumil Smída

Cinematography: Jaroslav Kučera

Screenplay: Věra Chytilová, Ester Krumbachova, Pavel Juracek

Starring: Jitka Cerhová ("Marie I") and Ivana Karbanová ("Marie II")

"The form of the film was really derived from the conceptual basis of the film. Because the concept of the film was destruction, the form became destructive as well."

—Věra Chytilová

Sometimes there are movies which defy easy categorization. They are experimental, they feel risqué; are about nothing, but also everything.

This is how I would describe *Daisies* by Věra Chytilová. It is a film with a deceptively simple plot, but its experimentation with content and form caused huge waves in Czechoslovakia at the time—and eventually, around the world.

First, some background: in 1945, the film industry in Czechoslovakia was nationalized, taking it from privately owned to being under the control of the state. By 1948, a communist government was in place, so the films being made in the 1950s were largely propaganda. Shot in the style of Soviet socialist realism, communist values were strongly depicted, the characters' struggles were rewarded with happy endings, and narratives proceeded in a very straightforward manner.

Meanwhile, FAMU, the national film school, had been established in Prague, and the teachers there showed their students films from around the world. These were arthouse films not distributed within the country, including works from the French New Wave and the Italian Neorealist movements by Jean-Luc Godard, Michelangelo Antonioni, Louis Malle, Robert Bresson, and more.

"Věra Chytilová was one of the most important women filmmakers of the 1960s. If Agnès Varda was the "mother" of the French New Wave, then Chytilová had the same role in Czechoslovakia."

Peter Hames, author of *The Czechoslovak New Wave*

By the time these students graduated in the mid-1960s, reform was underway and the restrictions on expression were slowly being loosened. The graduates turned their lenses on everyday life, infusing the experimentation of other cinematic movements with their own unique experiences. These films were often critical of the government, using metaphor and humor to speak out about the oppressive regime. They pushed the boundaries of filmmaking, and their free-spirited artistic tone was often seen as being dangerous to the ideals of communist Czechoslovakia. The films were smuggled out of the country to play at festivals around the world, and so the short but sharp "Czechoslovak New Wave" was born.

This movement lasted only a few years, starting around 1963 and ending in 1968 when the Soviet Union and other members of the Warsaw Pact invaded Czechoslovakia and toppled the President. After that, many filmmakers fled the country or struggled to find work. But within those five years there was a burst of intense creativity from filmmakers such as Miloš Forman, František Vláčil, and Věra Chytilová.

Chytilová was the only woman in the movement, often referred to as the "First Lady of Czech Cinema." Born in 1929 to a strict Catholic family, she studied architecture and philosophy at college before becoming a model, a draftsman, and a clapper girl at a film studio in Prague. That was where she developed an interest in making movies, and at twenty-eight years old she applied to study at FAMU. As the only female student in her class, she refused to let her gender be a barrier and often shocked her male peers with her confidence and ferocity. At FAMU, Chytilová experimented with improvisation and the use of non-professional actors and found she preferred work that was less structured.

She continued to play with form in her first feature film, which was released in 1963 and appropriately called *Something Different*. Here, Chytilová melded documentary and narrative to tell two parallel stories about two very different women. She also contributed to the omnibus film *Pearls of the Deep* made with several other Czech filmmakers in 1965, but it was her second feature *Daisies* that truly put her on the map.

To describe the plot of the film is to do it a disservice, because *Daisies* is more of an existential fever dream than a linear, narrative movie. In short, the story concerns two bored women, Marie I (Jitka Cerhová) and Marie II (Ivana Karbanová), causing havoc as they run amok through their city. They revolt against an oppressive society by treating symbols of wealth, such as money and food, with little care. Throughout the film they go out with wealthy older men, eating at expensive restaurants and leaving their unlucky dates to foot the bills.

Chytilová called the film "a philosophical documentary in the form of a farce," with the two Maries rebelling against a male-dominated society that views them only as objects. They believe that the world is meaningless and so do what they want. *Daisies* is also something of a rebellion against filmmaking itself—here Věra Chytilová rejects the standard approach to moviemaking by ditching a linear narrative and creating characters who are difficult to connect with. She uses striking images, jumping from black-and-white to color at unexpected moments, and weaves in surreal montages where the girls consider everything from romance to death.

"You always have to work as if what you're working on could be your last."

Věra Chytilová

The two girls do not behave the way young ladies "should." But the most controversial scene in *Daisies* actually involved a food fight. In the scene, the girls come across a rich banquet, which they happily destroy, wasting the decadent feast by throwing food at each other. It was this scene which led to the film being banned from playing in theaters, with the Czech Government citing food wastage as the reason for the decision. Appropriately, the film is dedicated "to those who get upset over a stomped-upon bed of lettuce."

Daisies feels like a bold feminist statement, with the women deciding they do not need men to complete their lives and using male sexual advances to get free food. But though her work often told stories about women and provided new representations of them onscreen, it is important to note that throughout her career Věra Chytilová rejected the label of "feminist" being attached to her films. She saw herself as an individual making a statement about her country, not her gender.

After 1968, many filmmakers of the Czechoslovak New Wave were blacklisted. Věra Chytilová released *Fruit of Paradise* in 1970 and *Kamaradi* in 1971, but didn't make another movie until the ban was lifted in 1976. Later, she turned to teaching, and found success with documentaries. Chytilová passed away in 2014 at the age of eighty-five and is remembered as a trailblazer for female filmmakers. She was an innovator and an uncompromising revolutionary artist and activist whose films dared to make a statement at a time when it was dangerous to do so.

☞ THE FEMALE GAZE

The two girls act the opposite to how young ladies are "supposed" to behave. Using their beauty and youth, they wage a feminine war on society, destroying the very things they are meant to hold dear—food, money, home, work. The male characters in *Daisies* are reduced to sugar daddies who do whatever the girls want and often end up in tears.

≡ FAST FACTS

★ Věra Chytilová was never officially classified as a blacklisted director, but the government made it nearly impossible for her to find work within Czechoslovakia. Secretly, she directed commercials under her husband's name, Jaroslav Kučera.

★ In the mid-1970s, "Year of Women," a US film festival, contacted Chytilová to get permission to screen *Daisies*. After she informed them that her government wouldn't let her attend or even make films in her own country, the festival petitioned the government on her behalf. This international pressure, plus a letter Chytilová wrote directly to President Gustáv Husák, encouraged the government to ease the ban so she could resume work.

★ Even her graduate film *The Ceiling* (1962) caused controversy. The movie was based on Chytilová's experiences as a fashion model and focused on exploitation and materialism. After a screening, one audience member stood up and said her film "undermines people's faith in socialism. If that is the way it really is, then none of it is worth it at all."

★ Chytilová married two cinematographers, Karel Ludwig and Jaroslav Kučera. Her two children with Kučera have followed in their footsteps and both work in the film industry—their daughter, Tereza Kucerová, is an actor and costume designer, and their son, Stepán Kučera, is a cinematographer.

Jenna Ipcar on *The Heartbreak Kid* (1972)

I've always felt stumped as to why we're even allowed to talk about *The Graduate* without also mentioning Elaine May's *The Heartbreak Kid*. Nichols and May had a past history as a comedic duo, and I've always felt that *The Heartbreak Kid* served as a more grounded and darkly comedic heightening of *The Graduate*. Under May's expert direction, *The Heartbreak Kid* is a supremely sharp commentary on the wake of destruction left behind by the follies of selfish men.

The Heartbreak Kid essentially starts where *The Graduate* leaves off: with a man realizing that his wedding hasn't fulfilled his spiritual desires, and therefore moving on to chase another whim. Lenny Cantrow is shown to be living purely on impulses, which have obvious repercussions that only he can't seem to anticipate. Similar to Benjamin Braddock, the film also ends with Lenny having a realization that doesn't extend beyond his own selfishness; he desires the chase more than the prize. While Nichols' film gently flirts with a dreamy existentialism, May's goes for some darkly realistic and fully grounded musings on male ego—taking the male fantasy of *The Graduate* and carrying it to its logical reality in *The Heartbreak Kid*.

May further flips *The Graduate* on its head by defining her main character primarily through the gaze of the supporting cast. It's the expressions and reactions of the people around Lenny that clue us in on how shallow this pursuit of his romantic ideal actually is. Neil Simon's script easily could have been a misogynistic (or questionably anti-Semitic) and boorish comedy about a man who tosses his nagging, confident Jewish wife, and obtains his ideal fantasy shiksa goddess through dogged persistence and enterprising bullshitting. Yet as the director, May pointedly makes the decision not to indulge the script in this way. She sets up most of the shots with her main character's back to us and with the camera's focus on the supporting cast's facial reactions toward him, keeping the audience from focusing solely on Lenny as the chief narrator. The result is that you truly learn who Lenny is through his wife Lila's hysterical weeping, his lover Kelly's bemusement at his advances, and her parent's simmering glares of disapproval.

The Heartbreak Kid is all at once a poignant, hilarious, and vicious retelling of the male romantic fantasy, the likes of which I feel only a woman could have been so acutely aware of in the 1970s. In the current climate of the #MeToo movement, it's a gift to see any film that shines a realistic light on the damage done by men who treat women like objects. A true triumph of female filmmaking!

Jenna Ipcar is a Brooklyn-based critic who has been writing about film for online publications since 2013. She co-founded Back Row (www. back-row.com), a female-run movie review website and podcast.

Jeanne Dielman, 23 Commerce Quay, 1080 Brussels

(Jeanne Dielman, 23, Quai du Commerce, 1080 Bruxelles)

Paradise Films, 1975, Belgium | Color, 201 minutes, Drama

Three days in the life of Jeanne Dielman as she cooks, cleans, and takes clients for sex.

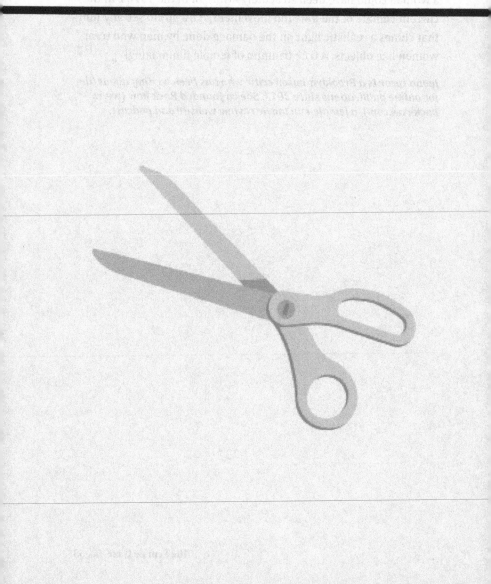

Director: Chantal Akerman

Producers: Evelyne Paul, Corinne Jénart

Cinematography: Babette Mangolte

Screenplay: Chantal Akerman

Starring: Delphine Seyrig ("Jeanne Dielman"), Jan Decorte ("Sylvain Dielman")

"I do think it's a feminist film because I give space to things which were never, almost never, shown in that way, like the daily gestures of a woman. They are the lowest in the hierarchy of film images. A kiss or a car crash comes higher, and I don't think that's accidental. It's because these are women's gestures that they count for so little."

—*Chantal Akerman*

Jeanne Dielman, 23 Commerce Quay, 1080 Brussels is a deceptively simple film which elevates a woman's domestic work to the level of high drama. A character study following three days in the life of Jeanne Dielman (Delphine Seyrig), the film invites its audience to observe her daily routine over the course of almost of three and a half hours. Jeanne cleans, run errands, visits a coffee shop, cooks dinner for her son—and, while the potatoes are boiling, she accepts afternoon clients who pay for sex.

On day one, we notice how meticulous Jeanne is about herself and her apartment. Everything has its place, and she is almost mechanical in the way she moves, adhering to a strict order in her routine. Day two starts out the same—waking her son Sylvain (Jan Decorte) for breakfast; a trip to the grocery store for that night's dinner; greeting her client at the front door and walking him to her bedroom. We don't see what happens inside the room, but as soon as they emerge, we sense that something is wrong. Jeanne's normally perfectly coiffed hair is slightly mussed. She forgets to turn on the light; she doesn't replace the top of the pot where she keeps her money. And when she returns to the kitchen, Jeanne realizes she has overcooked the potatoes. She takes the pot and staggers with it from room to room, shocked and unsure what to do.

Day three doesn't get much better for Jeanne. She drops a spoon while putting her cutlery away, messes up her cup of coffee, and can't find the right button to sew on Sylvain's jacket. Everything is out of alignment. As Jeanne sits in a chair, staring blankly into the distance, we feel her anxiety. Without spoiling the ending, all of this leads Jeanne to take drastic action.

This is a woman who clearly needs to be in control, perfectly played in a restrained performance by Delphine Seyrig. In later interviews, director Chantal Akerman explained that on day two, Jeanne had an orgasm with her client. That moment of loss of control was enough to form a crack in her perfect shield, making her desperate to regain her composure.

Even before its dramatic end, there is a sense of tension which builds slowly throughout *Jeanne Dielman*. Audiences are conditioned to watching films where many things happen. Here, Chantel Akerman shows us the unremarkable, in long takes shot on a fixed camera. There are no close-ups, no reverse angles. The camera is always positioned straight in front of the action—often from a low angle—and lingers on scenes even after the characters have exited. Chantal Akerman's camera is never voyeuristic, never peering through a window or keyhole.

Akerman has explained that she wanted to make sure the audience always knew where she, as the director, was. This was, she said, "the only way to shoot the film—to avoid cutting the action in a hundred places, to look carefully and to be respectful. The framing was meant to respect her space, her, and her gestures within it."

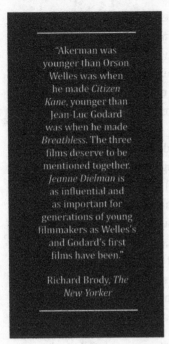

"Akerman was younger than Orson Welles was when he made *Citizen Kane*, younger than Jean-Luc Godard was when he made *Breathless*. The three films deserve to be mentioned together. *Jeanne Dielman* is as influential and as important for generations of young filmmakers as Welles's and Godard's first films have been."

Richard Brody, *The New Yorker*

As viewers, we go through a range of emotions. At first, we can't help but squirm uncomfortably, waiting for an edit or for something to happen. We are restless, suddenly aware of ourselves, and overcome with an instinct to reach for some kind of distraction. But if we stay the course, we find that we become absorbed in the details. We notice the color of the curtains, the pattern of the wallpaper, the coat Jeanne puts on to keep her clothes clean. It's a mesmerizing study of time, so understated for most of the movie—so that when things do start to shift, even a fallen spoon seems disastrous.

Much time and focus is given to watching Jeanne do simple tasks such as peeling potatoes, making meatloaf, and washing dishes. Yet the part of her day when she takes clients into her bedroom is never shown. By doing this, Chantal Akerman keeps the focus on Jeanne's daily work, making that the most important part of her instead of seeing her merely as a sexual object.

Jeanne Dielman, 23 Commerce Quay, 1080 Brussels has been called a masterpiece of feminist cinema. But the idea came to Chantel Akerman very quickly, and she wrote the script in just two weeks. "It all came very easily, of course," she explained, "Because I had seen it all around me." The "it" Akerman refers to could be the oppression of women; or perhaps it may be the anxiety of everyday life, that feeling we find so hard to communicate—that beneath the surface of our perfect veneer lies a deep well of melancholy, ready to take over at a moment's notice.

Chantal Akerman knew that feeling better than most. She was born in Brussels in 1950 to a Jewish family. Her mother and grandparents had been sent to Auschwitz, and only her mother made it back. At the age of fifteen, Akerman saw *Pierrot le Fou* by Jean-Luc Godard and immediately decided to dedicate her life to making movies. Three years later, she began studying film at the Institut National Supérieur des Arts du Spectacle et des Techniques de Diffusion (INSAS) but dropped out after a few months. She was eager to start making films, and her first venture was *Saute ma ville* (*Blow Up My Town*). This was a thirteen-minute, black-and-white 35mm film which starred Akerman as herself. "One day, I wanted to make a film about myself," she said. "That was *Saute ma ville*. I needed a camera, some film, some lights, and someone to operate the camera. I asked somebody I knew if he would help me make the film, and somebody else loaned me a camera, we bought a little film stock, and we made the film in one night. And then I edited it." As simple as that.

The film was a precursor to *Jeanne Dielman*, and it followed Akerman as she went to the kitchen to perform unremarkable tasks before abruptly committing suicide at the end. The film premiered at a short film festival in 1971, and that same year Akerman moved to New York. There she met director and cinematographer Babette Mangolte, and the two became friends and collaborators. They worked together on one of Akerman's first features, *Hotel Monterey* in 1972, an experimental documentary which used long takes to examine hotel corridors. *Hotel Monterey* was accepted to play at the Nancy Theater Festival, where it won a Jury Prize. And on that jury was the Lebanese-born French actress Delphine Seyrig, one of the icons of the French New Wave, who had worked with directors such as Alain Resnais and Luis Buñuel.

It was Seyrig's star power which made *Jeanne Dielman* possible. The budget was small, and the crew was almost entirely made up of women. Chantal Akerman was just twenty-four years old at the time, working outside of any studio system, pushing the boundaries of film format and length. The movie premiered at the 1975 Cannes Film Festival to critical acclaim, with the *New York Times* calling it the "first masterpiece of the feminine in the history of the cinema," and it has since become a cult classic.

After that success, Akerman said she felt she had to escape her own mastery and avoid repeating herself. She moved away from studying the effects of time in film and began making movies across all genres—musicals, comedies, and documentaries. Her final film was *No Home Movie*, released in 2015. This was a documentary featuring conversations between herself and her mother just before her mother passed away in 2014. Chantal Akerman suffered from grief and depression following her mother's death, and was briefly hospitalized. On October 5, 2015, at the age of sixty-five, Akerman took her own life.

Her life was short, but Chantal Akerman's legacy lives on, with filmmakers such as Gus Van Sant, Todd Haynes, and Apichatpong Weerasethakul citing *Jeanne Dielman* and Akerman as a powerful influence.

❧ THE FEMALE GAZE

Considered a masterpiece of feminist cinema, *Jeanne Dielman* was released during "second-wave" feminism—a time when women staying at home doing domestic tasks had begun speaking up about their feelings of isolation. This film tapped into the sense of alienation women were feeling at the time, which are present in Jeanne's anxiety and melancholy as a character. *Jeanne Dielman* has also been praised for the way it elevates a woman's domestic work to art by using long takes and a still camera which was purposely not voyeuristic in nature. Also, Akerman chose not to show Jeanne's other work as a prostitute, and the film does not shame her for it.

☰ FAST FACTS

★ Chantal Akerman made more than forty films during her career, filming in Belgium, eastern Europe, the US, Israel, Mexico, China, and more.

★ She was a multitalented artist. In addition to her films, Akerman wrote a play, published two books, and worked in the art world creating a series of video installations.

★ In the 1970s, while living in New York, Akerman was inspired by the video work of avant-garde artists such as Michael Snow, Yvonne Rainer, and Andy Warhol. She started to experiment with some of the techniques used by these artists, but turning her lens onto the daily life of women.

The Lost Honor of Katharina Blum

Bioskop Film, 1975, Germany | Color, 106 minutes, Drama/Thriller

A young woman's life is ruined after she is accused of aiding a terrorist.

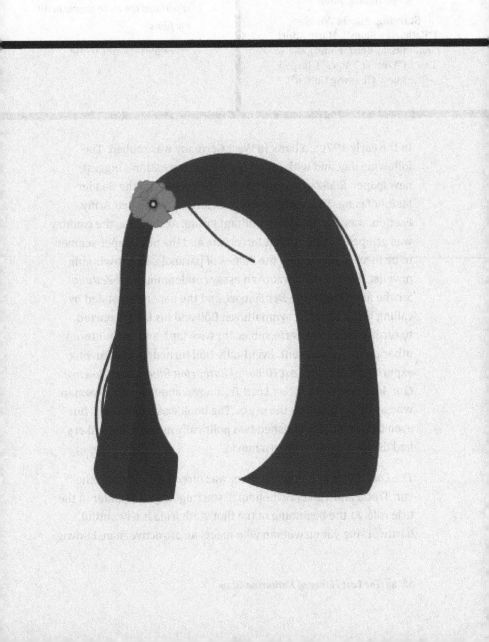

Director: Margarethe von Trotta (with Volker Schlöndorff)

Producer: Eberhard Junkersdorf

Cinematography: Jost Vacano

Screenplay: Margarethe von Trotta, Volker Schlöndorff, based on a novel by Heinrich Böll

Starring: Angela Winkler ("Katharina Blum"), Mario Adorf ("Kommissar Beizmenne"), Dieter Laser ("Werner Tötges"), Jürgen Prochnow ("Ludwig Götten")

"I am always attracted by a woman who has to fight for her own life and her own reality, who has to get out of a certain situation of imprisonment, to free herself. That is perhaps the main theme in all my films."

—Margarethe von Trotta

In the early 1970s, a bank in West Germany was robbed. The following day, and without any evidence, the nation's biggest newspaper, *Bild-Zeitung,* attributed the robbery to the Baader-Meinhof gang. That gang, sometimes known as the Red Army Faction, was a far left-wing militant group. At the time, the country was gripped by fears about terrorism, and the newspaper seemed to be focused on fanning the flames of paranoia. Nobel-winning novelist Heinrich Böll wrote an essay condemning *Bild-Zeitung* for the news magazine *Der Spiegel*, and the paper responded by calling him a terrorist sympathizer. Böll and his family started to receive hate mail, were subject to wire taps, and encountered other police harassment. Eventually Böll turned this harrowing experience into *The Lost Honor of Katharina Blum: How Violence Can Arise and What It Can Lead To,* a novel about a young woman whose life is ruined by the press. The book was a bestseller, but even before it was published two politically minded filmmakers had decided to turn it into a movie.

The Lost Honor of Katharina Blum was directed by Margarethe von Trotta and Volker Schlöndorff, starring Angela Winkler in the title role. At the beginning of the film, Katharina is a beautiful, hardworking young woman who meets an attractive man, Ludwig

Götten (Jürgen Prochnow), on a rare night out with friends. Their chemistry is immediate, and Blum leaves the party with him, taking him back to her place. In the morning she is startled by the police, who burst into her apartment looking for him. They claim that Götten is a terrorist and take Blum into custody on suspicion of aiding him.

> "Her work is of special interest because it is a woman-centered and woman-affirming cinema of a kind that is still a rarity—women looked at with intensity and love by the woman behind the camera, by one another on the screen, and by women like oneself in the audience...it is a major development in the experience of women in film."
>
> Barbara Quart,
> Film Critic

At the police station, Blum is subjected to hours of questioning by Kommissar Beizmenne (Mario Adorf) and his team. They taunt her for sleeping with Götten so soon after meeting him, but she refuses to flinch or play their games. As a form of punishment, Beizmenne leaks details about the case to a brash reporter from *The Paper*. Based on these scant details, Werner Tötges (Dieter Laser) begins to publish scathing articles about Katharina's love life, each becoming more sensational by the day. Blum starts to receive hate mail, obscene phone calls, and unwanted sexual advances. Her safety is threatened, her friends distance themselves from her, and she loses her job. All the while, *The Paper* prints more and more articles about Blum and her life, ruining her reputation and placing her under severe psychological stress.

Though this is a movie made over forty years ago, it feels as timely as ever. Watching it again, I was reminded of the book *So You've Been Publicly Shamed* by Jon Ronson, which explores the type of glee people seem to experience from watching and participating in online trolling and the devastating effects on the person targeted. Katharina's experience could also be likened to the invasive level of surveillance some individuals were subjected to following 9/11, or to how hate has been stoked by fake news posts and conspiracy theories circulated via social media.

In case von Trotta and Schöndorff's intentions were not sufficiently clear back in 1975, the film included a scathing epitaph which reads, "Should the description of certain journalistic practices bear any resemblance to the practices of the *Bild-Zeitung*, this is nether intentional, nor accidental, but unavoidable." It was a brave action on their part to speak up against such a powerful media company.

"We fought for so many years to get the same rights in filmmaking that men had or still have. We got attention, and all of a sudden our male colleagues said yes, yes, we have to understand and help the women to get their rights. And then came the backlash. Then all of a sudden it was silent, and it was just as if we didn't speak before... I have made films for forty years now, and I did a lot of fighting, and I was one of the first women in Germany to make films, and there are many, many more women—but there are not enough."

Margarethe von Trotta

The press in the *The Lost Honor of Katharina Blum* have zero regard for civil liberties, and the police are portrayed as morally bankrupt. There is little nuance on either side, with their actions exaggerated to make a point about the erosion of civil liberties and the dangers involved when authorities begin acting as if they are above the law.

Angela Winkler grounds the film with a singularly powerful performance. Her steadfast silence enrages the police, who expect her to be a "good girl" and cooperate— or at the very least, to be ashamed for having a one-night stand. It's not personal, they insist, but then decide to destroy her through the media. In this they are helped by the misogynistic Tötges, who is the type of person who believes any fame is good, even when it comes with vicious slut-shaming from members of the public. "You are news," he tells her proudly. Soon, it doesn't matter why the police questioned her in the first place. In the eyes of her community, Blum is guilty—her biggest crime being that she is a woman unashamed of her sexuality.

Much of the feminist point of view in *The Lost Honor of Katharina Blum* has been attributed to Margarethe von Trotta. This was her first feature film as a director, working alongside Volker Schlöndorff, who was her husband at the time. Though he had previously made several feature films, *The Lost Honor of Katharina Blum* gave Schlöndorff his first box office hit, and both he and von Trotta soon became a vital part of New German Cinema. It was to be their only directorial collaboration. After this success, Schlöndorff went on to make political films such as the Oscar-winning *The Tin Drum*, while von Trotta directed a string of feminist movies, joining a small but powerful group of European female filmmakers.

Margarethe von Trotta was born at a tumultuous time: the year 1942 in Berlin, Germany. After going through the war and graduating from high school, she studied business, art, philology, and drama. But in the early 1960s her world was changed by a visit to Paris, where she saw films by Ingmar Bergman, Alfred Hitchcock, and the directors of the French New Wave. As she later explained, "I came from Germany before the New Wave, so we had all these silly movies. Cinema for me was entertainment, but it was not art. When I came to Paris, all of the sudden I understood what cinema could be. I stood there and said, 'That is what I'd like to do with my life.' "

Unfortunately, it wasn't to be easy. There were few female directors working in the industry, so von Trotta started taking on small parts as an actress. She caught the attention of several directors, including Volker Schlöndorff, who later became her romantic partner and creative collaborator. She cowrote with Schlöndorff on several projects before getting the chance to prove herself as a director alongside him on *The Lost Honor of Katharina*

Blum. Because that film went on to be such a success, von Trotta was given more opportunities as a director and proved herself by making movies centering on women. She made *The Second Awakening of Christa Klages*, released in 1978, based on the true story of a kindergarten teacher who robbed a bank to keep the school open.

And then, beginning in 1979, Margarethe von Trotta made her famous trilogy of films about sisters. With *Sisters, or the Balance of Happiness*, *Marianne and Juliane* (sometimes known as *The German Sisters*), and *Three Sisters*, von Trotta became an important feminist director and one of the leading filmmakers in New German Cinema.

Throughout the '80s, '90s, 2000s, and to this day, von Trotta continues to make films about the struggles of everyday women. Her stories are sensitively told and depict complex, three-dimensional female characters, delving into their psychology, emotions, and inner life. Comparisons have been made between her work and the films of Ingmar Bergman, who Margarethe von Trotta has cited as a huge influence. She explored this personal connection in a documentary called *Searching for Ingmar Bergman*, which played at the 2018 Cannes Film Festival.

Despite her focus on the stories of women, the title of "feminist" or "female" filmmaker is one from which Margarethe von Trotta has shied away. As she explained in an interview with *The Observer*, this was more due to the reaction of a paying audience than her own views. "When I started to make films," she said, "I wanted to tell something about me and about us and about my experience and my knowledge. I felt also a little bit like a duty to speak about women, like I was a voice for other women who didn't have this possibility to speak. I have nothing against feminism, and surely I'm a feminist, but the word is used now mainly by men, in an ironic way. They say, 'Oh, that's just a women's film. You don't have to go in, it's not interesting for you as a man.' I'm very much against this."

And indeed, to view von Trotta as only a great female filmmaker would be to reduce her immense talents. With her remarkable body of work, unique perspective, and skills in telling engaging stories, there is little doubt that Margarethe von Trotta is one of the most important German directors in history and that she deserves to be talked about alongside the likes of Rainer Werner Fassbinder, Werner Herzog, Wim Wenders, and Volker Schlöndorff.

🎥 THE FEMALE GAZE

Katharina Blum is treated very differently than if she were a man. When she doesn't display the appropriate amount of shame at sleeping with someone she has just met, the male-dominated police force and a male reporter go out of their way to ruin her reputation—and show no remorse when she begins to receive anonymous hate mail calling her degrading names and threatening to ruin her life.

≡ FAST FACTS

★ *The Lost Honor of Katharina Blum* was one of the biggest hits of any German films in the 1970s and was released the same year as another political thriller, *Three Days of the Condor*, starring Robert Redford.

★ On set, Volker Schlöndorff looked after the technical side of directing, while Margarethe von Trotta took care of the performances—the aspect most praised by critics.

★ The success of this film led to a 1984 made-for-television remake called *The Lost Honor of Kathryn Beck*, starring Marlo Thomas and Kris Kristofferson.

★ In 1992, the great director Ingmar Bergman was asked by the Göteborg Film Festival to list the films that had most impressed him. Among names like Charlie Chaplin, Federico Fellini, and Akira Kurosawa, he included Margarethe von

Trotta. He particularly admired her film *Marianne and Juliane* and told her it had given him courage during a time of depression.

★ When Margarethe von Trotta won the Golden Lion at the Venice Film Festival for her film *Marianne and Juliane*, she was the first director to win that top prize since Leni Riefenstahl's win for *Olympia* in 1938.

Seven Beauties

(Pasqualino Settebellezze)

Medusa Distribuzione, 1975, Italy | Color, 114 minutes, Comedy/Drama

*An Italian man joins the army during World War II to avoid a
murder conviction, only to end up in a concentration camp after
deserting his unit.*

Director: Lina Wertmüller

Producer: Arrigo Colombo

Cinematography: Tonino Delli Colli

Screenplay: Lina Wertmüller

Starring: Giancarlo Giannini ("Pasqualino"), Fernando Rey ("Pedro"), Shirley Stoler ("Prison Camp Commandant"), Piero Di Iorio ("Francesco")

"What I hope to express in my films is my great faith in the possibility of man becoming human."
—Lina Wertmüller

"If *Swept Away* marks a considerable leap beyond Wertmüller's earlier, very fine films, *Seven Beauties* is an upward leap in seven league boots that propels her into the highest regions of cinematic art, into the company of the major directors. Not since I saw Ozu's *Tokyo Story* was I so overwhelmed by a film..."

John Simon, *New York* magazine

When Lina Wertmüller's *Seven Beauties* was released in 1975, it caused quite a bit of controversy. This was nothing new for Wertmüller, who was already one of the most talked-about filmmakers in Italy thanks to her scathing and provocative critiques of life there. But *Seven Beauties* asked the audience to do two unthinkable things: to follow the story of a man who murders, rapes, and is cowardly; and to laugh while being shown the horrors of World War II.

Right from the opening credits, we know we're in for an unconventional war film. *Seven Beauties* starts with a series of newsreel images from the war, set rather incongruously to the song "Oh Yeah" by Enzo Jannacci. The lyrics include: "The ones who vote for the right because they're fed up with strikes. Oh yeah.

The ones who vote white in order not to get dirty. The ones who never get involved with politics. Oh yeah."

This sets the tone for what we are about to see—a study of the contradictions of the people involved in World War II and how those who stood by and did nothing are as guilty as those who committed the atrocities.

And the central character of Pasqualino (Giancarlo Giannini) is certainly guilty. We are introduced to him at the very moment he deserts Mussolini's army, running through a dark, rainy forest in Germany. He boasts to fellow Italian soldier Francesco (Piero Di Iorio) that he stole bandages from a dead man in order to fake an injury and escape. When they later come across Nazi soldiers slaughtering a group of innocent Jews, Pasqualino refuses to intervene, fearing he might lose his own life in the process.

But he is not without his charms—or so he thinks. As the movie flashes back to the bright colors of pre-war Naples, we learn that Pasqualino ran a mattress company and considered himself quite a hit with the ladies. He gropes his female employees and flirts with women on the street, but is guilty of double standards when it comes to his many sisters. When he discovers that one of his sisters has started prostituting herself, he declares he will kill the pimp who has destroyed his family's honor. This turns out to be nothing but talk; when Pasqualino faces the pimp, Totonno, he is knocked out in one punch. Humiliated, Pasqualino sneaks into Totonno's bedroom and shoots the other man dead before he can defend himself. Things only get worse from there—Pasqualino then attempts to dispose of the body by cutting it up into pieces.

This, it turns out, is the crime which ultimately leads to his involvement in World War II. As the film jumps back and forth in time, we see Pasqualino sent to an insane asylum. Here, in a particularly brutal scene, he rapes a female patient who is strapped to a bed. As a way out of the asylum, he agrees to join

Mussolini's army, where after deserting his squad, he is captured by the Nazis and sent to a concentration camp.

Lina Wertmüller portrays the camp in realistic and horrific detail. She uses close-ups of mass executions of Jewish people to make it impossible to escape the brutality. Running the camp is a woman (Shirley Stoler) who seems devoid of humanity. She tortures innocent men and orders them to their death. Remembering some advice from his mother about appealing to women with love, Pasqualino decides that his only way out is to seduce her. In the most controversial scenes of the film, Pasqualino offers sexual favors to the Nazi woman, leading to another morally difficult situation.

In most movies, these types of moral conundrums would see the character search within himself and decide to change. This is not one of those movies. As film critic Roger Ebert observed, "*Seven Beauties* isn't the account of a man's fall from dignity, because Pasqualino never had any—and that's what makes it intriguing." At every turn, Pasqualino chooses to save his own life over anyone else's, and somehow, he keeps surviving.

Despite the material (or perhaps in defiance of it), *Seven Beauties* is a comedy—a very, very dark comedy. The tone switches throughout, from more broadly comedic to ironic and finally caustic. What keeps us watching is the charisma of Giancarlo Giannini. He is a handsome actor with a devilish smile who plays Pasqualino with glee, throwing himself unapologetically into this revolting character. He is so compelling that despite ourselves, we almost want Pasqualino to come out on top.

Featuring such a horrific character who inspires sympathy from the audience formed one part of the controversy surrounding *Seven Beauties*. The other was its comedic approach to World War II.

And yet, *Seven Beauties* went on to become one of Lina Wertmüller's most successful films and one of the few foreign films to be nominated for four Academy Awards. One of those nominations was for Giancarlo Giannini's performance. Another was for Wertmüller's direction, making her the very first female filmmaker ever to be nominated for a Best Director Oscar. In 2018, following the announcement of Greta Gerwig as the fifth woman up for the award, Lina Wertmüller reflected on how news reports in 1976 termed her nomination "historic." Though she was embarrassed at the time, "in hindsight, it was [historic]," she says, "especially for women all over the world. To this day I get thank-you letters from directors who say they have been inspired by my experience."

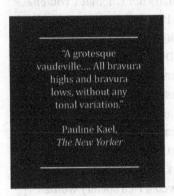

"A grotesque vaudeville.... All bravura highs and bravura lows, without any tonal variation."

Pauline Kael,
The New Yorker

Lina Wertmüller was born in Rome in 1928, a time when the country was ruled by fascist leader Benito Mussolini. She loved cinema from the start; she expressed her rebellious streak by sneaking out of class to watch movies and was expelled from fifteen different schools. "I was fascinated by stories on the big screen," Wertmüller later explained, "and I wanted to be involved in that kind of entertainment... Then, when I was a teenager, I met the actress Flora Carabella. She was a little older than me, but we became best friends, and she introduced me to the magic of theater. I was very young, but I immediately knew that I wanted to study at the Theatre Academy. That's how I started to be part of that world."

She graduated from the Academy in Rome in 1951, much to the chagrin of her father, who wanted her to be a lawyer. He was a controlling presence throughout her life and often fought with his daughter. But Lina Wertmüller was determined to succeed; she spent a decade working in experimental theater and puppeteering, where she used puppets to tell the stories of Franz Kafka. Then in 1961, Wertmüller got her big break when she met acclaimed director Federico Fellini and was hired as assistant director for *8½*. Working on this groundbreaking piece of Italian cinema gave her the inspiration, confidence, and financial backing to direct her first film, *The Lizards (I Basilischi)*, in 1963, about three men who spend their days chasing women. Both that debut and her second film, *Let's Talk about Men*, a look at misogyny released in 1965, were well regarded, yet Wertmüller still struggled to secure enough financing to keep directing.

"I was not the only one... Before me, there were many pioneer female directors. Since the silent era, we [have] had great filmmakers such as Elvira Notari, who was born in Salerno, and Alice Guy, who grew up at Gaumont. Elvira was one the first directors of all time. She started making films from the very beginning of the century with her own production company... I have to admit that I've never felt it was a problem that I was one of the few women making films."

Lina Wertmüller

She turned to television for work, but made her cinematic comeback with 1972's *The Seduction of Mimi*, a political satire which won her the Best Director award at Cannes. Wertmüller found even more success with her next three films. *Love and Anarchy* (1973) starred Giancarlo Giannini and earned her the attention of international critics. *Swept Away* in 1974 followed a rich society woman who becomes stranded with a crew member while on a cruise. This film earned much critical praise but also a great deal of backlash about the abusive treatment of the central female character, with Anthony Kaufman from *The Village Voice* writing that it was "possibly the most outrageously misogynist film ever made by a woman." The following year, *Seven Beauties* was released and earned both rave reviews and critical rants, particularly about the films' sensitivity toward its Holocaust subject matter.

After *Seven Beauties*, Lina Wertmüller struggled to make any more critical hits. Her first American film, *The End of the World in Our Usual Bed in a Night Full of Rain*, failed at the box office. But she continued to work in Italy, where she later had some success with her 1992 comedy, *Ciao, Professore!*

Though now in her nineties, Lina Wertmüller continues to direct, commanding her sets with a watchful eye from behind her trademark white-rimmed glasses. Throughout her career, Wertmüller has gained both fierce fans and critics and has been called alternately "essential" and "grotesque." But what is certain is that her divisive and daring work has forever cemented Lina Wertmüller's reputation as one of the most accomplished and controversial Italian directors in history.

✻ THE FEMALE GAZE

Seven Beauties pokes fun at men who see women as sexual objects, yet are also fiercely protective of the women in their own families. Here, Pasqualino expects his sisters to remain virgins and is extremely controlling over their lives. But he believes that all other women desire him sexually and treats them horrifically. There are two sex scenes that are very hard to watch—one involving a brutal rape, the other shot in a pointedly non-erotic fashion. Throughout *Seven Beauties*, Lina Wertmüller does not shy away from showing the audience the ugliest aspects of misogyny.

═ FAST FACTS

★ Lina Wertmüller first met Giancarlo Giannini in 1966, after casting him in *Rita the Mosquito* (which she made under the stage name George H. Brown). The two went on to collaborate many more times, with Giannini starring in several of her movies.

★ For the sequel to *Rita the Mosquito*—called *Don't Sting the Mosquito*—Enrico Job was the art director. Wertmüller and Job fell in love and remained married until his death in 2008.

★ Wertmüller planned for the story of *Seven Beauties* to be told in a linear fashion, but found while editing it that a non-linear approach worked even better.

★ After Wertmüller was nominated for Best Director at the Academy Awards, she remained the only woman to have received that distinction for nearly twenty years until Jane Campion was nominated for *The Piano* in 1994.

Tomris Laffly on *News from Home* (1977)

To be a fresh-off-the-boat immigrant is to dwell in a constant state
of melancholy. To adopt a new country is to split your identity into
two, wondering if it will ever be whole again while your physical
whereabouts clash with the invisible inner voices of family
members and friends from the past. Belgian filmmaker Chantal
Akerman, peerless in the craft of experimental filmmaking that
blurs the divide between documentary and fiction, grabs on to that
imperceptible (and by all means, un-filmable) emotional confusion
and turns it into poetry with *News From Home*. Call it a cinematic
essay, an homage to the New York City sleaze of the '70s, or a
languid portrayal of alienation. *News from Home* is all of that, as
well as an introspectively accurate illustration of being the *other*.
As an immigrant who once stood on the intimidating edges of this
well-oiled metropolitan machine called NYC (hoping to blend in,
and maybe even belong), I find the exquisite pain of loneliness
Akerman sketches out to be brutally exact.

In eighty-six meditative minutes, Akerman navigates the
headspace of one such cultural outcast (herself) via unfussy
methods. Along with cinematographers Jim Asbell and Akerman's
repeat collaborator Babette Mangolte, Akerman (never seen
on camera here) films various streets, avenues, storefronts,
and the graffiti-stamped subway cars of 1976 NYC through
uncompromising long takes, representing the city's estranging
reality in the midst of a historically grim crisis of decay. She
contrasts the eeriness of her purposely dim images with her own
voiceover (sweet, fragile, and knowingly monotonous), reading
a number of letters her loving mother wrote to her between
the years of 1971–73, when Akerman lived across various
neighborhoods of the city.

Not unlike her metronomic, precisely composed masterpiece
Jeanne Dielman, 23 quai du Commerce, 1080 Bruxelles or her
uncanny *Hotel Monterey*, *News from Home* pulls the viewer in

with an initially aimless appearance. But in time, the words of Akerman's over-worried, fretting mother—juxtaposed against (and sometimes drawn out by) the beats of an indifferent urban jungle of roaring engines and rattling trains—form an unmistakable narrative through repetition. Akerman, only twenty-six at the time, lets us observe the "Ford to City: Drop Dead" era of NYC in all its apathetic cruelty, while her caring mother continues to inform her of life's commonplace events: birthday parties, ordinary familial news, her father's health issues and so on.

Each letter inquires about Akerman's health and safety in near-desperation and begs for continued and increased communication. Every now and then, we learn about a twenty-dollar bill or a package of summer clothes her thoughtful mother has sent, while New Yorkers of a bygone period of grit either ignore her camera or intently stare at it with heartbreaking indifference. Among the most quintessential New York films, *News from Home* is an ever-timely statement on an immigrant's involuntary seclusion. Its final images, filmed from the Staten Island Ferry, especially leave a permanent scar, with the ghost of the Twin Towers cutting through a nostalgic mist.

Tomris Laffly is a New York-based film writer and critic. She regularly contributes to Time Out New York, RogerEbert.com, Film Journal International, *and* Film School Rejects, *and has bylines in a number of other outlets, including* Variety *and* Vulture. *She has a special interest in the awards season and covers various film festivals throughout the year.*

Farran Smith Nehme on
Desperately Seeking Susan (1985)

There aren't many genuine screwball comedies made after the
1930s heyday of such films, but Susan Seidelman's sparkling 1985
Desperately Seeking Susan qualifies. It's a romantic comedy whose
real love object is New York, a city built by immigrants, not all of
whom had to come through Ellis Island. Others have come from
the vast strip-mall desert of American suburbs, like unhappy New
Jersey housewife Roberta (Rosanna Arquette), who discovers the
wonders of the city across the Hudson River and thereby her true,
gloriously offbeat self.

Roberta is leading a drab existence in Fort Lee that includes a
loutish husband (Mark Blum). To distract herself, she reads the
personals, especially a series of ads that are "Desperately Seeking
Susan." Roberta gets a vicarious thrill from Susan (Madonna),
who roams the globe but always seems to come back to the lover
posting the ads. In a sudden fit of daring, Roberta decides to go to
Battery Park and witness the latest meeting—but when she does,
she gets hit on the head, develops amnesia, and is then mistaken
for the elusive Susan.

The delightfully complicated plot spins along, with nobody
recognizing anybody and a MacGuffin in the form of ugly but
valuable earrings. In *Desperately Seeking Susan*, the men take
the frequently female roles as objects and bystanders, in a nicely
executed gender-twist that also hearkens back to the great
romantic comedies of the Depression. Roberta's eventual love
interest, Dez (Aidan Quinn), doesn't know what the hell is going on
and spends a lot of time being charmingly bemused.

But while the scenes between Arquette and Quinn are adorably
sexy, Seidelman's greatest accomplishment is capturing this
particular moment in New York. It was dirty and occasionally
frightening, and you can see that in the movie. But it also had the
old Danceteria club, the vintage store Love Saves the Day, and the

Bleecker Street Cinema. The East Village had squatters, artists, and assorted bohemians, not bankers and trust-fund babies.

And then, of course, there's the fact that this remains Madonna's best performance on film. Her Susan is an "indolent, trampy goddess" as Pauline Kael so perfectly put it: the tough-girl accent, the snapping gum, and the larcenous flair as Susan eases toward the door to make a getaway as she tries on a pair of boots she likes.

Who knows—Susan herself was probably something of a Roberta at one point, practicing her wiles on the local lunks and thinking, "There've gotta be bigger fish to fry," until the day she hit Manhattan. That's the New York that *Desperately Seeking Susan* promises, a city where you can find your weirdness level, stick with it, and be accepted for it. One minute, you're a bored housewife wearing Peter Pan collars and button earrings, and the next minute you're sporting a ratty 1950s prom dress and you're doing a magic act with a bird. I love New York, and I love this movie.

**Farran Smith Nehme has written about film and film history for the New York Post, Barron's, *the* Wall Street Journal, Film Comment, Sight & Sound, *and* Criterion. *She writes about classic film at her blog,* Self-Styled Siren. *Her novel,* Missing Reels, *was published in 2014.*

My Brilliant Career

Greater Union Organisation/New South Wales Film Corp, 1979, Australia | Color,
98 minutes, Drama

A headstrong young woman decides to pursue a career over marriage in turn-of-the-century Australia.

Director: Gillian Armstrong

Producer: Margaret Fink

Cinematography: Don McAlpine

Screenplay: Eleanor Witcombe

Starring: Judy Davis ("Sybylla Melvyn"), Sam Neill ("Harry Beecham"), Wendy Hughes ("Aunt Helen")

"I think there is still a misconception that all directors are Cecil B. De Mille types with a loud voice and a whip. Perhaps maybe that's why there's always been some puzzlement about a woman in the director's role."

—*Gillian Armstrong*

"At her best...Gillian Armstrong cuts closer to the core of women's divided yearnings than any other director."

Molly Haskell, film critic and author

When Gillian Armstrong's picture *My Brilliant Career* was released in 1979, it was the first feature-length movie directed by a woman in Australia in almost fifty years. Since it was only her second feature film as a director, this meant a huge amount of pressure for Armstrong.

My Brilliant Career is based on a novel released in 1901 by a woman in her early twenties writing under the name Miles Franklin. The story is set just before the turn of the century in rural Australia, where a headstrong teenage tomboy named Sybylla Melvyn (Judy Davis) is determined to be independent. She wants to be a writer, or a pianist, or an opera singer—something more "brilliant" than her provincial existence on her family's farm, and something outside the societal expectations of marriage.

In the opening narration, Sybylla says, "Here is the story of my career. My brilliant career. I make no apologies for being egotistical, because I am." And she is indeed unapologetic about her focus on a career, much to the frustration of her mother (Julia Blake). Sybylla is sent to her maternal grandmother's house (Aileen Britton) to learn how to be a proper lady, and is soon courted by a potential suitor, the wealthy landowner Harry Beecham (Sam Neill). There is a palpable chemistry between them, and the two fall in love despite Sybylla's insistence that she only wants to be friends. Harry is entranced by her spirited temperament, and she in turn is able to truly be herself around him.

In any other film, this friendship would have turned conveniently into a courtship, with marriage following close behind. But *My Brilliant Career* is not that movie. After Harry proposes marriage, Sybylla slaps him across the face with her riding crop. She rejects his offer, opting instead to continue her own journey of self-discovery—to find out, "What's wrong with the world, and with me, who I am, everything." And, of course, to work on getting that brilliant career.

This is an ending which still feels revolutionary today, let alone in 1901 when the book was published, or even in 1979 when the film was released. The themes of going against the pressures of society, sexism, and classism and being true to yourself are timeless and remain inspiring. By choosing her own path, *My Brilliant Career* has rightly been hailed as a "feminist fairytale"—the story of a woman who saved herself.

The film features a tour-de-force performance from Judy Davis. It is hard to believe that this was only her second role in film, and her first as the lead. Gillian Armstrong fought hard to cast both her and another relative newcomer, Sam Neill. This choice was a perfect one, with Davis' wild hair and intense eyes embodying the determination of a young Sybylla who wants to make her own way in the world. "Don't you love me a little?" asks Harry. "Yes," Sybylla replies, "but I'd destroy you, and I can't do that."

Just like Sybylla, the film is fierce and free-spirited. The landscape of Australia is captured beautifully by cinematographer Don McAlpine, with lush, breathtaking wide-angle shots that almost look like paintings. Armstrong has said she was inspired by 1890s postcards of the Australian bush—a rugged landscape as unforgiving as her protagonist.

Armstrong's pacing keeps the period drama moving, and this energy helped *My Brilliant Career* to become a huge hit around the world. The film played at the 1979 Cannes Film Festival and went on to be nominated for an Academy Award for Best Costume Design. It's now viewed as being a seminal part of the Australian New Wave, a period of unfettered creativity which lasted from 1975 to 1985. This was spawned by the creation of special funding grants allowing filmmakers such as George Miller, Bruce Beresford, Peter Weir, Fred Schepisi, and Gillian Armstrong to make original movies.

"The most sensitive and accomplished woman director in the English-speaking world."

The Washington Post review of *My Brilliant Career*

The new wave reinvigorated the Australian film industry, which had been almost nonexistent during the 1940s, '50s, and '60s. Gillian Armstrong was born in 1950 in Melbourne and did not see an Australian movie on the big screen until she was eighteen. Even when she started studying art and film at a technical college, there was still no movie industry in Australia. After working briefly as an editor, she earned a scholarship to be part of the very first year at the newly created Australian Film and Television School. There were just twelve students in that cohort, including Phillip Noyce and Chris Noonan, who would also go on to be part of the new wave.

Meanwhile, producer Margaret Fink had discovered the little-known book *My Brilliant Career* when it was re-released in 1965. She spent thirteen years trying to get a film version made with various cast and crew. At one point, Fink had considered Roman Polanski as the director, but that all changed when she met Gillian Armstrong. After graduating from film school, Armstrong had started working in the art departments for several movies while making her own short films and documentaries on the side. One of the productions Armstrong worked on was produced by Margaret Fink, who had seen her shorts and knew she had real talent.

With Gillian Armstrong on board to direct, the film started to come together. And although it wasn't intentional, *My Brilliant Career* ended up with a lot of feminine power: alongside Fink and Armstrong, there was also writer Eleanor Witcombe, production designer Luciana Arrighi, and Anna Senior on costumes. The production supervisor, bookkeeper, and accountant were all women, too. But that didn't shield Armstrong from sexism while making the movie. Media reports wondered openly if a woman could survive on set in the heat and dust. During postproduction, editor Nicholas Beauman was often asked if the film was "cutting together," with many people apparently unable to believe that a female director could make a coherent movie.

> "The women that have got through over the years—Jane Campion and Jocelyn Moorhouse and so on—have worked ten times as hard as the men. They're ten times as good as the men. There won't be equality until there are as many mediocre women directors as there are mediocre men."
>
> Gillian Armstrong

Following the success of *My Brilliant Career*, Hollywood came calling for Gillian Armstrong, but she said no. "I got branded as a feminist director, because it was a feminist story," she later explained, "but then that's all I was offered: women achievers—first woman to fly a plane, climb a mountain, ride a camel. I really fought against that labeling. I like to say my characters, male and female, are complicated, and not formulaic, and have depth and layers." She did choose to make another female-driven story, but this was set in Australia and filmed on her own terms—the punk rock musical *Starstruck*, released in 1982.

Armstrong ended up going to Hollywood to make *Mrs Soffel*, released in 1984, and had another huge hit there ten years later with *Little Women*. And though she had started out as a rare woman working in the Australian film industry, she had not realized it was such a struggle as a career for other women. That changed when she saw the statistics for Australian movies directed by women versus men: just 17 percent of feature films in Australia had female directors, despite the percentage of female film school graduates being around 50 percent. That's when Armstrong decided to speak out for change and approached the Australian Directors' Guild to form a committee and support Screen Australia's Gender Matters initiative.

"I used to think, 'I did it, why can't all the other women?' " she said. "There were women's initiatives and film groups, and I was actually a bit snobby about all that. I was like, well, you've just to make a good film. It's about your individual talent. That's why this has been a big change for me to speak out about it."

Gillian Armstrong continues to work for more female representation in Australian film and makes movies across many different genres, all with her own unique wild spirit.

🎬 THE FEMALE GAZE

Sybylla Melvyn chooses a potential career over a husband during the late nineteenth century, a time when marriage was all that women were supposed to aspire to. Even in the late 1970s, this choice was still surprising to filmgoing audiences. *My Brilliant Career* offers no postscript about whether Sybylla was ultimately successful or not—the fact that she is trying is enough.

★ *My Brilliant Career* launched the brilliant careers of director Gillian Armstrong and star Judy Davis and relaunched the career of author Miles Franklin. Davis has since been nominated for two Oscars, for *A Passage to India* and *Husbands and Wives*. Before Armstrong, the last woman to have directed a feature film in Australia was Paulette McDonagh, with *Two Minutes Silence* in 1933. Paulette's two sisters were also filmmakers, Phyllis and Isabel, and the three often worked together throughout the 1920s and 1930s.

★ On *My Brilliant Career*, Armstrong is billed as "Gill Armstrong," her nickname.

★ The company who distributed and partly financed the film was concerned that a female audience would be upset that Sybylla didn't marry Harry. To appease them and make it more ambiguous, Armstrong added the line, "I'm so near loving you."

★ Armstrong's experience working in art departments is evident in the attention to detail in the sets and props used. Her production designer, Luciana Arrighi, went on to work with James Ivory and Ismail Merchant, and won an Oscar for her work on *Howards End*.

Amy Nicholson on *The Decline Of Western Civilization I & II* (1981 & 1988)

"It's not bullshit," says a teen punk in the first minute of Penelope Spheeris' monumental music doc franchise. It sure wasn't. Spheeris, a single mom with the forged-by-fire heart-strength to empathize with misfits, addicts, and creeps, steadily captured both the violence of a live Germs show—after they'd been blacklisted from every club in LA—and the intimate moments afterwards in singer Darby Crash's *Spiderman* sticker-covered apartment where he and his girlfriend got high and giggled about finding a dead body. *The Decline of Western Civilization* is so gritty it feels like a wad of gum Spheeris peeled off the street. It proved Spheeris was a fearless nonfiction filmmaker. By the time the documentary premiered in 1981, Crash was dead, too, and LAPD police chief Daryl Gates was so spooked by the spikey-haired crowds on Hollywood Boulevard, he tried to ban the film.

Just one more circus in Spheeris' wild life. She was literally born in a traveling carnival, where she had a front row seat to how oddballs create a family. Her father was the strong man, and when Spheeris was seven, he was murdered defending a black man from a racist attack. Spheeris grew up bold, brilliant, open-minded, and unflappable, perhaps the only director in Hollywood who was voted her high school's Most Likely to Succeed and had a Big Gulp full of urine dumped on her head at an Ozzy Osbourne show.

MTV launched one month after that first flick rampaged across screens. Eight years later, it had radically reshaped the LA scene. Crash had been terrified people would think he wanted to be a rock star. Back then, "rock star" was an insult. Now, rock stardom was the goal—and Spheeris was ready for a sequel: *The Decline of Western Civilization Part II: The Metal Years*. Music had changed, so her style did, too. *Decline Part II* is colorful, almost comic. Instead lording over chaos, her subjects worship cash, ambition, and their own cocks, boasting about all the groupies they've banged.

When Spheeris invited them to choose where they wanted to be photographed, Gene Simmons picked a lingerie store; Paul Stanley, a bed stuffed with babes. The girls were half-naked. The guys' egos were totally exposed. Her camera coolly absorbs their braggadocio. Dudes might think they were in charge. But she was the one in the editing room.

"I was just preserving it for history to let people know that that was a cool way to be back in 1987," Spheeris later told Pitchfork. Afterward, Spheeris attempted to go mainstream with big studio comedies like *Wayne's World* and *The Beverly Hillbillies*, but snuck back to the streets in the last years of the '90s to shoot a third *Decline* film about homeless kids. "I'm not good at selling out," she admitted. "It's the punk rocker in me." Rock on, Penelope. Rock on.

Amy Nicholson is a film writer and critic for **Variety**, **The Guardian**, *and the* **Washington Post***, and is the host of the movie podcasts* **The Canon** *and* **Unspooled***. Her first book,* **Tom Cruise: Anatomy of an Actor***, was published by Cahiers du Cinema.*

Miri Jedeikin on *Big* (1988)

When Penny Marshall's heartwarming comedy *Big* first hit theaters in 1988, it was hardly groundbreaking. A handful of films in the "age-change" comedy subcategory had already been released, to mixed results. *Big*, on the other hand, was a breakout hit, appealing to both crowds and critics alike.

When we first meet our protagonist Josh, he's a typical tween with a budding interest in girls who is still comfortably steeped in the innocence of childhood. After he's publicly embarrassed by the fact that he's too small to get on a roller coaster at the town fair, he discovers the dusty, dimly lit wish granting machine known as Zoltar. He pops a coin into the slot and makes his wish, which, understandably, is to be big. As it turns out, his wish is granted. Literally. Given that Josh is now the size of a grown man and unrecognizable even to his own mom, he heads to nearby New York City and gets a job at a toy company, which is when the fun really begins.

Whether it's watching Hanks show up to a company soirée decked out in a sparkling, rhinestone-encrusted white tux with tails, or grinning from ear to ear as he and Robert Loggia dance their way through an iconic rendition of "Heart and Soul" on a giant piano, *Big* is in equal measures wistful and warmly hilarious. And it stands the test of time. Thirty years after its release, it remains one of the world's most beloved and unique coming-of-age stories on film.

As a kid, *Big* filled me with a sense of wonder and excitement. It offered a special kind of magic, grounded in the reality of that heightened moment just before childhood ends, but when adulthood is still something mysterious and out of reach. To this day it presents an innocent, unabashedly buoyant world in which anything is possible. It offers a passing but profound glimpse into a "what-if" scenario that reminds us all to love where we are, but to keep our hearts and minds open and full of hope.

Many years after I first saw the film, I learned that with *Big*, Penny Marshall had made history. She became the first woman to direct a film that would go on to make more than 100 million dollars at the box office. That she did this on only her second film as a director is even more impressive. In 1988, Marshall showed the traditionally male-dominated film industry that women were not only capable of directing good films, but profitable ones too.

Miri Jedeikin is a film reporter, critic, and Masters of Clinical Psychology candidate. She lives in Los Angeles, CA, and hails from Montreal, Québec, the province that is also home to the almighty poutine.

Tiffany Vazquez on *Paris Is Burning* (1991)

Try to imagine being a gay man or a trans woman of color in 1987 New York City. Mainstream culture does not accept you. You can't walk into corporate America expecting a welcoming smile, let alone a job, so your employment options are limited and undesirable at best. Your family has most likely disowned you for being who you are. Finally, you are losing all of your friends and significant others to a disease your own government doesn't understand or is unwilling to find a cure for. You are an outcast; an unwanted member of society. How do you channel this overwhelming pain? Where can you go not just to survive, but to live? You show off and show out at the ball.

Paris Is Burning, the 1991 documentary by Jennie Livingston, details ball culture in the LGBTQIA community in late 1980s NYC. The title of this film comes from an annual ball hosted by drag performer Paris DuPree, who is also credited as one of the inventors of voguing. Besides explaining all the details of ballroom culture, *Paris Is Burning* highlights the lives of members of the LGBTQIA community, some of whom are now praised as trailblazers in culture and activism. This film is important for many reasons. One theme is that of "realness" and identity. Balls are competitions comprised of categories. Whoever can successfully transform themselves into the archetype of said category wins. At face value, this may all sound like shallow competition, but this was the only safe space where members of this community could pull off being whatever they wanted to be, whether that was a character on *Dynasty*, a member of our country's armed forces, or a "Wall Street executive." Within the walls of the ballroom, one could finally become a wealthy socialite or a high fashion model with no judgment, and no system designed to tell you "no." It is unspeakably important to be able to have a safe space for marginalized people to express themselves and support each other. But most importantly, this was a space for trans men and women to be valued and supported as real men and women—a conversation that is still happening today.

Gay and trans black and latinx youth who were oppressed on every sociopolitical and economic level channeled their talent and ingenuity into a culture that has been consistently borrowed but even more often stolen. I still marvel at the excellence marginalized people have created despite how every systemic force was not designed with them in mind. This is how hip-hop was created. More current examples of marginalized people leading cultural trends can be found in the best content coming from Vine, Twitter, and Instagram. Ballroom culture is a huge result of this same ingenuity—this thirst for the socially, politically, and economically oppressed to have safe spaces. These are the main figures in *Paris Is Burning*, and we should recognize them as major cultural contributors: Paris DuPree, Angie Xtravaganza, Venus Xtravaganza, Willi Ninja, Octavia St. Laurent, Dorian Corey, Pepper Labeija, Sol Pendavis, and many more. Without these figures, neither RuPaul, Madonna's whole *Blonde Ambition* tour, nor the incredible breakout television series *Pose* would have existed.

Film is a reflection of the human experience, which is why watching films like *Paris Is Burning* is important. The subjects of this film have not always been respected as human beings simply because of their lifestyle. This documentary lets us into the world of talented men and women and their hopes, dreams, desires, and love. And nearly all of them paid for their right to equality with their lives. I had a cousin who died from AIDS in the 1990s, and he was part of this culture. This film makes me feel closer to him, and if that's not the power of art, I don't know what is.

Tiffany Vazquez is the Senior Content Manager of Film at GIPHY. Before GIPHY, she worked at the Film Society of Lincoln Center and earned two Masters degrees, one in Cinema Studies from NYU and the other in International Communications from St. John's University. She obviously likes film a lot, and she has appeared on Turner Classic Movies as a Saturday Daytime host.

Daughters of the Dust

American Playhouse, 1991, USA | Color, 112 minutes, Drama

Set at the beginning of the twentieth century, an African American family plans to move from their island home to the mainland.

Director: Julie Dash

Producers: Julie Dash and Arthur Jafa

Cinematography: Arthur Jafa

Screenplay: Julie Dash

Starring: Cora Lee Day ("Nana Peazant"), Alva Rogers ("Eula Peazant"), Adisa Anderson ("Eli Peazant"), Barbara-O ("Yellow Mary"), Trula Hoosier ("Trula"), Kai-Lynn Warren ("The Unborn Child")

"I decided to let the story unravel itself in a way in which an African griot would tell the story, since that's part of our tradition. So the story kind of unfolds throughout this day and a half in various vignettes. It unfolds, comes back, it unfolds and it comes back."

—*Julie Dash*

It's difficult to accurately describe the experience of watching *Daughters of the Dust* by Julie Dash. In some ways it is more akin to inhabiting a dream or hearing a collection of somebody else's memories than it is to watching a movie.

Daughters of the Dust is a richly crafted tone poem: quietly absorbing, completely affecting, and hard to shake. The narrative is not told in a linear structure. Instead, the film has been crafted to feel like a long-told tale in the oral African American tradition. The story involves a family of Gullah-Geeches, the Peazant family. They are patois-speaking descendants of slaves who live on the Sea Islands off the coast of Georgia and South Carolina. The year is 1902, and the family is getting ready to migrate north to the mainland, leaving their home behind.

The film begins with two women from the Peazant family returning to the island from the mainland, bringing guests in tow. Viola (Cheryl Lynn Bruce) arrives from Philadelphia with a photographer (Tommy Redmond Hicks) who wants to document the isolated group. "Yellow Mary" Peazant (Barbara-O) arrives with a young woman, Trula (Trula Hoosier), who some suspect of being Yellow Mary's lover. They have come to ready the group for their relocation, though not all of the members of the family want to leave.

The head of this matriarchal family is perfectly happy to stay where she is with the "old souls" on the island. Great-grandmother Nana Peazant (Cora Lee Day) is the living embodiment of their cultural history and memories who tells stories of their ancestry and carries mementos with her at all times. Nana is superstitious, and her traditional beliefs are not welcomed by some of the younger members, who view it almost as a kind of paganism.

This story is narrated by Nana and an Unborn Child (Kai-Lynn Warren) who is racing to join her parents, Eula (Alva Rogers) and Eli (Adisa Anderson), before it is too late. Eula and Eli are dealing with a massive amount of grief after Eula is raped by a white man. Among the other stories woven into the plot, there's Iona (Bahni Turpin), who falls in love with a Cherokee man living on the island, and Bilal Muhammad (Umer Abdurrahman), an elder who remembers the slave ships that came to the island. All of this unfolds over the last day and a half on the island for the Peazant family, culminating with their boarding of the boat.

Daughters of the Dust has been called "visual poetry," which feels like an apt description. There are dreamlike images of women in

> "People tell each other about it. 'I've seen it three times,' a woman told me the other night at the Film Center. 'I get something new out of it every time.' It is all a matter of notes and moods, music and tones of voice, atmosphere and deep feeling. If Dash had assigned every character a role in a conventional plot, this would have been just another movie—maybe a good one, but nothing new. Instead, somehow she makes this many stories about many families, and through it we understand how African American families persisted against slavery and tried to be true to their memories."
>
> Roger Ebert

flowing white dresses on the beach and shots of sunlight filtered through haze-filled air. Julie Dash and cinematographer Arthur Jafa stage scenes with the family in a series of tableaux, where the women are arranged in a way suggestive of formal paintings. There is also a great deal of African symbolism in the film. Colors such as indigo are also used as a nod to the past—the hands of some of the older members of the community are stained dark blue, indicating that they were former slaves of indigo plantations. Sound also plays a major role, with the score combining African drums and '90s synthesizers. It all feels quite magical, especially with the lyrical narration from the two central characters—the youngest and oldest members of the family.

The past and the future are threaded all the way through *Daughters of the Dust*. Women are the heads of this family, the carriers of belief and African tradition. They tell stories that are a patchwork of memories and ancestral tales, such as how the Igbo people walked on water to escape slavery and return to Africa. The women demonstrate ancient rituals and traditional cooking, and the family members speak a mixture of English, French, and the Gullah (or Geechee) language. There are times when the dialect is difficult to follow, but the emotion behind the words is easy to translate. Julie Dash said later that she "wanted to take the African American experience and rephrase it in such a way that whether or not you understood the film on the first screening, the visuals would be so haunting it would break through with a freshness about what we already know."

There's a particularly powerful scene toward the end of the film when Eula lets loose in a fierce monologue. She displays through her emotions how the sorrow of the past continues to wound the present. And even though the film is set in 1902, it feels as if she is talking about the present day.

Daughters of the Dust is now over twenty-five years old, but the genesis of the idea came long before that. In 1975, Julie Dash decided she wanted to tell a story about black women at the

beginning of the century. She decided to focus on the Sea Islands because they "are sacred ground; they represent our Ellis Island." Her father came from a Gullah background, and Dash was eager to learn more. Armed with this idea, Dash spent years doing research and learning about the descendants of slaves, their culture, language, and rituals. Once she had the necessary financing and had cast her actors, they spent months in pre-production learning the Gullah language.

This is Julie Dash's first and only feature film to date. She was born in 1952 in New York and later studied film at several institutions. Dash earned a film degree from City College of New York and then went to the American Film Institute's Conservatory in Los Angeles to study screenwriting. But she truly hit her creative stride when she attended UCLA's School of Theater, Film and Television. There she found herself part of a diverse class, alongside many other students of color. Together they decided to work together to create the kind of cinema that was more reflective of their lives and backgrounds. Later, this class was dubbed "the LA Rebellion," and their work has since been studied and exhibited in museums.

Daughters of the Dust premiered at the 1991 Sundance Film Festival, where it won the Best Cinematography award, and went on to play in arthouse theaters. The theatrical release was small but attracted positive attention, with critics such as Roger Ebert writing favorably about it. Afterwards, however, Julie Dash wasn't given many opportunities to make another feature film. She worked steadily—directing television shows, writing a novel, working in commercials, teaching at universities—all the while pitching ideas to all the movie studios, both large and small. But the doors remained closed to her, even though *Daughters of the Dust* was entered into the Library of Congress's National Film Registry in 2004 and remains a favorite among film lovers.

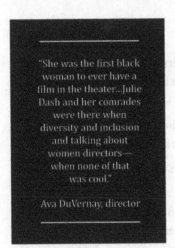

"She was the first black woman to ever have a film in the theater...Julie Dash and her comrades were there when diversity and inclusion and talking about women directors—when none of that was cool."

Ava DuVernay, director

And then along came Beyoncé. In 2016, *Daughters of the Dust* experienced a resurgence in popularity and gained major exposure when it was noted that parts of the visuals for Beyoncé's album *Lemonade* seemed to be influenced by the film. Audiences noted the similarities in her diffused images of black women wearing white dresses on the beach and in the symbolism and tableaux arrangements. On the night the singer released *Lemonade*, *Daughters of the Dust* began trending on social media. Beyoncé has not publicly acknowledged the film as her inspiration, but the speculation was enough to make her massive fan base curious about it. Fortuitously, at the time, Julie Dash was just about to re-release her film, complete with a new digital restoration.

And so audiences are finally discovering the groundbreaking work of pioneer Julie Dash. Meanwhile, she continues to work as a director, with Ava DuVernay and Oprah Winfrey recently hiring her to direct several episodes of their television show *Queen Sugar*.

✹ THE FEMALE GAZE

Julie Dash's film is a celebration of African American womanhood, of motherhood, and of heritage. The structure of the Peazant family is matriarchal, with the women acting as the keepers of tradition and storytelling. She repeatedly poses the family of women in striking tableaux, making them appear as living works of art.

≡ FAST FACTS

- ★ *Daughters of the Dust* was the first full-length movie given a theatrical release that was written and directed by an African American woman.

- ★ Dash worked for a decade conducting research for *Daughters of the Dust* with funding from a grant.

- ★ After months of pre-production, the film was shot over three weeks on a budget of $800,000.

- ★ Much of the funding for the film came from PBS' *American Playhouse*, which insisted on theatrical distribution rather than a run on television.

- ★ The visuals for Beyoncé's *Lemonade* album feature many references to *Daughters of the Dust*; and though she has never publicly credited it as an influence, the similarities between the two are undeniable.

Point Break

Largo Entertainment, 1991, USA | Color, 120 minutes, Drama/Action

A rookie FBI agent tries to capture a group of criminals responsible for a string of bank robberies.

Director: Kathryn Bigelow

Producers: James Cameron, Peter Abrams, Robert L. Levy

Cinematography: Donald Peterman

Screenplay: W. Peter Iliff, Rick King

Starring: Keanu Reeves ("Johnny Utah"), Patrick Swayze ("Bodhi"), Gary Busey ("Angelo Pappas"), Lori Petty ("Tyler")

"Thrill-seeking adrenaline addicts have always fascinated me. The idea seems to be that it's not until you risk your humanness that you feel most human. Not until you risk all awareness do you gain awareness."

—Kathryn Bigelow

There are many ways to approach the films of Kathryn Bigelow. We could start right at the beginning with *The Loveless*, starring Willem Dafoe as a member of a motorcycle gang. Or we might look at what came after, the vampire film *Near Dark*. Or we can head straight to *The Hurt Locker*, the war movie that made Bigelow the first (and to date, the only) woman to win the Academy Award for Best Director. She is a filmmaker who has made a career from giving a feminine twist to genres long thought to be exclusively the preserve of men. For that reason, it's especially interesting to look at her work through the macho '90s action cult classic *Point Break*, starring Keanu Reeves and Patrick Swayze.

The film's plot is fairly ridiculous but also a lot of fun. Reeves plays Johnny Utah, a former football hero who joins the FBI following a knee injury. As a new recruit, he is partnered with veteran agent Angelo Pappas (Gary Busey) and saddled with a seemingly impossible case—to capture the criminals behind a string of recent bank robberies. This gang leaves little trace behind, and they are known as the "ex-Presidents" because each wears the mask of a former US President: Ronald Reagan, Richard Nixon, Jimmy Carter, and Lyndon B. Johnson. (In a nice touch, after a robbery the Nixon character yells, "I am not a crook!")

The only leads that Utah and Pappas have to go on are a grainy piece of video footage (showing one of the criminals mooning the camera) and a strand of hair. Because the hair contains the same pollutants as a local beach, and the exposed buttocks feature a stark tan line, Utah and Pappas guess that the criminals must be surfers. It's decided that Utah should go undercover to find out the truth.

This is how Utah meets Tyler (Lori Petty), a surfer girl who reluctantly agrees to teach him how to surf. Through Tyler, Utah encounters Bodhi (Patrick Swayze) and his surfing buddies. The name Bodhi, Tyler explains, is short for "Bodhisattva," a Buddhist term for an enlightened being who has delayed reaching nirvana in order to save others. It's an apt name for Bodhi, who sees himself as an enlightened soul—albeit one who robs banks and surfs big waves as a way to fight the system. "We stand for something," he tells Utah earnestly. "To those dead souls inching along the freeways in their metal coffins, we show them that the human spirit is still alive."

Bodhi's big dream is to surf an impossible wave brought about by an upcoming record storm. Tyler thinks, "Big wave riding is for macho assholes with a death wish." But to Bodhi, it represents a sort of nirvana—the melding of man and the environment. "If you want the ultimate," he says, "you gotta be willing to pay the ultimate price. No sacrifice to die doing what you love."

Technically, Bodhi is the villain of the film. Patrick Swayze and Kathryn Bigelow make him so enticing, however, that it's no wonder Johnny Utah can't resist being around him. This moral ambiguity is one of the ways in which *Point Break* veers away from the formulaic action films that came before it. Following the Vietnam War, many of the heroes of 1980s Hollywood became muscle-bound men, boosting morale by literally embodying the strength and power of the nation. These characters were armies of one with a clear sense of right and wrong, shooting or punching their way through the ranks of bad guys. Actors such as Sylvester Stallone, Arnold Schwarzenegger, and Chuck Norris became hugely popular during this period, reshaping the popular idea of masculinity.

On paper, the character of Johnny Utah in *Point Break* seems cut from the same cloth: an all-American football hero who joins law enforcement. But instead of casting an overly masculine actor, Kathryn Bigelow was determined to hire Keanu Reeves. This was long before *Speed*, *The Matrix*, or his role punching through bad guys in *John Wick*; at the time, Reeves was known only for playing sensitive, innocent characters.

In one interview, executive producer James Cameron remembered how hard Kathryn Bigelow fought to get Reeves approved. "We had this meeting where the Fox executives were going, 'Keanu Reeves in an action film? Based on what? *Bill & Ted's Excellent Adventure*?' They were being so insulting. But she insisted he could be an action star. I didn't see it either, frankly. I supported her in the meeting, but when we walked out, I was going, 'Based on what?' But she worked on his wardrobe, she showed him how to walk, she made him work out. She was his Olympic coach. He should send her a bottle of champagne every year to thank her."

Patrick Swayze was the bigger name of the two, having played both sensitive lovers in *Dirty Dancing* and *Ghost* and action heroes in *Road House* and *Red Dawn*. But Swayze was attracted to *Point Break* because he could see from the beginning that it would be something different. "Rarely do you get a film about two guys that isn't just slap-ass, macho, jokey crap," he said in an interview. "And the dynamics were very interesting because I wanted to play it like a love story between two men, which is exactly how it does play."

The idea of a macho bond is one that is celebrated in many Hollywood action films, with the importance of male "buddy" relationships heavily romanticized. The masculine body is typically fetishized, shown in close-ups and slow motion as men perform athletic acts. One such example is the oiled-up volleyball scene in *Top Gun*, which was released just a few years earlier. In *Point Break*, Bigelow almost pokes fun at cinema's fascination with bromance, using lines of dialogue which seem right on the edge of parody. "I know you want me so bad it's like acid in your mouth," Bodhi says to Utah.

Gender identity is also something Bigelow plays with. Bodhi has long, blonde hair, while Tyler—both in her name and her short black hair—is purposely androgynous. In one scene shot from above, Utah and Tyler lie in bed together, looking almost like twins. By the end of the film, Tyler is reduced to handcuffs and white silky pajamas—a feminized object left waiting while her two ex-boyfriends figure themselves out.

With *Point Break*, Kathryn Bigelow became a rare female director succeeding in an area of Hollywood to which not many women had previously been allowed access. Not only could she stage an exciting, memorable, cinematic foot-chase, she was equally interested in exploring the existential reasons that drive men to seek dangerous thrills.

Needless to say, Bigelow was not the first choice to direct. She got her hands on the project only after the original director Ridley Scott left and the production had lagged for years. James Cameron was eager to produce the film and brought it to her attention. The two were married at the time, and while Cameron was the bigger name—known for *The Terminator*, *The Abyss*, and *Aliens*—Kathryn Bigelow had by then established herself as an interesting filmmaker in the genre space.

> "Film critics wrongly called Kathryn Bigelow's *Point Break* 'a dose of macho claptrap' (*Sight & Sound*) and 'intellectually shallow' (*The Guardian*). But *Point Break* is a rare, wondrous thing: a fun, smart, sincere action film. It's a Western, a heist film, a buddy film unafraid of its homoerotic undertones—and overtones. It revolutionized the action genre."
>
> Priscilla Page, *Birth.Movies.Death.*

Bigelow was born in California in 1951 to a father who liked to draw cartoons in his spare time. She inherited his artistic spirit, studying painting after graduating from high school first at the San Francisco Art Institute and then at the Whitney Museum of Art in New York. After realizing the limitations of painting in terms of its ability to explore issues with a broad audience, Kathryn Bigelow decided to switch to film. Her first short came out in 1978. Called *The Set-Up*, its study of violence between two men does indeed "set up" the tone of Bigelow's work to come. A year later, she attended Columbia University and graduated with a master's degree in film theory and criticism.

Her debut feature in 1981 was *The Loveless*, inspired by the 1953 classic film, *The Wild Ones*. Set in the late 1950s, the two films share a motorcycle gang and a complicated guy at the center of the story—but instead of Marlon Brando, *The Loveless* stars a young Willem Dafoe. This film brought Bigelow enough success to direct a second feature six years later. *Near Dark* was a vampire drama which played with the idea of gender roles by featuring a woman as the blood-thirsty killer and a man as the innocent victim. Bigelow experimented further with this idea in *Blue Steel*, her first major studio production, which was released in 1990. Jamie Lee Curtis starred in the type of role usually reserved for a male actor, playing a rookie New York police officer who falls for a murderer.

When *Point Break* was released a year later, it was met with lackluster box office returns and a few scathing reviews. But soon afterwards the film started to find a cult audience. Decades later, it stands out as a particularly influential action film, inspiring everything from a scene in *Hot Fuzz* to a 2015 remake to the entire *The Fast and The Furious* franchise.

Following *Point Break*, Bigelow went on to direct a series of action thrillers. There was *Strange Days* from 1995 starring Ralph Fiennes, *The Weight of Water* in 2000 with Sean Penn, and *K-19: The Widowmaker* in 2002 with Harrison Ford and Liam Neeson. In between, Bigelow directed television, and it was on a TV project called *The Inside* that she met her most important collaborator, Mark Boal.

Boal was a journalist whose articles had been adapted into television specials and films. He'd spent time embedded with bomb squads during the Iraq War, and this was what interested Bigelow. The two teamed up to write *The Hurt Locker*, which was released in 2008. Their script drew on Boal's experiences, focusing on the men who make up an Army Explosive Disposal Unit, some of whom become addicted to the danger involved.

The Hurt Locker became Kathryn Bigelow's most well-received movie of her career to that point, winning six Academy Awards and making history when Bigelow became the first woman in the eighty-two years of the Oscars to take home the Best Director statue. Somewhat ironically, she was chosen for the award over her former producer and ex-husband James Cameron, who was nominated that year for *Avatar*.

Bigelow and Boal reunited for another war thriller—2012's *Zero Dark Thirty*, starring Jessica Chastain as a CIA agent working to find and kill the terrorist Osama Bin Laden. In 2017, the two teamed up again to make *Detroit*, a tense drama set during the 1967 riots in Detroit, when a group of racist police officers abused their power. Though set in the past, the film was timely, following a string of reports about racially charged police brutality.

Throughout her impressive career, Kathryn Bigelow has eschewed the idea of being labeled a "female" filmmaker, insisting her work is not about her gender. Criticism of her films point to the way they sometimes sideline female characters or reinforce stereotypes. But simply by virtue of being a woman who makes the sort of films she does, Bigelow represents a rare example of a female filmmaker focusing on male subcultures, and by so doing, hopefully paving the way for a future where women can tell male stories, female stories—or any kind of stories they want.

✽ THE FEMALE GAZE

With *Point Break*, Kathryn Bigelow made many choices which gave an interesting twist to what could have otherwise been a forgettable action thriller. We can see this in the casting of Keanu Reeves, who gave a layer of sensitivity to an otherwise standard American hero character. Similarly, Patrick Swayze's Bodhi is portrayed as a likable villain who has an undeniable chemistry with Utah. And in stark contrast to Bodhi with his long blonde hair, the female love interest, Tyler, is somewhat androgynous. Tyler is visibly more capable than Utah for most of the film, and the fact that as soon as she takes on a more "feminine" appearance she is relegated to the background seems to be making a point about the way women are treated in action films.

≡ FAST FACTS

★ The original title for *Point Break* was *Johnny Utah*, and then it was changed to *Riders on the Storm* for most of its shooting. The idea for the story came from Rick King, who dreamt it up while lying on the beach. He then hired W. Peter Iliff, a waiter at the time, as its writer. Iliff followed this success with screenplays for *Patriot Games* and *Varsity Blues*.

★ Kathryn Bigelow and James Cameron made their own rewrites of the script before shooting but were not able to get credit from the Writers Guild.

★ At various points in pre-production before Kathryn Bigelow came on as director, both Charlie Sheen and Matthew Broderick were signed to play Johnny Utah. Patrick Swayze also auditioned for the role of Utah, but was eventually cast as Bodhi.

★ To prepare for the role, Keanu Reeves spent time with real FBI agents, learned how to fire guns with the Los Angeles Police Department, trained with football coaches from the University of California Los Angeles team, and learned to surf.

★ Patrick Swayze was an experienced skydiver who performed his own stunts for the movie, jumping over fifty times.

★ To capture the foot-chase, Bigelow's camera crew used a special Steadicam device called a "Pogo Cam" which allowed the operators to run behind the actors while filming.

★ For one part of the foot-chase, stunt double Scott Wilder wears the Ronald Reagan mask to fill in for Swayze, who had to leave the set for a *Ghost* press tour in Europe.

Orlando

Adventure Pictures, 1992, UK | Color, 93 minutes, Comedy/Drama

The journey of an English aristocrat over 400 years, as a man and then as a woman.

Director: Sally Potter

Producer: Christopher Sheppard

Cinematography: Aleksei Rodionov

Screenplay: Sally Potter, based on a novel by Virginia Woolf

Starring: Tilda Swinton ("Orlando"), Billy Zane ("Shelmerdine"), Quentin Crisp ("Queen Elizabeth I"), Lothaire Bluteau ("The Khan")

"It's the first film that I've made that I'm pleased with, the first time in my filmmaking life when I've begun to feel a sense of mastery of the form... It makes me remember why I am on earth."

—Sally Potter

"Do not fade. Do not wither. Do not grow old." These are the words spoken to Lord Orlando (Tilda Swinton) by Queen Elizabeth I (Quentin Crisp), the words that begin an epic, magical journey through 400 years of English history following Orlando, who indeed never fades, never withers, and never grows old. He merely changes gender halfway through.

Orlando begins life as a he, a young aristocrat living with his parents in late sixteenth-century England. He becomes a favorite of Queen Elizabeth I, who gives him permission to own his family's sprawling estate. Orlando longs to be a poet but is ridiculed for this dream. Skipping forward to the seventeenth century, Orlando falls for a beautiful Russian princess (Charlotte Valandrey) during a lavish dinner party held on the frozen River Thames before spending a decade as a British ambassador at the court of the Khan (Lothaire Bluteau) in the Middle East.

It is here that Orlando wakes up one day to find that he has turned into a she. This moment comes after the male Orlando balks at the idea of killing others in war. The female Orlando wakes up and looks first into the mirror at her new body, and then at the camera, saying, "Same person, no difference at all. Just a different sex."

But there is a difference in the way she is treated. Though Orlando essentially feels like the same person, she spends the eighteenth century fighting to keep her house. As a woman, she is not entitled to own an estate, and as someone who has been around for two hundred years, she is legally dead. "You are a female. It amounts to the same thing," Orlando is told. Her writing is not taken seriously by the great literary figures, and she grows bored in the company of Alexander Pope and Joseph Addison.

In the nineteenth century, she explores sex with handsome American adventurer Shelmerdine (Billy Zane), who breezes in and out of her life, leaving Orlando pregnant with a daughter. By the twentieth century, the daughter is still young, and Orlando is seen zipping through London on a motorcycle, being asked to do rewrites on a book based on her life.

"In many ways, *Orlando* helped to bring art back to the art house, so that today's quality film landscape doesn't just include gritty, low-budget dramas of social import but movies that mix high art and high camp in challenging and pleasurable ways. You can see the impeccably designed vignettes of Orlando in Wes Anderson's filmed dioramas, or in Sofia Coppola's new-wave Marie Antoinette."

Dan Kois,
Slate magazine

The real basis for the story is Virginia Woolf's novel of the same name published in 1928—a time when women were beginning to rise up and question why their gender precluded them from having certain rights, such as voting. This book has been called "the longest and most charming love letter in literature," because both its inspiration and the male-female character of Orlando came from Woolf's admiration for a bisexual aristocrat named Vita Sackville-West. Like the fictional character, Vita was an aspiring writer who was not afforded the kind of reverence she desired. Similarly, Woolf's book was dismissed upon its release, with critics claiming it was "not one of her more serious works."

But the book, like the film, explores many interesting and timeless themes over the course of its sprawling story: literature, the pursuit of writing as art, English history, royalty, fashion, war— and of course, gender identity. Through the character of Orlando, the audience is given permission to wonder what life might be like as the other sex or during another era. The role of women changes throughout the decades, yet much unfortunately remains the same, with a male publisher giving present-day Orlando notes on her own story.

As a man, Orlando enjoys many privileges that are later taken away when Orlando is a woman, but beneath lies the same person. Director Sally Potter explained, "I am trying to restore to people that sense of themselves which has nothing to do with gender, time, or circumstance;" in other words, the true essence of ourselves.

The idea of playing with gender, essence, and identity is also reflected in the choice of casting. Alongside the magnificent Tilda Swinton as the omni-sex Orlando, Quentin Crisp plays Queen Elizabeth I with wonderful tongue-in-cheek wit, and writer Heathcote Williams juggles dual roles as a poet in one era and a book publisher in another.

When *Orlando* was released in the early 1990s, Tilda Swinton wasn't yet known outside her native England. She began her career working with British filmmaker and gay activist Derek Jarman, with roles in *Caravaggio*, *The Last of England*, and *Edward II*. Interestingly, just before playing the gender-bending Orlando, Tilda starred in John Maybury's *Man to Man*, as a woman who assumes her husband's identity. Even before that role, Sally Potter knew she wanted Swinton for the lead role in *Orlando*, and talked to Swinton about it before financing was secured. And Swinton is extraordinary as this intelligent, curious character—her serene, androgynous face is captivating as she talks directly to the camera, inviting the audience to come with her on this adventure.

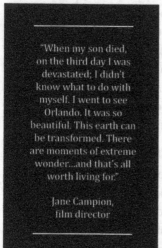

"When my son died, on the third day I was devastated; I didn't know what to do with myself. I went to see Orlando. It was so beautiful. This earth can be transformed. There are moments of extreme wonder...and that's all worth living for."

Jane Campion, film director

Visually, *Orlando* is breathtaking. The costumes Swinton wears are sumptuous and the settings are beautiful—creating a whirlwind of color and movement as Orlando leaps and bounds through time, all elegantly directed by Sally Potter. It's difficult to believe she was able to do so much on such a limited budget. After fighting for many years, Potter ended up with only a small portion of the money she needed, even after agreeing to coproduce with companies from Russia, France, Italy, and Holland. When production began, she had just ten weeks to shoot four hundred years of time across three continents.

Sally Potter had read Virginia Woolf's book as a teenager and even back then thought it should be made into a film. She was born into an artistic family in London in 1949 and made her first 8mm film at just fourteen years old. By sixteen, Potter had decided to be a film director while also studying dance and choreography, her other artistic passion. Her first films were a series of shorts made in the late 1960s and early '70s in which she experimented with form. *Play* from 1970 showed children playing in the street on two side-by-side screens, and *Thriller*, released in 1979, was a feminist take on the heroine of *La Bohème*.

It was *Thriller* which earned Potter enough attention to be able to make a feature film. The result was a production now cited as one of the best feminist films ever made. Using an all-female cast and crew, *The Gold Diggers* examined the relationship between money, power, and fame. Unfortunately, the film itself didn't attract either money or fame and was not well received on its release in 1983. Though it eventually found a cult audience, the criticism made it much harder for Potter to find funding for her next project.

"The effect of *The Gold Diggers* was to throw me into the wilderness," Sally Potter explained in an interview. "It became absolutely impossible to raise money. I made a short film called *London Story* as a test...and I couldn't even raise money for that without using my own credit card. After all that, I think it was actually because of the inherent difficulty that I decided to take on something as ambitious as adapting Virginia Woolf's book, a process that took seven years of writing and rewriting."

"[*Orlando* is] Ms. Potter's triumph. With the firmest but lightest of touches, she has spun gossamer."

Vincent Canby,
The New York Times

A decade later, Sally Potter finally released *Orlando*, her second feature, which became her first mainstream hit. The film won numerous awards at film festivals and went on to be nominated for two Academy Awards for Costume and Set Design. After that first success for Potter, more followed. *The Tango Lesson* from 1997 was a personal film which looked at the imbalance of power between men and women and starred Potter as a film director who learns how to tango. Later *Ginger and Rosa*, released in 2012, took a complex look at female relationships in 1960s London.

During her impressive career, Sally Potter has made both commercial hits and experimental short films; she has garnered mainstream success as well as underground cult status. Throughout it all, she has maintained her own unique artistic spirit. Her ambitious work combines her love of cinema writing, dance, music, and art as tools to explore important themes of gender, identity, performance, and the plight of women throughout the ages.

🎥 THE FEMALE GAZE

Through the character of Orlando, Sally Potter explores the way the genders are treated differently. While the male version of Orlando espouses—from his privileged vantage point—a view that the sexes are essentially the same, the female Orlando soon discovers that women are not granted the same level of freedom.

☰ FAST FACTS

★ In addition to film, dance, and choreography, Sally Potter tried her hand at being a musician. She also worked alongside David Motion to compose the score for *Orlando*.

★ Twenty years later, Tilda Swinton says *Orlando* is still the name she is known by in Russia, and she is happy to answer to it. She also owns two costumes from the film.

★ *Orlando* was the film debut of actor Toby Jones, who has a small role as a valet.

★ Sally Potter was made an Officer of the Order of the British Empire (OBE) in 2012 for her services to film.

★ Potter's film *Yes* in 2004 was written entirely in iambic pentameter. It seems that poetry runs in her family, as her father was also a poet.

Jen Yamato on *A League of Their Own* (1992)

With director Penny Marshall at the helm of the based-on-the-incredible-true-story of the All-American Girls Professional Baseball League (AAGPBL), *A League of Their Own* knocked one out of the park as one of cinema's most enduring and loving odes to sports history, women, and sisterhood. It's also arguably one of the most quotable movies of the decade—with dozens of lines, moments, and scenes forever etched into the hearts of a generation of fans.

"Lay off the high ones!"

"I like the high ones!"

"Mule!"

"Nag!"

Geena Davis and Lori Petty star as Dottie Hinson and Kit Keller, the farm-raised sisters turned rival baseball phenoms who anchor the Golden Globe-nominated period dramedy. But a sprawling ensemble of talented women (Megan Cavanaugh, Rosie O'Donnell, Ann Cusack, and Madonna among them) bring further vibrancy to this fictionalized ode honoring the talent, grit, and legacy of the female athletes who were recruited in real life by a chewing gum magnate to play hardball in skirts on teams with names like the Rockford Peaches, Racine Belles, and the Grand Rapids Chicks during World War II.

Sweeping photography by Oscar-nominated cinematographer Miroslav Ondříček captures the textured beauty of a wartime American heartland traversed by our barnstorming heroines; the rapid-fire patter of a script by Lowell Ganz and Babaloo Mandel (from a story by Kim Wilson and Kelly Candaele, whose mother, Helen Callaghan, was a center fielder in the AAGPBL) takes flight from the mouths of a stellar supporting cast, including Tom Hanks in a career-best performance as washed-up team manager Jimmy Dugan.

And between scenes of good, old-fashioned, pulse-quickening baseball, between those hard-earned raspberries from sliding into base, Marshall never forgets to remind us there was more at stake for these women than just a game. They were ball players, sisters, mothers, wives, dreamers, doers, and trailblazers fighting for their turn at bat at a time when others still would never get the chance.

Rare is the Hollywood studio movie that centers so pointedly on the lives of women like these, who defied gender norms and swung for greatness while still having to prove their mettle to skeptical male owners and the public alike. Whether you saw yourself in Dottie, Kit, fast-talking "All the Way" Mae, tomboy slugger Marla Hooch, sweet right fielder Evelyn Gardner, or Betty "Spaghetti," you probably had a favorite Rockford Peach.

The tears you shed watching Kit round third belie the misguided notion that there's no crying in baseball—not when your heart is truly in the game. And when you hear that familiar refrain, the rest of the words fall right into place: "We are the members of the All-American League / we come from cities near and far..."

Jen Yamato is a film reporter and critic for the Los Angeles Times *who has covered Hollywood and pop culture for outlets including* Movieline, Deadline Hollywood, *and* The Daily Beast. *She is a member of the Los Angeles Film Critics Association, and once upon a time could throw a bullet to home plate all the way from center field.*

The Piano

**CiBy 2000/Australian Film Commission, 1993, New Zealand |
Color, 121 minutes, Drama**

*In the mid-nineteenth century, a mute woman and her young daughter
move for an arranged marriage to New Zealand, where she loses her
beloved piano.*

Director: Jane Campion
Producer: Jan Chapman
Cinematography: Stuart Dryburgh
Screenplay: Jane Campion
Starring: Holly Hunter ("Ada"), Anna Paquin ("Flora"), Harvey Keitel ("Baines"), Sam Neill ("Stewart")

"I feel a kinship between the kind of romance that Emily Brontë portrayed in Wuthering Heights and this film. Hers is not the notion of romance that we've come to use, it's very harsh and extreme, a gothic exploration of the romantic impulse; I wanted to respond to those ideas in my own century."

—*Jane Campion*

The main theme from the musical score for *The Piano* is almost as recognizable as the film itself. It only takes a few bars of composer Michael Nyman's haunting *The Heart Asks Pleasure First* to transport us to a rugged beach in nineteenth-century New Zealand, watching a woman who speaks with her music rather than her voice. It might come as little surprise, therefore, that when director Jane Campion hired Nyman to create the music, she gave him a script annotated with emotions rather than dialogue.

The film's main character Ada (Holly Hunter) is mute; she explains through her voiceover narration that, "I have not spoken since I was six years old. Nobody knows why, least of all myself. My father says it is a dark talent, and the day I take it into my head to stop breathing will be my last." Ada is in her thirties now, with a young daughter named Flora (Anna Paquin) with whom she communicates by using a special sign language. They have arrived on the shores of New Zealand, where her father has arranged for Ada to marry a local bachelor Stewart (Sam Neill), a man she has never met. Stewart instructs the Maori tribesmen to take their belongings from the boat to the beach and then up the hill to their new home—all except Ada's beloved piano, which is deemed too large to carry. Ada is distraught at the idea of leaving it behind, but her new husband is unmoved.

Their marriage is one without any intimacy or love, and Ada escapes to the beach whenever she can to play her piano. One day her rough-mannered neighbor Baines (Harvey Keitel) hears her music and offers to transport the instrument off the beach if she can teach him how to play—and play with him. "There's a way you can have your piano back," Baines tells Ada. "You see, I'd like us to make a deal. There's things I'd...like to do while you play. If you let me, you can earn it back. What do you think? One visit for every key."

Slowly, these piano lessons turn into something much more. Ada and Baines begin an affair as Baines falls in love with her. Stewart discovers them together, but instead of anger, he feels surprise...and arousal. It is during these scenes that Jane Campion differs from other directors. *The Piano* is full of erotic restraint, where just a flash of bare flesh through a hole in a stocking becomes both shocking and sexy. As Campion told the late film critic Roger Ebert, she was "trying to re-examine what erotic is. To see if you can create it in a half-centimeter square [of] flesh."

Campion juxtaposes these scenes of Ada, Baines, and Stewart discovering their repressed sexual desires with sequences of the native Maori people, who speak freely about body parts and find it amusing when they are asked to shield an older white lady relieving herself in the forest. This also speaks to the destructive nature of colonization, where European settlers tried to keep and enforce the traditions of their society rather than adapting to their new surroundings and the native people. The result is both farcical and cruel.

Loneliness is a major theme in the film, with each of the main characters locked within his or her own mind. Ada can't speak, and her immense pride means she refuses to show emotion even when in excruciating pain. In any case, her attempts at communication are rarely heeded. The only place she is able to truly let go is in front of her piano.

Watching the film now, it's difficult to imagine anyone else but Holly Hunter in the lead role. She is strong, yet petite and vulnerable, with a piercing gaze that cuts right through whomever she is looking at. But despite being both an accomplished actor and a skilled pianist, Hunter had to fight for the role. Campion had originally conceived Ada as a "tall woman with a strong, dark, eerie Frida Kahlo sort of beauty."

When she was finally cast, Holly Hunter threw herself into the creation of Ada. For four months before filming began, Hunter took piano lessons and practiced playing Michael Nyman's score. She was determined to be able to play well enough that she would not be dubbed over in the final cut. She wasn't, and what we hear as a viewer is Hunter's real playing. She also created a whole new sign language for the role, because back in 1850, an official language hadn't yet been established. Hunter worked with an American Sign Language interpreter to make up a language that she could perform well enough to make it look as if she had been signing all her life.

Holly Hunter in turn taught Anna Paquin this language, and by doing so, created a secret communication between the two women which helped them to form a real bond. This was Paquin's first film role, and she brought a cheeky precociousness to Flora that seemed well beyond her young years. Harvey Keitel was another unexpected choice, much like his portrayal of Baines: unkempt and wild, his face covered in Maori tattoos, concealing a romantic nature beneath.

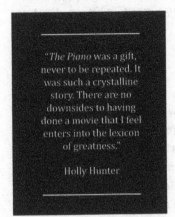

"*The Piano* was a gift, never to be repeated. It was such a crystalline story. There are no downsides to having done a movie that I feel enters into the lexicon of greatness."

Holly Hunter

The Piano was screened at the 1993 Cannes Film Festival, where Jane Campion became the first (and as of now, only) woman to win the festival's major award in competition, the Palme d'Or. More prizes followed at the 1994 Academy Awards, where the movie received eight nominations and won three. Holly Hunter, Anna Paquin, and Jane Campion walked away with Oscars, making eleven-year old Paquin the second youngest winner in history of the Best Supporting Actress Award.

These wins came ten years after Jane Campion began writing the script, originally titled *The Piano Lesson*. She had begun working on it even before she completed her first feature film in 1989, *Sweetie*. Campion was born in Wellington, New Zealand, in 1954 and studied anthropology and painting before turning to film. While she was at the Australian Film, Television and Radio School in Sydney, Australia, she began to make short films. Her third short was called *Peel: An Exercise in Discipline* and was about a young boy who is forced to pick up the orange peel he has thrown out of a car. That short ended up being accepted for the Cannes Film Festival and won the Short Film Palme d'Or in 1986. *Sweetie* also went on to be screened at Cannes, where it was not so well received. Campion earned rave reviews for her next movie, *An Angel at my Table*, about New Zealand writer Janet Frame. Then came her breakthrough with *The Piano*.

Throughout her career, Jane Campion has continued to focus on the stories of women who aren't usually the stars of movies. These are messy, complicated, and misunderstood women on the fringes of society, often living within dysfunctional families. Since that initial premiere at Cannes, *Sweetie* has been reclaimed among the best of Jane Campion's impressive filmography, which also includes *The Portrait of a Lady*, *Holy Smoke*, *In the Cut*, and *Bright Star*.

⚸ THE FEMALE GAZE

There has been some debate over whether or not *The Piano* should be considered a feminist film. The argument against is based on the violence to which Ada is subjected and how she is coerced into a sexual relationship in order to regain her piano. On the other hand, this is a film which depicts female desire and a woman rebelling against the men in her life. Ada is branded as being "crazy" or "mad"—labels often given to non-compliant women. And it is in the film's love scenes that Jane Campion's female gaze is most clearly on display, with the eroticism coming primarily from what isn't seen, rather than what is.

⚌ FAST FACTS

★ Jane Campion's Palme d'Or win at the 1993 Cannes Film Festival was shared in a tie with *Farewell My Concubine* by Kaige Chen.

★ At the 1994 Academy Awards, *The Piano* won three Oscars: Best Actress for Holly Hunter, Best Supporting Actress for Anna Paquin, Best Original Screenplay for Jane Campion. It was nominated for another five Oscars, with Campion becoming only the second woman ever nominated for Best Director.

* Because Anna Paquin was so young, she was only allowed to watch the first twenty minutes of the film and didn't receive a full script.

* *The Piano* has been claimed as an Australian film and a New Zealand film and was mainly financed by a French production company. Though the film is set and shot in New Zealand, it was deemed eligible for the Australian Film Institute awards because Campion studied at the Australian Film, Television and Radio School in Sydney.

Roth Cornet on *The Piano* (1993)

"The voice you hear is not my speaking voice, but my mind's voice," says Holly Hunter's Ada in the initial impressionistic moments of Jane Campion's *The Piano*, inviting us into her inner world. As with so many great films, its beating heart can be found within the first minute. That soft, sweet, distant, untouchable inflection, combined with the accompanying images of a sunlit world obscured and made more beautiful—transformed into art—by a woman's hands and fingers, set the stage for what is to come. We are placed directly in Ada's perspective as she observes the world, and it stares back with dispassion, lust, confusion, condemnation, and eventually, a small grace of understanding.

This is the story of a woman's voice, which is her power as much as it is her prison. Seduction, acquiescence, subtle yet precise cruelty, joy, and rage held back by a thread are all found in a woman's speech—and in Ada's time, she would have owned none of it. Free of the burden of intellectualized rationalization, young Ada looked ahead and saw a future in which her words were not her own and her silence was demanded, so she stole silence and made it her weapon. Ada rejects the tool that she knows she cannot own and forges her own. Her hands, the stories they tell, her music, her wild, irrepressible daughter, and even her very refusal to utter a single soul-diminishing syllable allow her to speak with liberation. When she chooses to cut off verbal expression, Ada chooses herself more fully than most of us ever will, or than we imagine we have permission to, while words, if forced, would stifle and strangle until there would be no Ada. Her body tells her story until such time as someone is willing to truly listen. Then, and only then, will she speak.

Jane Campion gave Ada a voice. As a director, she revealed her own via her art. When I saw this film as a young girl, it showed me that I might one day have my own as well.

Roth Cornet is the Editor-in-Chief of the popular digital media brand ScreenJunkies News. She has worked in production, acquisitions, criticism, and entertainment reporting. In other words, she's traveled the fields of the entertainment industry, where she hopes to eventually bump into herself.

Marya Gates on *Little Women* (1994)

Gillian Armstrong's *Little Women* was the first movie I fell in love with. I was about eight years old when I saw it in theaters with my mother, and it was a magical experience. I had never connected with a character as deeply as I did with misfit Jo March. She doesn't fit with her family or those around her, and she feels everything just so passionately. I loved her immediately. In the nearly twenty-five years since its release, I have watched this movie more than any other film, and each time I revisit it, I fall even more in love with its world and with its protagonist.

Director Armstrong's career is full of complex women, from Sybylla in *My Brilliant Career* (1979) to Jackie in *Starstruck* (1982) to Lilli in *High Tide* (1987), all of whom I feel were able to exist on celluloid because they had a director who fought to tell their messy and decidedly female stories right. There had been two earlier major adaptations of Louisa May Alcott's novel in 1933 and 1948. Those productions were directed and produced by men, though the screenplays for both counted Sarah Y. Mason as a cowriter. What makes the 1994 production shine is not just Armstrong at the helm but also the strong vision of producer Denise Di Novi and screenwriter Robin Swicord. With the combination of these three women behind the scenes and a superb lead in Winona Ryder, who received a Best Actress Academy Award nomination for her performance as Jo, you can feel the female energy coursing through the film's veins.

It's got fiery women, girls rebelling against societal norms, cats in bonnets, and everything else you could ever want in a movie. Plus you'll never find a man more perfect than Gabriel Byrne's Prof. Bhaer. I guarantee this movie will wrap itself around your heart and never let go.

Marya E. Gates has a BA in Comparative and French Literature from the University of California, Berkeley and an MFA in Screenwriting from the Academy of Art University. She has been blogging, vlogging, and podcasting about film and feminism for over ten years.

Piya Sinha-Roy on *Clueless* (1995)

From bugging over high school boys to ruining a red Alaia, there are few films that are as steeped in 1990s American pop culture and as quotable as Amy Heckerling's 1995 teen comedy *Clueless*.

Based loosely on Jane Austen's *Emma*, New York native Heckerling drew a wealth of inspiration from sitting in at a Beverly Hills high school to bring to life her heroine, Cher Horowitz (Alicia Silverstone) and her group of attractive, entitled friends: Dionne (Stacey Dash), Tai (Brittany Murphy), Murray (Donald Faison), Elton (Jeremy Sisto), and the dreamy Josh (Paul Rudd).

Growing up in England in the 1990s, I watched as Cher and her friends dressed like the glamorous celebrities I saw in magazines; school was really an afterthought for these American teens, who were rollin' with their homies to rowdy Valley house parties and setting their teachers up with coffee and Cliff's Notes sonnets to get good grades.

If you're an Angeleno, Heckerling weaves wonderful little Los Angeles insider nuggets into *Clueless*, such as the back-and-forth between Cher and Elton after the "val party" on the freeways and boulevards one might take to get back to Beverly Hills. And then there's that Cranberries CD (likely 1994's *No Need to Argue*) that Elton left on the quad and the memorable slang—"He's kind of a Baldwin," and, "She's a full on Monet"—that Heckerling tapped to capture the intricacies of a Beverly Hills girl in 1995.

I never realized until I started covering Hollywood that there were so few female filmmakers working in Hollywood. Kathryn Bigelow had directed Jamie Lee Curtis in 1990's cop thriller *Blue Steel* and then Keanu Reeves in 1991's crime action *Point Break*. Mira Nair explored culture clash in the 1993 comedy *Bhaji on the Beach*. Sofia Coppola made her debut with 1999's *The Virgin Suicides*.

But it was the words "Written and Directed by Amy Heckerling"—projected in bright neon green letters against a blue background as the end credits of *Clueless* started rolling—that were seared into my mind. I never questioned that Heckerling might have been one of a tiny minority in Hollywood, struggling in a male-dominated industry. Her name always stuck with me as I watched and rewatched *Clueless*.

More than a decade before *Clueless*, Heckerling made her feature-length debut with 1982's *Fast Times at Ridgemont High*, which chronicled the trials of a group of Southern California high school students over the course of a year. Heckerling brought the true story by Cameron Crowe to the screen and captured compelling portrayals from her cadre of young actors such as Jennifer Jason Leigh, Judge Reinhold, and specifically, a breakout performance from Sean Penn as the stoner surfer Jeff Spicoli.

When the movie was selected for the National Film Registry in 2005, the organization described the film as "the finest teen comedy of recent decades" and praised the "tender, compassionate treatment of adolescence with hilarious performances."

Clueless has yet to receive the same recognition as *Fast Times at Ridgemont High*, but one could argue that its legacy has outshone that of Heckerling's debut as it transcends the twenty-plus years to resonate with a new generation that hails Cher as a quote-worthy heroine and creates memes of scenes such as her debate speech:"May I please remind you that it does not say RSVP on the Statue of Liberty."

Who's to say how Heckerling's life might have differed had she been a male director with a hit like *Clueless*. But in the veteran filmmaker's own words from a 2016 profile in Interview Magazine, Heckerling leaves us with this: "As a female, you can't just say, "I think I want to explore. You're always trying to figure out how to just stay in the game."

Piya Sinha-Roy is a journalist in Los Angeles covering film, industry news, and representation in Hollywood.

The Watermelon Woman

Dancing Girl, 1996, USA | Color, 83 minutes, Comedy/Drama

A video store clerk makes a documentary to uncover the hidden history of a black actress from the 1930s.

Director: Cheryl Dunye

Producers: Alexandra Juhasz, Barry Swimar

Cinematography: Michelle Crenshaw

Screenplay: Cheryl Dunye

Starring: Cheryl Dunye ("Cheryl"), Valarie Walker ("Tamara"), Lisa Marie Bronson ("Fae Richards"), Guinevere Turner ("Diana")

"I did the research, I did look in black film history and found nothing but homophobia and omission. I did look at queer film history, I read Vito Russo and found no mention of race. So I hope that my film spurs these younger people to think about their identities within the context of representation in the media."

—*Cheryl Dunye*

"It's a powerful piece of art that allows us to think about who has access to representation and who has access to archives, and why women, people of color, and queer people have not had access to these powerful instruments. That's Cheryl's power, she's funny. And she opens doors, but the doors she's opening are complicated."

Alexandra Juhasz, producer and "Martha Page"

At the end of *The Watermelon Woman*, there is an epigraph which reads, "Sometimes you have to create your own history." This is in fact a perfect way to describe not only this landmark independent film but the filmmaker herself. When Cheryl Dunye released *The Watermelon Woman* in 1996, she became the first black lesbian to ever direct a feature film. Even today, the movie remains a vital piece of the New Queer Cinema movement.

Dunye not only directs but also stars in the film, playing a version of herself—also called Cheryl. In this role, she is a film buff and aspiring filmmaker who works at a video store in Philadelphia alongside her best friend and fellow lesbian Tamara (Valarie Walker). After watching a movie from the 1930s, Cheryl becomes intrigued by a black actress playing a mammy in a small role. The actress is billed only as "The Watermelon Woman," and in this pre-internet world, Cheryl decides to make a documentary to find out who she was.

She searches film archives and records interviews with experts, discovering that "The Watermelon Woman" was a singer-turned-actress named Fae Richards (Lisa Marie Bronson). Richards was also from Philadelphia and was involved in a relationship with a white lesbian director, Martha Page (Alexandra Juhasz). As Cheryl becomes more and more obsessed with this forgotten star, her own story begins to mirror Fae's—especially though her new relationship with a white customer at the video store, Diana (Guinevere Turner).

"Twenty years later, it still feels so urgent, very contemporary, like it was made yesterday. I think that says a lot about [Dunye's] legacy and her foresight about issues that still aren't resolved in the film industry and media making."

Erin Christovale, curator of the Hammer Museum film program *How to Love a Watermelon Woman*

Right until the very end of the film and that epigraph, you'd be forgiven for believing that Fae Richards was a real actress from early Hollywood. *The Watermelon Woman* is a fascinating mixture of narrative and documentary-style storytelling, switching between the story of Cheryl and the documentary she is shooting. It even features "archival" footage of Richards, complete with fictional classic films and staged photos created by photographer Zoe Leonard. The talking head "interviews" are so well-acted they seem real, and there's even a funny cameo by famous feminist philosopher Camille Paglia.

In fact, the film is filled with smart, nuanced humor which speaks to many issues that are still timely today. There's a scene where Cheryl is stopped by the police, who call her a male "crackhead freak," even though she tells them she's a woman and isn't doing anything but walking down a street. In another scene, Cheryl visits an archive devoted to lesbian history, only to find the information about African-Americans carelessly stored in a box in a corner. These scenes are woven so naturally into the plot that even though the film doesn't take itself very seriously, the messages about racism are clear. This is particularly the case when it comes to the cultural history of black actors, their confinement to small, stereotypical roles, and their continued invisibility in history, thanks to a lack of historical records. As the character of Cheryl explains, her films "have to be about black women, because our stories have never been told."

> "The Watermelon Woman is a vital example of New Queer Cinema, but it's more than a time capsule. Funny and smart, full of biting humor and astute observations about identity and history, Cheryl Dunye's audacious, joyous debut feature captures the process of falling hopelessly in love with the movies."
>
> Serena Donadoni,
> The Village Voice

At its heart, The Watermelon Woman is about Cheryl Dunye's own search for identity and love. Like her fictional character Fae Richards, the Cheryl in the film struggles with the career parameters set by others because of the color of her skin. Also like Fae, she faces judgment for her interracial relationship. Cheryl Dunye brings so much light and charisma to this lead role that it's easy to root for her and become frustrated on her behalf.

The Watermelon Woman is a self-assured, audacious piece of work that plays with form and new ideas. This was an incredible debut feature for Dunye, and it quickly became an integral part of the New Queer Cinema movement—a time in the 1990s when young queer filmmakers embraced independent film as a way to finally tell their own personal stories. This was a rare moment in cinema history, buoyed by a surge of activism around queer politics in which the goal was to explore ideas rather than necessarily make a commercial product. The experimental aspect of the filmmaking was very important, not only in changing the *type* of stories being told but the *way* they were being told.

The film was not released without controversy. Cheryl Dunye was awarded a $31,500 grant by the National Endowment for the Arts (NEA) to make *The Watermelon Woman*. After reading a review of it describing the "hot" lesbian sex scene, congressman Peter Hoekstra wrote an amendment to try and reduce funding to the NEA. Dunye wasn't allowed to be part of this debate—"I was sort of like The Watermelon Woman," she later said, "talked about, but I didn't have a real face"—but luckily she was defended by a Texas representative. Sheila Jackson Lee argued for the film as a piece of art, not pornography. "To hear a black congresswoman represent," Dunye said, "and actually get to see it was a beautiful moment, really, ultimately."

Cheryl Dunye was born in Liberia, but grew up in Philadelphia. She attended art school before making *The Watermelon Woman* as her first feature film, the premise of which was inspired by her own research into whether she could find a black openly lesbian actress in Hollywood history. The film received critically acclaim and went on to win the Teddy award at the Berlin International Film Festival in 1996. It has recently been restored for its twentieth anniversary by UCLA's Legacy Project. After this initial success, Dunye went on to make many more movies, including a studio film released in 2004 called *My Baby's Daddy*.

But she soon realized commercial filmmaking wasn't what she wanted to focus on, and a break in Amsterdam led to her working with the Binger Filmlab, where she reignited her passion for telling black stories. "I am so tired of not seeing black queer lives in the future. I'm so tired of the 'magical negro' syndrome," Dunye explained later. "I want to be able to tell stories as a filmmaker, and have the rights to do what every filmmaker is allowed to do."

Now with fifteen features and shorts under her belt, as well as a career as a Professor at the San Francisco State University School of Cinema, Cheryl Dunye has managed to stay true to her original voice. She remains an integral part of film history and an inspiration to young filmmakers. When asked what she wants audiences to continue to get from her debut film, Dunye said, "Step up to the plate of your lives and your Watermelon Woman, whomever that might be for you, and do it. It's a call for action in that sense and [for] putting yourself in the picture. I think that's one thing that I want these younger audiences to feel and do."

❦ THE FEMALE GAZE

The Watermelon Woman (sadly) remains an outlier in cinema history, as a film made by and about an African American lesbian. The entire movie is shown through the eyes of the character Cheryl, who also films herself in the documentary sections. It shows how she would like to be represented as well as commenting on how black actresses have been portrayed throughout cinema history.

═ FAST FACTS

★ *The Watermelon Woman* cost $300,000 to make, financed by a grant from the National Endowment for the Arts, plus donations from friends. Dunye describes the financing process as an early crowdfunding project.

★ Having found no archives for black lesbian actresses in cinema history at the Library of Congress and the Lesbian Herstory Archive, photographer Zoe Leonard took seventy-eight photos of the fictional Watermelon Woman to create a mock archive to use in the film.

★ The film's title is a play on the Melvin Van Peebles film *Watermelon Man* from 1970.

★ Guinevere Turner, who plays Diana in the film, was cast by Dunye after starring in the film *Go Fish* in 1994, a groundbreaking lesbian indie film which Turner also cowrote. Turner went on to cowrite 2000's *American Psycho* alongside director Mary Harron.

★ In 2017 Ava DuVernay hired Cheryl Dunye to direct episodes in the second season of her TV show *Queen Sugar*, in addition to another queer filmmaker, Aurora Guerrero.

Jamie Broadnax on *Eve's Bayou* (1997)

"Memory is a selection of images, some elusive, others printed indelibly on the brain." One of the most incredibly beautiful films I have ever experienced as a fan was the Southern Gothic classic *Eve's Bayou*, directed by Kasi Lemmons. The story was told with such authenticity and the cinematography was so remarkable it inspired me to study film in college. Seeing a film told through the lens of a young black girl and with such a compelling performance led me to study more about Kasi Lemmons.

When I went to film school—and majored in film directing, I wrote a term paper about Kasi and her work as a filmmaker, because it was the first time I saw film that reflected women like me whose family lineage was one I felt deeply connected with as someone who grew up and was raised in the south. To see that the auteur of this production was also a woman of color like me was refreshing. It also gave me hope that I, too, could direct movies.

Although ultimately filmmaking didn't end up becoming the career I fell into, sharing stories about women like Kasi and writing news stories about their work actually did. And I'm grateful for the film *Eve's Bayou* for what it did for me personally, culturally, and professionally. It's rare that nuanced and complex stories about black women are told with such artistic beauty and genius. *Eve's Bayou* was revolutionary for me.

Jamie Broadnax is the founder and creator of the online publication **Black Girl Nerds.** *She executive produces the* **BGN** *podcast and has a book due out soon about the community of nerdy women of color.*

Monica Castillo on *Eve's Bayou* (1997)

Kasi Lemmons' directorial debut, *Eve's Bayou*, is built out of the memories of its main character. The voice of an older Eve guides us into the swampy marshlands of Louisiana she and her family called home, and to the summer of 1962 where her childhood memory goes dark with anger, resentment, and sadness.

Through the eyes of a ten-year-old Eve (Jurnee Smollett), the audience returns with her to the scene of the crime. After a big party at her home, Eve catches her father Louis (Samuel L. Jackson) messing around with a woman who isn't her mother. The young girl is confused about what to do, and the emotional tension leads her to rebel against both her parents. She finds some comfort in the arms of her thrice-widowed Aunt Mozelle (Debbi Morgan), as they both have the gift of premonitions—or is it a curse?

Memory is both a blessing and a burden for the Batiste family. It's never as reliable as it needs to be, and it's not so easily conjured up when you need it. People's recollections of events are different from one another's. In the film, the memories of the Baptiste family's ancestors are invoked fairly frequently because these stories still feel interconnected through the generations. The environment, both physical and familial, that surrounds Eve will haunt her memories in ways she doesn't fully yet see.

The Batiste family drama lingers in the Louisiana air like humidity—inescapable and suffocating. The number of scandals and betrayals in the family history seems endless. Despite her naivete, Eve tries to make sense of the grown-up problems around her. In her effort to fix things while emotionally hurt, she thrashes around until she finds a solution that has irreparable consequences.

Lemmons explores the terrain with an observant eye: capturing the creeping stillness of these waters, the Spanish moss blowing in the wind, and Eve's rebellious spirit scorching the earth behind her. Perhaps it was Lemmons' experience as an actress that helped her young star give an unforgettable performance as a young girl trying to make sense of grown-ups' misdeeds. The story she tells has a Southern Gothic twist and the occasional visual hint of a film noir during shadowy night sequences. *Eve's Bayou* is as gorgeous and enchanting as it is heartbreaking and shocking—a work of art from a director who should have many more movies to her name.

Monica Castillo is a writer and critic based in New York City. Her work has appeared in The Washington Post, The New York Times, The Village Voice, RogerEbert.com, Cosmopolitan, Remezcla, NPR, *and* The Boston Globe.

The Virgin Suicides

American Zoetrope, 1999, USA | Color, 97 minutes

In a small Michigan suburb in the 1970s, five sisters mysteriously take their own lives.

Director: Sofia Coppola

Producers: Francis Ford Coppola, Julie Constanza, Dan Halsted, Chris Hanley

Cinematography: Edward Lachman

Screenplay: Sofia Coppola, based on the book by Jeffrey Eugenides

Starring: Kirsten Dunst ("Lux Lisbon"), James Woods ("Mr. Lisbon"), Kathleen Turner ("Mrs. Lisbon"), Josh Hartnett ("Trip Fontaine"), Giovanni Ribisi ("Narrator")

"There wasn't much poetic filmmaking that spoke to me as a girl and a young woman and also treated us with the respect I felt that audience deserved..."

—Sofia Coppola

In the opening scene of *The Virgin Suicides*, a young girl is rushed to an ambulance after slitting open her wrists. At the hospital, the doctor (Danny DeVito) looks at her and asks a touch condescendingly, "What are you doing here, honey? You're not even old enough to know how bad life gets." At this, she gives him a withering look and answers, "Obviously, you've never been a thirteen-year-old girl."

We know her name is Cecilia (Hanna Hall) because the narrator (Giovanni Ribisi) tells us so. She is one of five sisters from the Lisbon family living in a suburb in Michigan in the early 1970s. Though the narrator is just one voice, he uses the pronoun "we." He represents the collective memories of a group of neighborhood boys who are transfixed by the five beautiful blonde girls living across the street—five girls, we are told, who will all soon be dead.

The sisters are Cecilia, Mary (A.J. Cook), Bonnie (Chelse Swain), Therese (Leslie Hayman), and Lux (Kirsten Dunst). Their mother, Mrs. Lisbon (Kathleen Turner), is strict and religious. She panics about her blossoming girls and does her best to keep them covered up, inside, and away from trouble. Their father, Mr. Lisbon (James Woods), is more of a pushover, a high school math teacher who talks to plants and loves explaining his model airplane collection to anyone who will listen.

After Cecilia's trip to the hospital, Father Moody (Scott Glenn) recommends the girls should start socializing with boys, and a small party brings the neighborhood kids face-to-face with these dreamlike women—girls that they will always love but never truly understand.

Dreamlike is precisely the mood of the film, a collection of indistinct memories where the characteristics of the people remembered have been heightened and improved over time. These girls are not three-dimensional, complex people, because this is a fantasy version of how the boys imagine them to be. The film moves languidly between visions of the girls to flashbacks of real events, creating a sort of pastiche of '70s suburbia and teen idealization. It's a similar experience to watching the classic Australian film *Picnic at Hanging Rock*: entrancing visions of blonde girls dressed in white, forever remembered in this way after they go missing. The central mystery here is the suicides. We are told they will all end their own lives before the film is over. We don't know how or why, and though it is inevitable, we want to save them—just like the boys in the film. And like those boys, the girls live on through our memories: young, beautiful, and perfect.

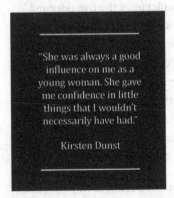

"She was always a good influence on me as a young woman. She gave me confidence in little things that I wouldn't necessarily have had."

Kirsten Dunst

The sister with the most distinct character arc is Lux, played by Kirsten Dunst with equal parts innocence and sexiness, albeit with a deep sense of sadness behind her large blue eyes. She is soon noticed by the best-looking guy at school, Trip Fontaine (Josh Hartnett), who goes out of his way to prove to her parents that he is a worthy date for their daughter. He manages to convince them to let him take Lux and her sisters to the prom. During the dance, Trip takes Lux out to the school field, where she loses her virginity to him. Despite claiming to have the best of intentions toward her, Trip leaves her alone on the field, and she wakes up there afterwards, confused. It's a sad—and sadly relatable—scene. Our first time is rarely as good as we hope it will be, and things do change afterwards. As present-day Trip (Michael Paré) explains, "She was the still point of the turning world then," but also that, "[O]ut there on the football field, it was different."

After this, the girls are more confined than ever, and the film moves inescapably toward their death. No matter how the neighborhood boys try to save the Lisbon girls, they can't. In these scenes, director Sofia Coppola captures perfectly how it is to be a teenager—our troubles feel huge and inescapable, as if we will be saddled with them for the rest of our lives. But things do get better. We grow up, and soon we start to mourn the death of our youth, looking back at our romanticized memories for comfort.

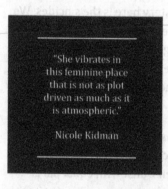

"She vibrates in this feminine place that is not as plot driven as much as it is atmospheric."

Nicole Kidman

The Virgin Suicides was an impressive feature film debut for Sofia Coppola. She adapted her screenplay from the book of the same name, a 1993 novel written by Jeffrey Eugenides. Like the film, the book views the five doomed sisters through the memories of the neighborhood boys. "The girls are seen at such a distance," Eugenides once explained; "They're created by the intention of the observer, and there are so many points of view that they don't really exist as an exact entity." This all meant that when it came to an adaptation, the director would need to convey more of a mood based on images rather than characters and a defined story.

The book spoke to Sofia Coppola in such a powerful way that she decided to write an adaptation even though she wasn't necessarily looking to direct a movie at the time. There was already a deal in place for the book with a different director and writer attached, but when that fell through, Coppola got to work on her version and won the chance to make it. "When I was in my mid-twenties, I came across *The Virgin Suicides*," Coppola said in an interview. "It felt like Jeffrey Eugenides, the writer, really understood the experience of being a teenager: the longing, the melancholy, the mystery between boys and girls. I loved how the boys were so confused by the girls, and I really connected with all that lazing around in your bedroom. I didn't feel like I saw that very much in films, not in a way I could relate to."

Her father, acclaimed director Francis Ford Coppola, helped by producing the film through his company, American Zoetrope. But Sofia Coppola had to prove herself as a filmmaker in her own right, with the added pressure of the expectations attached to her family name. Like the girls in the book, she needed to find her own voice in a male-dominated world.

Sofia Coppola grew up in New York. She was born in 1971, the year her father was making *The Godfather*. Her mother Eleanor is also a director who makes narrative films and documentaries, and her brother Roman is a producer and writer who works with Wes Anderson. Sofia's aunt is actress Talia Shire, her cousins are actors Jason Schwartzman and Nicolas Cage, and her niece Gia Coppola is also a filmmaker. Film is the family business; before she ever stepped behind the lens, Sofia Coppola appeared in several of her father's films.

Her role in the third *Godfather* film would be her last as an actress, thanks to some particularly scathing reviews. She turned to other art forms, studying first painting, then doing some modeling, photography, and fashion design. In 1996, her first film was released, a short movie called *Bed, Bath, and Beyond*, followed two years later by another short, *Lick the Star*. "I never thought I would be a filmmaker," Coppola later explained, "It wasn't something I ever planned, despite the fact I loved hanging around on sets...I had so many interests—design, photography, music—but I just couldn't find one medium that really clicked for me. Then I made a short film, *Lick the Star*, in 1998, and it brought together all the things I loved."

Just a year after that second short film came *The Virgin Suicides*, her first feature-length film. This production announced the arrival of a vital new voice in the American film industry and proved Coppola adept at translating the spirit and emotions of the novel. Critical acclaim followed, but the movie was hamstrung by a small release, reportedly due to worries that it would encourage teen suicides.

The biggest success for Sofia Coppola came with her second film, *Lost in Translation*, in 2003. With this movie, she became the first American woman to ever be nominated for a Best Director Academy Award, and only the third woman of any nationality to be nominated in that category. *Lost in Translation* was a huge hit both commercially and critically. She followed that up with *Marie Antoinette* in 2006, *Somewhere* in 2010, *The Bling Ring* in 2013, and *The Beguiled* in 2017, for which she won the Best Director award at the Cannes Film Festival. She was only the second woman to have ever won that honor, fifty-six years after the first.

Though *The Virgin Suicides* only found a small audience upon its initial release, its popularity has grown over the years. As Sofia Coppola told *The Guardian*, "A couple of years ago, a bunch of teenage girls told me how much they loved *The Virgin Suicides*. I thought: How do they even know about that? They weren't even born. Through the internet, it's had a second life. It's nice to know that it still speaks to some young women."

✤ THE FEMALE GAZE

The Virgin Suicides is interesting to study in terms of its "gaze," in that the story is told through the perspective of teenage boys.

As such, it could be seen as an exploration of masculine desire and the idealization of first love. But in the gentle hands of Sofia Coppola, the movie offers a look at femininity and the complex emotions of teenaged girls. The girls are also not overtly and overly sexualized in the way many American teen films tend to do. Instead, they appear as ethereal beauties in golden meadows—unrealistic, yes, but not exploited.

≡ FAST FACTS

★ Sofia Coppola made her first appearance onscreen as a male baby, in a baptism scene in *The Godfather*.

★ Three generations of Coppolas have won Oscars; Sofia is one of the three. Her grandfather Carmine Coppola won for Best Original Score for *The Godfather Part II*, her father won five times plus an honorary Oscar, and she has won once, for Best Original Screenplay for *Lost in Translation*.

★ *The Virgin Suicides* marked the first collaboration for Coppola and Kirsten Dunst. The two went on to make *Marie Antoinette* and *The Beguiled* together, and Dunst had a cameo in *The Bling Ring*.

★ Sofia has been nicknamed "The Velvet Hammer" by Bill Murray for her tough but gentle approach to directing.

Clarke Wolfe on *American Psycho* (2000)

Confession time: I love Mary Harron's *American Psycho*. There are some movies that when you catch them on TV or put them on in the background, you find yourself captivated, unable to focus on anything else. For most people those movies are *The Shawshank Redemption*, *Forrest Gump*, or *Big* (OK, most things with Tom Hanks, really). But for me, that movie is *American Psycho*.

For my money, Christian Bale gives the performance of a lifetime at just twenty-five years old—he was barely twenty-six when the film was released. The supporting cast, which includes Justin Theroux, Josh Lucas, and Jared Leto as Patrick Bateman's yuppie douchebag "friends," is still laugh-out-loud funny, the movie is endlessly quotable ("I have to return some video tapes"), and it seems to get better every time I watch it thanks to the countless layers lurking in the visuals and throughout the screenplay.

When you think about it, Mary Harron's super dark comedy breaks all of the rules that we think we know (consciously or unconsciously) about female filmmakers: women don't make scary movies, women just don't get comedy, women don't shoot action well, and women don't direct men in iconic performances.

Now, let's be honest here: *American Psycho* works, and it endures, because Harron and cowriter Guinevere Turner recognize that Patrick Bateman and all of his friends, despite their youth, their good looks, their wealth, and their privilege, are losers. It's not simply that they're deplorable, they're also morons. As screenwriters, Harron and Turner are not afraid of making fun of the Patrick Batemans of the world to their faces while simultaneously recognizing a painful and horrifying truth: Patrick Bateman is invincible and he will get away with whatever transgression he decides to commit, because when you're a Patrick Bateman, people choose not to hold you accountable.

I understand a film like *American Psycho* isn't for everyone, but even so, it is one I would encourage any cinephile to experience. It is topical, funny, scary, edgy, incredibly thoughtful, and timeless. It is dark and violent and aggressive and upsetting; and in less than twenty years since the movie premiered to a soft box office take, over time, it has achieved cult classic status.

American Psycho ridicules toxic masculinity, which is still (unfortunately) thriving. And while there is no way to know what might have been had the countless other proposed adaptations of Bret Easton Ellis' novel made their way to the big screen, I am willing to bet that they wouldn't—and probably couldn't— have succeeded in satirizing the vapid, party boy lifestyle that is deliciously raked over the coals throughout the film. This is because of one last painful and horrifying truth: most of us aren't ready to eradicate and condemn the Patrick Bateman ideal.

Clarke Wolfe is an actress, a host, and a producer. She founded her production company, Rocket Ships and Dreams Productions, in 2013 and currently resides in Los Angeles, California.

Jessie Maltin on *Songcatcher* (2000)

Songcatcher is one of the most intricately beautiful films I have ever seen—and I mean beautiful in every sense of the word. The music is enchanting, the scenery is whimsical, the costume design is perfection, the script is thoughtful, and the acting is superb.

Maggie Greenwald wrote and directed this incredible story about a musicologist (played by Janet McTeer) who decides to venture into the Appalachian mountains in order to capture and document their soulful ballads for posterity. Her sister (Jane Adams) is a teacher there and has started to gain the trust of the locals. Of course, intelligent women were not necessarily understood or respected in 1907, regardless of the location. McTeer must approach each and every resident with caution—and she eventually recruits a mountain girl (Emmy Rossum) to assist her. This strong, vibrant doctor of music rattles the community, and they can't help but react in an extreme and chaotic way.

The soundtrack is akin to that of *O Brother, Where Art Thou?*— real and gritty and sung from the heart. Pat Carroll, Iris DeMent, Rossum, and so many others breathe life into these homespun songs handed down from generation to generation. Greenwald has created a film that is singular by bringing together a cast of magnificent women who command the screen and the story and by choosing both a subject unlike any other and a location you can't help but fall in love with.

This is not a summer blockbuster, a fast-paced action flick, or a loud and bombastic crowd pleaser. This is an expertly crafted piece of art, and we are lucky to have it.

Jessie Maltin is a proud member of the mighty Maltin Empire, running www.leonardmaltin.com and co-hosting the **Maltin on Movies** *podcast. She was raised in the wild by cinephiles and lived to tell the tale.*

Whale Rider

South Pacific Pictures, 2002, New Zealand | Color, 101 minutes

A young girl is denied her rightful place as chief of a Maori tribe because of her gender.

Director: Niki Caro

Producers: Bill Gavin, Linda Goldstein Knowlton

Cinematography: Leon Narbey

Screenplay: Niki Caro, based on the book by Witi Ihimaera

Starring: Keisha Castle-Hughes ("Paikea"), Rawiri Paratene ("Koro"), Cliff Curtis ("Porourangi"), Vicky Haughton ("Nanny Flowers")

"As a filmmaker I wish to make a connection with my audience. I want to tell stories that deserve to be told."

—*Niki Caro*

Part fairytale, part intimate family drama, *Whale Rider* weaves fable, cultural history, and gender politics together to create a truly special movie. Set in a remote coastal town in New Zealand, Keisha Castle-Hughes stars as Paikea, or Pai for short. She was named after the original chieftain of her Whangara Maori tribe, who as ancient legend tells it, arrived in New Zealand on the back of a whale. Every subsequent male heir of the family line has taken up the mantle as chief, but during Pai's birth, her mother and Pai's male twin die. "There was no gladness when I was born," says Pai's voiceover. Her father, Porourangi (Cliff Curtis), doesn't want to take his rightful role as the next chief, so Pai's grandfather Koro (Rawiri Paratene) is distraught at the death of his male grandson. Koro refuses to go against tradition by acknowledging a girl as a worthy heir. While Pai is still a child, Porourangi leaves New Zealand to be an artist, leaving his daughter in the care of Koro and Nanny Flowers (Vicky Haughton).

Koro is tough on his family. He loves Pai but dismisses her as "just a girl." He is also disappointed in his son and does not understand why he would choose to travel overseas instead of being the tribal leader. "I can't be what he wants," Porourangi says at one point. "Me neither," says Pai, though she decides not to go to Europe with her father, but rather to stay and prove herself. She feels a weight of guilt for surviving when her brother did not and has a strong, willful personality. So when Koro starts to train the young boys in the village for the leadership role, Pai listens in and does some training on her own.

"Among the other qualities Caro... brings to the mix are a willingness to let this story tell itself in its own time and the ability to create emotion that is intense without being cloying or dishonest. She is also able, and this is critical, to leave the mundane behind and steer the film to a higher level when the story demands to go there."

Kenneth Turan,
Los Angeles Times

Pai is courageous and naturally talented. It is obvious to everyone but Koro that she is more capable than any of the boys in the village. Her gender is the only thing holding her back, and Niki Caro points to the double standards applied to girls and boys in various ways. For example, Pai is described as "bossy," while the boys are taught during their training to be angry—they are taught that "anger is part of your battle."

With this role, Keisha Castle-Hughes became the youngest actress ever nominated for Best Actress at the Academy Awards up to that time. She was just eleven years old at the time of filming after being selected from a pool of 10,000 child actresses. And she is remarkable here; she infuses Pai with a sense of spiritual connectedness beyond her years while also allowing her to be a young girl simply trying to impress her grandfather.

Whale Rider is also somewhat of a cautionary tale against blindly following tradition. It suggests that perhaps the "old ways" are not always the only ways to live life. There is a clear generational difference between grandfather and granddaughter, and this relationship is the most potent and complex in the film. These ideas about tradition and gender are wonderfully balanced within *Whale Rider*'s delicate script. Niki Caro's writing avoids the expected clichés and gently moves the story toward an unexpected and beautiful ending—a full-circle moment concerning birth and death.

The source material for this film was the book *Whale Rider* by Witi Ihimaera. In order to adapt it into a screenplay, Niki Caro (a non-Maori New Zealander) had to do a lot of research. Like the character of Pai, she had to convince the members of a Maori tribe that she was worthy of telling this beloved story. She got to know the Ngati Konohi community, who alongside her cast, made sure that the details and language used were correct. There was a small outcry in the press when a Maori publication learned that Caro would be adapting their story, but the film was later embraced. In New Zealand it remained number one at the box office for many weeks, and it was critically acclaimed internationally. *Whale Rider* played at the Sundance Film Festival and the Toronto International Film Festival and went on to win a BAFTA (British Academy of Film and Television Arts) award, as well as receiving nominations for Keisha Castle-Hughes' work in it from the Screen Actors Guild and the Academy.

Whale Rider wasn't the first film directed by Niki Caro, who was born in Wellington in 1967. She grew up watching a variety of movies from many different countries but didn't think of directing as being a viable option. "My diet was incredible European cinema," Caro said in an interview. "But I never saw my own world onscreen until I saw [Jane Campion's] *Sweetie*...I loved its familiar accent, the weird way it was framed, and that it had female protagonists. It was revelatory to me that you could do this."

Caro studied at the Elam School of Fine Arts in Auckland, and while there, changed her focus from sculpture to filmmaking. But the school didn't have much in terms of a film department, so she "learned to make films by figuring it out." One of her scripts earned her a place at Swinburne's Film and Television School in Melbourne, Australia. Then Caro went back to New Zealand, where she "waitressed for ten years [and] assisted on music videos or whatever was in production—small films, you name it," until slowly, she began to get work writing and directing several TV dramas.

One of those dramas, *The Summer the Queen Came*, received two nominations at the 1994 NZ Film and Television Awards. That same year, her short film *Sure to Rise* was selected to play at the Cannes Film Festival. In 1998, Caro went back to Cannes with her first feature film, *Memory and Desire*, about a Japanese couple traveling around New Zealand. But *Whale Rider* was the film which really earned Niki Caro some attention, and soon after its success, Hollywood came knocking.

> "I was secretly stalking Niki. And I realized that there were only two choices: prison or being cast in this film. So I'm very glad it turned out to be the second. I'd gone to see Whale Rider like everybody else, and really fell in love with Niki through that film. And so I stalked her—I was trying to see what she was doing next."
>
> Charlize Theron, on why she wanted to do *North Country*

Her debut American film was *North Country* from 2005, starring Charlize Theron as a woman fighting back against the sexual harassment she endures in her job as a miner. The film was nominated for two Oscars: a Best Actress for Charlize Theron and

Best Supporting Actress for Frances McDormand. Caro followed that up with *A Heavenly Vintage*, set in nineteenth-century France, which reunited her with Keisha Castle-Hughes. After that came *McFarland USA*, released in 2015, with Kevin Costner as the coach of a cross-country running team, and *The Zookeeper's Wife* from 2017, based on a true story of a couple who shielded Jews during World War II inside a Polish zoo and starring Jessica Chastain. Her next big screen project is set to be the live-action version of *Mulan*, the animated 1998 Disney hit.

Throughout the course of her career, Niki Caro has made films about outsiders who refuse to let society dictate what they can and cannot do and who are inspirational in their willingness to keep pushing onwards. This could also be an accurate portrayal of Niki Caro herself. She is a female filmmaker from New Zealand making Hollywood movies on a large scale at a time when only 4 percent of women get to do that, making her a vital role model for up-and-coming female directors.

✽ THE FEMALE GAZE

In *Whale Rider*, the character of Pai, played by Keisha Castle-Hughes, is shown as a strong, self-sufficient, capable young girl. She is not idealized or scrutinized in terms of her beauty, yet she maintains her femininity throughout her heroic journey. The film deals with gender biases in the Maori tradition, which are also found in other cultures where girls are seen as being lesser than boys. Pai's character arc in the movie points out how these biases are often false.

★ *Whale Rider* had its debut at the 2002 Toronto International Film Festival, where it won the People's Choice Award. It also picked up the World Cinema Audience Award at the Sundance Film Festival and the Canal Plus Award at the Rotterdam Film Festival.

★ *Whale Rider* remains New Zealand's fifth most financially successful movie as well as the biggest box office hit for a local female filmmaker.

★ Charlize Theron won Best Actress in the same year that Keisha Castle-Hughes was nominated for an Oscar, and when Theron was nominated again two years later, it was for her work with Niki Caro on *North Country*.

★ When Niki Caro was hired to direct *Mulan* (slated for release in 2020), she became only the fifth woman to ever direct a movie with a budget of over $100 million, joining Kathryn Bigelow (*K-19: The Widowmaker*), Patty Jenkins (*Wonder Woman*), Jennifer Yuh Nelson (*Kung Fu Panda 2*), and Ava DuVernay (*A Wrinkle in Time*).

Real Women Have Curves

LaVoo Productions, 2002, USA | Color, 93 minutes

Ana is a first generation Mexican-American girl caught between her desire to go to college and her parents' wish for her to work in the family business.

Director: Patricia Cardoso

Producers: Marilyn R. Atlas, Effie Brown, George LaVoo

Cinematography: Jim Denault

Screenplay: George LaVoo, based on a play by Josefina López

Starring: America Ferrera ("Ana"), Lupe Ontiveros ("Carmen"), Ingrid Oliu ("Estela"), George Lopez ("Mr Guzman"), Brian Sites ("Jimmy"), Soledad St. Hilaire ("Pancha")

"You have to know your strengths and your stretches. It is hard. But if you have persistence and you have patience, you are going to be able to tell your stories."

—Patricia Cardoso

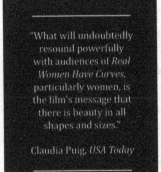

"What will undoubtedly resound powerfully with audiences of *Real Women Have Curves*, particularly women, is the film's message that there is beauty in all shapes and sizes."

Claudia Puig, *USA Today*

There's a scene in *Real Women Have Curves* which remains surprising even sixteen years after its debut. Inside a hot sewing factory in East Los Angeles, a group of Mexican-American women sweat over their machines. They are making formal satin dresses which they sell to a department store for $18, where they are then marked up to $600. The youngest woman of the group is Ana (America Ferrera), a teenager just out of high school. Ana complains about the heat as she steams the dresses, so she decides to take off her clothes. Ana's mother Carmen (Lupe Ontiveros) is shocked at seeing her daughter proudly flaunting her curvy figure. Soon the other women start to strip too, comparing their stomachs, cellulite, and curves in a proud display of ownership over their bodies. These are bodies they have long been taught to cover up; these women have been told they are too curvy for men to desire.

Throughout all of this, Ana gives her mother—the only one now fully clothed—a defiant look. Ana is not model thin, and that is perfectly fine with her. She loves herself as she is. She knows she's worth more than just what is on the outside, and she accepts herself even when her mother Carmen does not.

Just as the title of the film suggests, positive body image is a major theme in *Real Woman Have Curves*. But it is just one of the ways this feature remains an outlier in American film history. Another major point of departure is who is represented onscreen. Ana is a first generation Mexican-American caught between the two cultures. This is illustrated in her daily bus trip to high school, which takes her from the colorful streets of East LA to the perfectly manicured lawns of Beverly Hills.

> "I'd never seen a movie like it, and I'd never seen a character like this portrayed in film before.... What's special about the film is that so many people can watch it and see themselves and the dream they have for themselves that their parents, family, or friends didn't see for them. The specificity of it made it feel universal."
>
> America Ferrera

Ana's teacher, Mr. Guzman (George Lopez), encourages her to apply for a Columbia University scholarship, but Ana's family will not hear of it. They expect her to follow the family tradition and work at the sewing factory run by her sister Estela (Ingrid Oliu), where her mother also works. Carmen sees Ana's future in simple terms—she will work and get married. "It's a matter of principle," Carmen says, "I've worked since I was thirteen years old and Ana is eighteen years old. Now it's her turn." Why should Ana want anything else? But the teenager has other plans for herself and resents her mother's traditional way of thinking.

Mother and daughter butt heads on most topics, from Ana's body—which Carmen believes will stop men from liking her—to her future and her decision to grow up on her own terms. This is especially clear when Ana decides to lose her virginity. She's got no delusions about love, so she picks the nice, sensible Jimmy (Brian Sites) to sleep with. Again, she's proud of her body. "Turn on the light, I want you to see me," says Ana; "This is what I look like."

If this demonstrates a confidence beyond her years, Ana is also a typical teenager in other ways. She is stubborn, storming off in tantrums about the "sweatshop" they are working in without having had any real-world experience for comparison. Ana rolls her eyes constantly at Carmen, especially when her mother declares that she is pregnant, a move calculated to try and guilt Ana into staying at home.

The fact that this relationship works so well is a credit to the two actors at the center of *Real Women Have Curves*. Lupe Ontiveros is an established actress who brings a strong sense of motherly love to Carmen's antics. Meanwhile, it's remarkable to note that this was America Ferrera's first film—her natural talent is clear in how she displays a variety of complex emotions. Her Ana feels real and lived in, and she is inspiring because she is so very relatable. I can only guess how it must have felt for young Latina girls to see themselves reflected in her character, given such a historic lack of such positive female roles. Sadly, years after this movie was released, this still remains the case.

The relationships in *Real Women Have Curves* are authentic, as is the location. Director Patricia Cardoso refused to stoop to clichés in creating Ana's predominantly Latinx suburb. It's not "dangerous" or stereotypically filled with gangs; there's real beauty in the mix of families, colorful buildings, and cultural history.

This was important to Cardoso, who grew up in Bogota, Columbia, watching movies from the USA and Europe. She moved to Los Angeles in 1987 to go to film school at UCLA, and it wasn't until she was twenty-one that she saw her first Colombian film. "I remember being like, 'Oh my God, it's so amazing: my own streets—my own people. That's my moon!'" Cardoso says, "I hadn't been aware I wasn't seeing my own people onscreen...I was blown away."

She had never originally intended to move to Hollywood to make movies. After high school, Patricia Cardoso studied archeology and anthropology at a university in Bogota, publishing her findings in many academic journals. It was when she realized that there might be a bigger platform to tell her stories that she switched to studying cinema.

At film school in the United States, Cardoso showed real talent, winning the 1990 Best Student Film Award at the Sundance Film Festival with her short *The Air Globes*. After graduating, Cardoso applied six times for an internship at Sundance and got in on her final try. This led to an internship for documentarians Freida Lee Mock and Terry Sanders and eventually to work at the Latin American Screenwriters Lab. This organization held workshops with leading Latinx filmmakers such as Guillermo del Toro and cinematographer Emmanuel Lubezki, so Cardoso had the opportunity to learn from the best.

> "[The percentage of] Latina women and ethnic minority women in television is 2 percent, and in feature films, there is 0 percent. There is basically Patricia Cardoso and nobody else."
>
> Maria Giese, filmmaker and activist

By the time she made *Real Women Have Curves*, Patricia Cardoso had already been directing films for a decade and had written multiple unproduced screenplays. In a full-circle moment, *Real Women Have Curves* was selected to premiere at the Sundance Film Festival, twelve years after her original short was screened there. The film quickly became a critical hit, winning the Audience Award and Special Jury Prize for Acting for both America Ferrera and Lupe Ontiveros. More accolades followed, including an Independent Spirit award and the Humanitas Prize, which honors entertainment that promotes human dignity.

Since *Real Women Have Curves* was released, Patricia Cardoso has struggled to get subsequent feature films made and has lost out on several big jobs to white male directors. But her film remains a favorite among many audiences, and Cardoso still gets thanked for her honesty—by, she says, "Women who look like me, women who don't look like movie stars. Women who have real bodies, which 98 percent of women in the world have."

🎥 THE FEMALE GAZE

Instead of perpetuating the usual beauty ideals of whiteness and thinness, *Real Women Have Curves* celebrates the natural body of Mexican-American Ana. She accepts and loves herself, even while her mother Carmen tells her she needs to lose weight to find a husband. The scene inside the sewing factory when the women strip off and proudly display their ample curves still feels revolutionary. Through the eyes of Patricia Cardoso, this scene invites viewers to celebrate with them, not to look upon them as sexual objects. Similarly, when Ana takes control of losing her virginity, she asks the boy to look at her as she is. Rather than reinforcing a societal message that women only have value if they are liked by men, the film shows that true acceptance of yourself is vastly more important.

≡ FAST FACTS

★ *Real Women Have Curves* is based on a play written by Josefina López, who was inspired to write it after being told she should be ashamed of her own body and culture. She decided that if there were "no stories about chunky girls getting laid, or being heroes, then I'm going to write those stories." It took eleven years to get it to the big screen.

★ Director Patricia Cardoso was the first Columbian woman to win a Fulbright scholarship to study film in Los Angeles. Despite her established filmography, Patricia Cardoso had to audition to direct the film, which involved doing an interview with the producers and studio. Her strong identification with the themes in the story led her to be successful in securing the role.

★ Patricia Cardoso wanted to make sure the neighborhood portrayed in the film was beautiful and celebrated the meaningful lives of everyday Latinos, so she worked with cinematographer Jim Denault to create sun-drenched, colorful frames, in a stark contrast to the "grittiness" of other films set in East LA.

★ Similarly, Cardoso refused to make the sewing factory a "grim sweatshop," because for the characters, this was respectful and enjoyable work.

★ Fifteen years after the release of the movie, some critics and writers have noticed similarities in terms of the mother-daughter dynamics between *Real Women Have Curves* and 2017's *Lady Bird*, written and directed by Greta Gerwig.

★ Despite the success of this film, director Patricia Cardoso has struggled to get more directorial work, saying she was almost hired to helm various feature films.

Bend It Like Beckham

Kintop Pictures, 2002, UK | Color, 112 minutes, Comedy/Drama

A young English girl from a Punjabi Sikh family battles for the right to play on a women's soccer team.

Director: Gurinder Chadha

Producer: Deepak Nayar

Cinematography: Jong Lin

Screenplay: Gurinder Chadha, Guljit Bindra, Paul Mayeda Berges

Starring: Parminder K. Nagra ("Jesminder"), Keira Knightley ("Juliette"), Jonathan Rhys Meyers ("Joe"), Anupam Kher ("Mr. Bhamra"), Shaheen Khan ("Mrs. Bhamra"), Archie Panjabi ("Pinky"), Juliet Stevenson ("Paula")

"I tell stories about people audiences might think they have nothing in common with, but then they emotionally connect with them and find they're not different at all."

—Gurinder Chadha

Inside the bedroom of Jesminder Bhamra (Parminder K. Nagra) hangs a giant poster of David Beckham. The handsome soccer star looks down on Jess as she daydreams of being on the British team and scoring a goal for her country. She envisions a televised game, with the commentators agreeing that Jess is just the savior the team needs...well, all except Jess' mother (Shaheen Khan). When the panel turns to Mrs. Bhamra for her opinion, she says Jess is wasting time playing the sport, she is showing too much leg, and she really needs to find a dress for her sister's wedding.

This daydream sets up the central conflict of *Bend It Like Beckham*: passion versus family duty. Soccer-loving Jess belongs to a traditional Indian family; her parents are Sikhs who moved from Uganda to England. She loves soccer but is forbidden to play the sport. Her parents want Jess to focus on learning how to cook, finding a nice Indian man, and upholding their traditional ways. But one day while secretly playing soccer in the park, Jess is spotted by Juliette (Keira Knightley), who encourages Jess to join their woman's team. The Hounslow Harriers are coached by a handsome Irishman called Joe (Jonathan Rhys Meyers); and Juliette has a crush on him. To make things really complicated, soon Jess does as well.

Jess soon begins to live two lives: one for her mother, where she claims to be working a steady job and helping her sister Pinky (Archie Panjabi) plan her wedding, and the other for herself, where she sneaks off to play on the soccer team and hang out with Juliette. Meanwhile, Juliette is also having trouble with her mother, Paula (Juliet Stevenson), who believes soccer is too "masculine." She's dismayed at Juliette's short hair, tomboy nature, and fondness for athletic wear. "There's a reason why Sporty Spice is the only one without a boyfriend..." Paula laments.

The title of the film refers to David Beckham's trademark kick, which curves the ball's flight in order to evade the opposing team and score a goal. It's used as a metaphor here for the way Jess has to bend the rules in order to follow her heart, all while maneuvering between two separate lives. And while she needs to stick to traditional Sikh values, this is a universal theme—one that as director Gurinder Chadha explains, is particularly applicable to girls. "We can see our goal, but instead of going straight there, we too have to twist and bend the rules sometimes to get what we want," she says, "no matter where we reside [and] no matter what group we claim or do not embrace as part of our ethnic lineage."

> "I think the great thing about *Bend It Like Beckham* was that it managed to be amazingly optimistic.... And I'd love to find that again."
>
> Keira Knightley

And with *Bend It Like Beckham*, Chadha herself does just that. She takes a dependable plot formula (living a double life, parental conflict) and gives it a twist by focusing on bigger themes of tradition, generational clashes, racism, sexism, and romance. Like a soccer game, the movie kicks back and forth between Jess' family life and her sports life. We see the joy she discovers playing soccer and how it spills out into other areas of her life. Parallels are made between Jess and Juliette, who both have mothers who disapprove of the masculine sport. With Juliette's story, Chadha shows how this experience is not limited to certain cultural backgrounds. Instead, this is a wider gender bias forced upon girls that dictates how they are supposed to act in order to "perform" some version of femininity. In Juliette's case, her mother wants her to wear lacy bras, dresses, and high heels, whereas Jess' mother wants her to show less skin and cover up her "shameful" body.

> "What makes it special is the bubbling energy of the cast and the warm joy with which Gurinder Chadha, the director and cowriter, tells her story. I am the first to admit that Gurinder Chadha is not a name on everybody's lips, but this is her third film, and I can promise you she has an unfailing instinct for human comedy that makes you feel good and laugh out loud."
>
> Roger Ebert,
> *Chicago Sun-Times*

Both girls have a crush on their coach, but eventually he falls for Jess. In order to date her, Joe also needs to bend the rules (of coach/player relations) as well as convince her family that he is worthy. This sets up another conflict, as Jess is expected to date an Indian man. As her sister Pinky says, "Do you really want to be the one that everyone stares at at every family do because you married the English bloke?" Never mind that Joe is actually Irish.

There's a further parallel drawn between Jess and her father (Anupam Kher), who comes to see her play and witnesses a racist slur being used against Jess. Mr. Bhamra admits that he too was the target of racism when he moved to England and tried to join a cricket team. Unlike Jess, who kicks up a fuss when she hears the racist word, Mr. Bhamra regrets that he never complained when "those bloody English cricket players threw [him] out of their club like a dog."

In the end, of course, the answer to the conflict is balance. Jess has to find a way to align her Indian and English sides—to come up with a cultural blend of her own making, one which reconciles family duty with her own independent passions.

The reason why this resolution feels authentic in *Bend It Like Beckham* is because it is precisely the same balance that director Gurinder Chadha had to find. She was born in Africa to Indian parents who moved to England when she was young. Growing up, she felt British but was also expected by her family to behave like a traditional Indian girl. When Chadha made her way into directing in the 1990s, she explored these themes of identity and culture in television specials and movies. Her second feature film *What's Cooking?* from 2000 wove together the stories of four families preparing a Thanksgiving dinner. The families were of Hispanic, Vietnamese, African American, and Jewish descent. Her goal was to show, through the making of a meal, the many similarities these different families shared. "As you become emotionally invested," Chadha said about the film, "you forget about where they come from. You stop seeing difference and realize they all want the same thing, to keep their families together."

> "*Bend It Like Beckham* offered an optimistic message of cultural wholeness I needed as I entered the thick of middle school, 4,000 miles from England and 7,400 from my grandparents' rural Indian villages. It made me realize I didn't have to try so hard to fit in and could work on reveling in the moments when I didn't."
>
> Rajpreet Heir,
> *The Atlantic*

What's Cooking? gave Gurinder Chadha some success, opening the door for her to release *Bend It Like Beckham* two years later. The film was made for $6 million and wasn't expected to be a hit. There were no movie stars attached, and the title referenced a UK soccer star who was not well known outside his own country—apart from fans of the pop group the Spice Girls, who knew David Beckham as "Mr. Posh Spice." When the film was released, some critics dismissed it as just another cultural comedy, but *Bend It Like*

Beckham quickly became popular with audiences. It grossed over $75 million worldwide to become one of the biggest British films of 2002. It also launched the careers of its two young female stars; Keira Knightley went on to achieve movie stardom, and Parminder Nagra had the longest run of any actor on the TV show *ER*.

"No one imagined that the movie was going to be so huge," said Gurinder Chadha in an interview, "and everywhere I went, people were like, 'Why don't you do a sequel?'" But in the end she decided against that. Instead, her next movie was a Bollywood version of Jane Austen's *Pride & Prejudice* in 2004, which was called *Bride & Prejudice*. After that came the teen film *Angus, Thongs and Perfect Snogging* in 2008, the comedy *It's a Wonderful Afterlife* in 2010, and the period drama *Viceroy's House* in 2017. Throughout, she has remained true to her original voice, with most of her movies continuing to feature stories about people of Indian heritage. In 2006, Chadha was made an Officer of the Order of the British Empire for her services to the British film industry.

In 2015, Gurinder Chadha did return to the world of *Bend It Like Beckham* with a stage musical version that played in London on the West End. In revisiting the film, Chadha reflected on its lasting success and related one particularly memorable experience to *The Guardian*. When she was in the hospital about to give birth, a doctor told Chadha about the doctor's own childbirth story. "She said, 'You know, when I had my child, I could take three possessions," explains Chadha, "and the one thing I wanted to take was *Bend It Like Beckham*. I watched the film over and over, and my child came into the world with the goodness of this movie.' "

❋ THE FEMALE GAZE

Director Gurinder Chadha gives her female characters complexity as they battle the restraints put on women's behavior. We see this clearly in other characters' reaction to Jess and Juliette's love of soccer. Both their mothers disapprove of women playing the sport, and both mothers perpetuate a narrow view of female sexuality. For Jess, being part of the Sikh culture means she is required to cover up her body and not encourage sexual interest, while Juliette is encouraged to try and attract more attention to her body within the confines of what is considered to be "feminine" clothing. Ultimately the message Chadha infuses into the film is one of women creating their own personal identity and not simply doing what is expected.

≡ FAST FACTS

★ With her 1993 debut *Bhaji on the Beach*, Gurinder Chadha became the first British Asian woman to ever direct a feature film.

★ The scar on Parminder Nagra's leg is real, and though she worried she wouldn't be cast in the film because of it, Gurinder Chadha embraced it by writing her scar into the script.

★ Keira Knightley was sixteen when she filmed *Bend It Like Beckham*, and though she had appeared in a few small roles, this was her breakthrough. A year after the release, she starred in the first installment of the *Pirates of the Caribbean* mega franchise.

★ Most of the female soccer players in the film were professionals, and both Parminder Nagra and Keira Knightley performed all of their own playing. They each trained for three months before filming, and their coach said that Knightley was naturally talented at the sport.

★ Because David Beckham wasn't a household name outside of England, the film distributor in the United States considered changing the name to *Move It Like Mia*, a reference to the American soccer player Mia Hamm.

★ In 2004, *Bend It Like Beckham* played at the Pyongyang Film Festival in North Korea, making it the first western film to be publicly screened in that country—though it was heavily edited due to censorship.

Alana Wulff on *Thirteen* (2003)

Tucked away in the sanctity of a teenage bedroom, two young girls take turns inhaling the nitrous oxide from an empty can of whipped cream. High and astonished at their newfound inability to feel pain, the girls giggle as they punch and slap one another—each strike more powerful than the last. It's a moment of confrontation, not just because of the self-abuse perpetrated by these seemingly harmless adolescent girls, but because it's a moment that forces the audience to acknowledge the terrifying desire we've all had to push the boundaries.

This also happens to be the opening scene of Catherine Hardwicke's directorial debut, *Thirteen*—a brutal yet tender story of two Year 7 students, Tracy (Evan Rachel Wood) and Evie (Nikki Reed), both age thirteen, who spiral into a world of drugs, crime, sex, and self-harm.

Hardwicke doesn't pull any punches (no pun intended). The film dives headfirst into the sensitive complexities of high school friendships and takes a raw approach to themes of desperation and betrayal. We see the lengths to which "good girl" Tracy goes in the hopes of earning the respect of Evie, the popular yet troubled leader of the pack. It's neorealism in a tank top and hoop earrings, and while we know how things are set to unfold, it's still shocking to see them play out in such an intense way.

This film is fast, emotional, and filled with teen angst—just like growing up. Hardwicke's approach isn't moralizing or judgmental, it's an honest and bracing look at the realities of adolescence—how desperate it can feel to fit in and prove ourselves and what it means when we know we're in too deep.

As an audience, we watch this film hating what happens to both girls, but not hating the actual movie itself. Inevitably, we feel for Tracy and her recovering alcoholic mother (played flawlessly by Holly Hunter). This could in large part be due to the fact that the semiautobiographical script was written by Reed at the age of fourteen. Combined with Hardwicke's almost documentary approach to filming, it's as realistic as it gets.

Think quick cuts, footage shot almost entirely by handheld cameras, and a tactile approach to lightning that becomes darker and grittier as Tracy descends further and further into oblivion. By the final scenes, the film is almost entirely black and white, providing us with no real answers to the problems posed throughout the movie—but giving viewers a sense that the chaos has finally come to a halt and that peace might eventually be around the corner.

This film is dark, hard to watch at times, and filled with passionate extremes, but this was always going to be the case. Those shocked by the movie's in-your-face approach to the subject matter clearly haven't dealt with teenage girls before, as voiced in the poignant sentiment of Cecilia Lisbon in *The Virgin Suicides*, "Obviously, doctor, you've never been a thirteen-year-old girl."

Alana Wulff is a writer, editor, and author with a deep love of pop culture and some might say an unnatural obsession with Christina Ricci. Alana's latest book, GIRLISH, is a guide to feminism for tween and teen girls the world over.

April Wolfe on *Innocence* (2004)

Lucile Hadžihalilović's *Innocence* acts as both an extended metaphor for female sexual awakening and an effectively chilling science fiction tale. In the world of *Innocence*, little girls arrive at a remote French boarding school in their very own caskets. They awake like adorable Draculas, immune to the sunshine, surrounded by their peers, and questioning why they're there. Each is given a different colored ribbon to signify their age, with the youngest in red and the oldest in purple.

Though this is only Hadžihalilović's sophomore feature film, she confidently withholds information about this world and these people and allows only trickles of details to fill in the picture: there are no boys, the girls must rigorously practice ballet, and the eldest girls disappear to an unknown destination at night. During the first moments of the film, we are submerged underwater—this world is confusing, and we do not yet know whether we should accept the tranquility of the water or struggle in its confines. There's no clear way of telling what or who is the danger, which is perhaps the perfect summation of adolescence and the feeling that *something* unknown and frightening is on the horizon: the unfamiliar.

What is most striking about *Innocence* is its dreamlike quality. Hadžihalilović's camera rarely moves. Instead, our vision of this world is fixed, stationary, and often peeks down on the girls from odd angles, not necessarily like surveillance but in the way that we might peek in on the goings-on of a dollhouse. In these carefully composed scenes, modernity abuts the natural world, as when a girl walks down a wooded path at night and electric lamps loom above her, lighting the way. Hadžihalilović juxtaposes warmth and coldness, and the result is an uncomfortable friction, a sense that—though all seems perfect on the surface—something is very wrong.

April Wolfe is a writer, filmmaker, and film critic in Los Angeles. She hosts the genre-film podcast Switchblade Sisters *on the Maximum Fun network.*

The Headless Woman

(La Mujer Sin Cabeza)

Aquafilms/El Deseo, 2008, Argentina | Color, 87 minutes, Drama/Thriller

After a hit-and-run accident, a woman struggles with the idea that she may have killed someone.

Director: Lucrecia Martel

Producers: Pedro Almodóvar, Agustín Almodóvar, Esther García

Cinematography: Bárbara Álvarez

Screenplay: Lucrecia Martel

Starring: María Onetto ("Verónica"), Claudia Cantero ("Josefina"), Inés Efron ("Candita"), Daniel Genoud ("Juan Manuel"), César Bordón ("Marcos")

"In the film, I show a social mechanism...whereby a social group as a whole tries to alleviate the suffering of one of its members. They gather together and cover up what happened in order to protect one of their own, even though it is possible that the person has committed a crime."

—Lucrecia Martel

Near the beginning of *The Headless Woman*, Verónica (or Veró for short, played by María Onetto) is driving down an isolated country road. Her cellphone rings, and she momentarily looks down to find it. That's when it happens. There is a loud bang as her car hits something...or someone. The camera remains on Veró's face as she processes what has just happened. In her side-view mirror, there is what appears to be a dog lying motionless in the middle of the road. After what feels like an eternity, Veró, disoriented, drives on.

Prior to this scene, director Lucrecia Martel sets up some key details told in brief glimpses. First, three boys and a dog play alongside a road in the bright sun. Then a group of women that includes Veró talks in a parking lot about a pool and chlorine. After the accident, Veró goes to the hospital in a daze and later is comforted by sex with a man named Juan Manuel (Daniel Genoud). But when she returns home the next day, it is to her husband, Marcos (César Bordón). Soon, Veró starts to worry that she may have hit a person, not just a dog. Both men, along with the people around her, quickly reassure her that she's just confused. "Don't worry, nothing happened," says Juan Manuel dismissively, even as a body is found in a nearby canal.

Confusion is exactly what viewers of *The Headless Woman* may feel as they too try to work out what has happened. Lucrecia Martel intentionally gives us disparate pieces of information, thereby evoking the amnesia that Veró may be experiencing. The camera stays tightly on Veró's head as Martel tries to put the viewer inside it. Most of what we come to know about her is pieced together from fragments of dialogue. This may prove exasperating for many, but it's a great example of what Martel does so well—she layers imagery, dialogue, and sound design together while trusting the audience to come to their own conclusions.

"In its depiction of willed amnesia and collusion to conceal a hidden current of remembrance, *The Headless Woman* recalls Antonioni's *L'Avventura*, in which a woman's disappearance on a boating expedition is quickly forgotten once the mainland is reached. Like that same director's *Blow-Up*, *The Headless Woman* is a metaphysical ghost story in which enigmatic clues are dropped about a possible crime that is never solved. The more closely you study *The Headless Woman*, the deeper and more unsettling are its mysteries.

Stephen Holden, *The New York Times*

This aesthetic gives us much to feast on in every frame, with little clues and misdirections scattered throughout. There's a small handprint on the side of Veró's car and snippets of information about a body blocking the canal. Seventies music plays in the background, conjuring up a time when Argentina was under a dictatorship and many turned a blind eye to what went on.

Putting aside whether Veró did or did not kill anyone, what is most telling is how she and everyone around her deals with it. Veró is tall, white, and blonde, so she stands out from the people who work for her. They are purposely relegated to the margins of the film while Veró stays front and center. This is a statement of class entitlement, which is made especially clear in how quickly her friends work together to clean up any traces of the accident. There also seem to be few consequences for the possible crime, and we conclude that this is because she is white and the boy was not. Slowly, even Veró starts to convince herself that it couldn't possibly be true. With a new hairstyle, she is a different person from the woman who had the accident and is able to forget.

Of course, we can all relate to wanting a clean slate after a traumatic event. But hair dye is not enough to get rid of ghosts. And Lucrecia Martel makes sure the audience doesn't forget about the boy who may have lost his life. In one scene, an elderly woman, Aunt Lala (María Vaner), claims that her house is full of the dead. "Shh!" she says to Veró; "They're leaving now. Don't look at them. Ignore them and they'll leave." In the background, running out the door, is a young boy, roughly the same age and height as the one who may have died. But of course it's not the same boy—this one is the son of a servant.

"She is nothing less than one of contemporary cinema's true visionaries. Almost every shot in her work shows you something in a way you've never seen it before. Simply put, her films look, sound, and move like no one else's."

Dennis Lim, Film Society of Lincoln Center

"Ignore them and they'll leave," could be a good metaphor for what Lucrecia Martel wanted to say about her country in this film. "I see people that still carry the weight of the really bad stuff that they did not denounce back when it happened under the dictatorship," Martel has said in an interview. "And now the same process is occurring, but it's in relation to poverty. A lot of people pretend they do not see that a huge part of the country is becoming poorer and poorer and is undergoing great suffering. And what we try not to see is that the entire legal system, health system, and education system are structured by social class."

The Headless Woman is one the most political movies in Lucrecia Martel's impressive filmography. She has made a career of crafting mysterious and mesmerizing films, often set in her home province of Salta in Argentina, where she was born in 1966. During her teenage years, she often picked up a camera to document her family's life, and she later studied at two film schools: animation at Avellaneda Experimental and film at the National Experimentation Filmmaking school in Buenos Aires. She was one of a group of young students who eschewed more traditional ways of making movies in favor of social realism. Together, these directors, who included Martel, Martín Rejtman, Pablo Trapero, Adrián Caetano, and Lisandro Alonso, formed the basis of the New Argentine Cinema movement.

Lucrecia Martel's solo debut feature was *La Ciénaga*, released in 2001, which told the story of a family spending their summer at a country house. Martel used metaphors and tragicomedy to comment on Argentina's economy, an approach which earned her awards at both the Berlin and Sundance Film Festivals. Her follow-up in 2004, *The Holy Girl*, was also critically well received. This story followed two teenage Argentinian girls, and Martel's visual style creates a tantalizing mix of innocence and desire.

> "Lucrecia Martel is the elusive poet of Latin American cinema, missing believed lost, the Mary Celeste in human form. She made *La Ciénaga* and *The Holy Girl*; [then] split the Cannes audience in two with her brilliant, maddening *The Headless Woman*."
>
> Xan Brooks,
> *The Guardian*

The Holy Girl competed for the Palme d'Or award at the Cannes Film Festival, as did *The Headless Woman* four years later. But critical reception for this later film was mixed, and its premiere met with boos from the audience. Eventually, *The Headless Woman* secured a small distribution outside of Argentina and slowly began to gain a cult following in places like the USA.

Now, a decade after its initial release, *The Headless Woman* has come to be regarded as an important addition to feminist cinema, largely for the way Lucrecia Martel takes the audience inside the mind of a complex, flawed woman. Martel followed this up with several short films and made a comeback in 2017 with her feature *Zama*, which examined class dynamics and colonialism in its story about a Spanish officer awaiting transfer to Buenos Aires in the seventeenth century.

Lucrecia Martel's unique style of layering dialogue and imagery creates a distinctive mood; she trusts the audience to be able to fill in the blanks. It is no surprise, then, that Martel's initial inspiration for filmmaking grew out of a mixture of women and memories. "My love of storytelling comes from oral tradition," Martel says, "the stories from my grandmother and conversations with [my] mother. The world is full of discussions of condensation, drifts, misunderstanding, repetition. These are the materials I work with. My debt is to these women."

✿ THE FEMALE GAZE

Though the title of the film is *The Headless Woman*, Lucrecia Martel's camera rarely strays from María Onetto's head. We follow the character of Veró closely as she tries, through a layer of amnesia, to process what she may have done. Rarely do we see films which allow access to a woman's thoughts in this way—even more rarely still when it concerns a problematic female character. Veró's actions, in cleaning up any signs of her possible crime and attempting to move on with her life, speak of a privilege which only a member of her class is allowed.

≡ FAST FACTS

★ Lucrecia Martel cites *The Silence* (1963) by Ingmar Bergman as having had a major influence on her career.

★ Martel cast María Onetto because of her aura of mystery. "Secrets enchant me," Martel says, "and Maria can make a sea of secrets out of nothing."

★ Following *The Headless Woman*, Martel began to write a sci-fi script based on an Argentinian comic book. After falling out with the producer, Martel found herself depressed and jobless, so she bought a boat and sailed up the Paraná river with two female friends and a box of books. One of these books was *Zama* by Antonio di Benedetto, which was to become her next feature film.

★ *Zama* was released nine years after *The Headless Woman*, and Martel worried she wouldn't live to see it released in cinemas. After completing the first cut of the film, she was diagnosed with cancer, and she had to stop production to seek treatment. Thankfully, her cancer is now in remission.

★ Martel's film *Zama* was not eligible to play at the 2017 Cannes Film Festival because one of the producers was Pedro Almodóvar, who was President of the Cannes Jury that year. Almodóvar was also a producer on *The Headless Woman*.

Wendy and Lucy

Field Guide Films/Film Science, 2008, USA | Color, 80 minutes, Drama

A young homeless woman loses her dog while passing through a small Oregon town.

MISSING

Director: Kelly Reichardt

Producers: Joshua Blum, Todd Haynes, Phil Morrison, Rajen Savjani

Cinematography: Sam Levy

Screenplay: Kelly Reichardt, Jonathan Raymond

Starring: Michelle Williams ("Wendy"), Will Patton ("mechanic"), Will Oldham ("Icky"), John Robinson ("Andy")

"We decided we were going to make a film about the economic situation in America... It came together post-Katrina. A lot of the victims down there [were] being condemned for letting their life become sort of precarious. So we just started with this idea—wondering what it takes to improve your situation and is this idea that in America anybody can improve their lot in life true?"

—*Kelly Reichardt*

Kelly Reichardt's *Wendy and Lucy* is the type of disquieting film which haunts the viewer long after it is over. It's a small movie about a large problem, one that could easily happen in many of our lives. And it illustrates a perfect marriage between a director devoted to realism and an actor willing to go there.

"Is *Wendy and Lucy* the *Bicycle Thieves* of the New Recession Cinema? Like De Sica's neorealist tragedy about postwar Italy, *Wendy and Lucy* expertly (and presciently) illustrates the current American climate by telling a very small-scale story—the micro in the macro—about the stranglehold of poverty and how bad luck begets bad decisions."

Kimberly Jones, *The Austin Chronicle*

Michelle Williams stars as Wendy, a young woman on the verge of homelessness who is passing through an Oregon town. Wendy's only companion is her dog Lucy, and while she is an expense Wendy can't afford, Lucy gives her a valuable tie to normalcy and a sense of safety as a girl traveling alone. But while they are in Oregon, things go horribly wrong. Wendy's car breaks down, and she gets caught stealing cans of dog food. In a heartbreaking scene, Wendy is taken away from the grocery store in the back of a police car, watching helplessly out the window as Lucy, tied up outside the store, is left behind. When Wendy comes back, Lucy is gone.

The bulk of this eighty-minute movie is spent following Wendy's attempts to find her dog and fix her car. Kelly Reichardt doesn't explain all the details of Wendy's situation; Reichardt provides only small glimpses that allow us to put together what she is going through. This is helped by a powerful and understated performance from Michelle Williams. Williams' Wendy rarely speaks, and her smiles are reserved for her dog. Only once, in a rare display of emotion, does she let her fear and anguish show. There's mention of a plan to travel to Alaska, where she hopes to find a job in a fish cannery. We see Wendy tallying up her money, subtracting the $50 shoplifting fine from her meager total. A phone call to Indiana reveals a sister unwilling to help. Wendy knows her situation is impossible, but she has come too far to go back.

Wendy and Lucy is a film in which not a lot happens on the surface. There are only a few characters and one location. But it all speaks to a larger problem—that of economic disparity in America. Kelly Reichardt and her cowriter Jonathan Raymond wrote the story after Hurricane Katrina hit the Gulf coast of the USA in 2005. The economic impact of the natural disaster hit the people who couldn't afford it the hardest. Then, the very same year that *Wendy and Lucy* was released, the financial crisis arrived. The housing bubble burst, leading to widespread economic decline, homelessness, and unemployment. With the gap between rich and poor widening ever further, the idea of the American Dream—that anyone can improve their life, and that if you're suffering from poverty, it's your fault—seems increasingly false.

Wendy's plight shows just how perilous life on the edge of homelessness can be. She is trapped by her situation, so much so that a small piece of bad luck becomes disastrous. She has some money, but no breathing room when things go wrong. And with no credit card or cellphone to her name, we presume Wendy has purposely cut herself off from society. This suggests how it is almost impossible to live outside of the system.

But Reichardt and Raymond wanted to infuse Wendy with ambition and spirit, so her desire to find work in Alaska plays on the American mythology of heading West for a better life. In an interview, Reichardt explained that they wanted to know whether this would be enough. "Could she really improve herself by just having that spirit? If you don't have a decent education, a trust fund, a social net, social skills...[or] any kind of financial net? Is all you really need the gumption to do it? That was sort of the seed of the idea."

Wendy and Lucy premiered at the 2008 Cannes Film Festival, where the dog who played Lucy won the unofficial "Palm Dog" award. Reviews from the festival praised the sparse, tense style of the film, along with the performance given by Michelle Williams.

This was Kelly Reichardt's fourth feature film, coming fourteen years after her debut, *River of Grass*. By this time, Reichardt had already established herself as an important voice in American neorealism, known for her minimalist, realistic style showing characters living on the edge of society in transit to a better life.

> "There was some talk of an Oscar nomination for Williams.... But *Wendy and Lucy*...would have looked a little awkward alongside the other Academy Award nominees. It's true that the big winner, *Slumdog Millionaire*, concerns itself with poverty and disenfranchisement, but it also celebrates, both in its story and in its exuberant, sentimental spirit, the magical power of popular culture to conquer misery, to make dreams come true. And the major function of Oscar night is to affirm that gauzy, enchanting notion. The world of *Wendy and Lucy* offers little in the way of enchantment but rather a different, more austere kind of beauty."
>
> A.O. Scott,
> *The New York Times*

Born in 1964 in Miami, Florida, Reichardt moved to Boston to attend the School of the Museum of Fine Arts. After graduating, she worked in the industry, releasing *River of Grass* in 1994. It was very well received and earned nominations at the Sundance Film Festival and the Independent Spirit Awards, but still Reichardt struggled to get her next film funded. So she started making short films instead. "I had ten years [starting] from the mid-1990s when I couldn't get a movie made," Reichardt explains. "It had a lot to do with being a woman. That's definitely a factor in raising money. During that time, it was impossible to get anything going, so I just said, 'F*** you!' and did Super 8 shorts instead."

In the end, it was an old friend who helped Reichardt secure financing for future projects—director Todd Haynes. The two had met in 1991 when Reichardt worked in the art department of Haynes' film *Poison*. "Kelly was in charge of props and set dressing," Haynes told *Bomb* magazine. "She made me laugh, and we've been friends ever since. I just didn't know what a great filmmaker she was until four years later, when I first saw *River of Grass*. It's an amazing first film. And it's full of the sardonic humor and spritely self-possession that those who know Kelly know are the staples of her personality."

After realizing how much of a struggle Reichardt had been facing, Haynes offered to be executive producer on her next project. His position in the industry combined with Reichardt's incredible talent opened the door for her to make *Old Joy*, released in 2006. This was also her first time working with cowriter Jonathan Raymond. He had been introduced to her by Todd Haynes after Haynes learned that Reichardt was a huge fan of Raymond's novels and short stories. "She asked if I had any smaller stories to potentially adapt, because the novel [his 2004 novel *The Half-Life*] was beyond her resources at that time," Raymond recalled in an interview. "I had the story *Old Joy*, which incredibly, she liked also and decided to adapt into a film. That experience was really fun for both of us, and we just kind of went on from there."

Two years after *Old Joy* was produced, Reichardt and Raymond began *Wendy and Lucy*, which was based on another of his short stories, *Train Choir*. They collaborated again on *Meek's Cutoff* from 2010 and wrote an original screenplay for it based on a true story. This film also reunited Reichardt with Michelle Williams, who starred in the Western as a settler who defends a Native American.

Jonathan Raymond and Kelly Reichardt worked together again on 2013's *Night Moves*, a rare genre entry in their filmography. The thriller follows a small group of radical environmentalists who plan to blow up a hydroelectric dam. Michelle Williams was absent from this film, but joined Reichardt again for *Certain Women*, released in 2016. This time around, Reichardt turned to the short stories of Maile Meloy to create three interconnected vignettes about women in Montana. *Certain Women* won praise from both festivals and critics and marked a return to the quieter films of Reichardt's early career.

"Director Kelly Reichardt has a style that is both contemplative and straightforward, unfolding at a pace closer to real life than most films. Reichardt draws strikingly natural performances from the cast and uses silence as powerfully as words."

Claudia Puig, *USA Today*

In an industry which consistently perpetuates the ideal of the American Dream, Kelly Reichardt's work stands out. She is a filmmaker who is not afraid to delve into the realism and despair of everyday life. She makes small stories in order to create larger conversations. And as Todd Haynes points out, she's done it all despite the added obstacle of her gender. "Kelly's besieged, aimless characters give new meaning to the word antihero," says Haynes; "And Kelly herself, battling tooth and nail to get her film made, did so without any of the benefits usually afforded first-time directors, i.e., a film school background, a calling-card short, some connection to money, or a penis. I don't think many male directors care to acknowledge the advantages their gender affords them, even at rock bottom."

☞ THE FEMALE GAZE

In diametric opposition to the vacuous female characters sometimes shown in Hollywood cinema, *Wendy and Lucy* features a female drifter struggling to stay afloat. Through a quiet performance marked with tiny gestures, Michelle Williams and Kelly Reichardt craft a three-dimensional woman whose complexity is on the inside. We learn more about her from her stoic determination than through what she says. Wendy's goals seem simple—find her dog and get her car fixed—but in this stark, realistic world, every penny counts, and we find ourselves willing her on. Wendy isn't sexualized as a character; she wears no makeup and covers her body with a sweatshirt. And Reichardt doesn't shy away from showing the danger faced by women alone on the streets and how even if they try to stay hidden, their gender still makes them a target.

≡ FAST FACTS

★ As well as directing, Kelly Reichardt is also often the editor of her films, including *Wendy and Lucy*.

★ Because it was so hard to secure financing, Kelly Reichardt had all but given up when she made 2006's *Old Joy*, thinking of it at the time as an art project which wouldn't go anywhere.

★ Michelle Williams had seen Kelly Reichardt's film *Old Joy* and knew she wanted to work with the director, coming directly from the set of Charlie Kaufman's *Synecdoche New York*.

★ *Wendy and Lucy* was reportedly made on a budget of only $300,000; it was filmed over twenty days with the smallest crew possible in order to enhance the realism.

★ The dog in *Wendy and Lucy* was Kelly Reichardt's own pet, who was also called Lucy. When Lucy passed away, Reichardt dedicated *Certain Women* to her late friend.

★ The film played at the Cannes, Toronto, and New York Film Festivals. It was eventually distributed by Oscilloscope Laboratories, an independent film company created by Beastie Boy Adam Yauch.

★ Reichardt's 2016 film *Certain Women* won the Best Film award at the London Film Festival.

Women Without Men

(Zanan-e Bedun-e Mardan)

An Essential Filmproduktion/Coop99/Parisienne de Prod, 2009, Iran | Color, 95 minutes, Drama

During the 1953 coup in Iran, four women's lives intersect as they try to find independence.

Director: Shirin Neshat (in collaboration with Shoja Azari)

Producers: Susanne Marian, Martin Gschlacht, and Philippe Bober

Cinematography: Martin Gschlacht

Screenplay: Shirin Neshat and Shoja Azari, based on the novel by Shahrnush Parsipur

Starring: Pegah Ferydoni ("Faezeh"), Shabnam Toulouei ("Munis"), Arita Shahrzad ("Fakhri"), Orsi Tóth ("Zarin")

"I've never been one of those artists who's been immediately accepted. There have been a lot of doubts. I think the impact hopefully can be on the younger generations and Iranian youth, as they look for new ways of communication and taking more classic and ancient ideas and transforming them into something contemporary."

—Shirin Neshat

In 1953, an American-led, British-backed coup in Iran brought down the elected Prime Minister and reinstalled the Shah to power. This coup effectively ended democracy in the country, damaged relationships with the West, and led to the Islamic revolution in 1979, the effects of which are still being felt. This historical moment is the setting for Shirin Neshat's *Women Without Men*, which follows four fictional women who are each struggling for independence from the men in their lives.

At the very beginning of the film, Munis (Shabnam Tolouei) jumps from a building, attempting to end her own life. She is seeking freedom from her brother, who restricts her access to any news and insists on marrying her off. He is aggressive and dominant, yet Munis' friend Faezeh (Pegah Ferydoni) wants to marry him. Then there is Fakhri (Arita Shahrzad), a woman unhappy in her marriage, who longs for an old lover. And Zarin (Orsi Tóth), who is desperately sad in her job as a prostitute, where she can't even look at her male clients. These four women converge in a dreamlike garden that is part of the estate Fakhri buys to escape her husband. This garden becomes a sort of Eden for them—an oasis where they can find solace without men.

The title of *Women Without Men* comes from the book it is based on, a popular Iranian novel by Shahrnush Parsipur. This title also serves as a nice play on the Ernest Hemingway novel *Men Without Women*. Like the source material, the film adaptation features a mixture of sociopolitical themes and magical realism. The historical facts of the coup and protests are embedded in the story, but so too are characters who seem to possess otherworldly abilities and several scenes which feel like dreams or nightmares.

The four central women come from different backgrounds and social classes, but all represent the historical repression of women in some way. Munis faces death in order to use her political voice. Faezeh struggles with shame and trauma after being sexually abused. Zarin feels like she can't get her body clean of all the men she's slept with; at one point, she scrubs her skin until she bleeds. And Fakhri is told her vast intelligence amounts to nothing because she is not young and no longer beautiful.

Director Shirin Neshat uses a great deal of metaphor and symbolism in the film, particularly when it comes to the garden. "In Iranian culture, the garden has also been regarded in political terms, suggesting ideas of 'exile,' 'independence,' and 'freedom,'" Neshat explains. "In *Women Without Men*, the garden is treated as a space of exile, refuge, oasis, where one can feel safe and secure."

When the four women meet there, they find true friendship, support, and a sense of autonomy for the first time.

The use of the chador (veil) in the film is also a symbol, alternating between representing both the oppression of women and a possible liberation for them, in terms of offering a brief freedom from scrutiny. In the 1950s, women in Iran could still choose whether they wanted to wear a chador or not. The character of Fakhri is seen without one, while Munis and Faezeh are often veiled. This freedom of choice gives the viewer a window into what Iran was like before the coup.

Women Without Men is the debut feature film from director Shirin Neshat, but it was not the first time she had been inspired by the book of the same name. Neshat is a visual artist and photographer who had previously exhibited video installations based around the characters in *Women Without Men*. This background in visual art is very apparent in her filmmaking, with certain images so strikingly composed they would not be out of place on the wall of a gallery, like the stark frames of Munis wearing her black chador, a lone woman in a sea of male protestors all dressed in white; or the garden scenes, which are almost painterly in their composition— fog illuminated by sunlight streaming through the trees, dancing through patches of brightly colored wildflowers.

Color plays an important role throughout the film. In some scenes it is overly saturated, evoking a dreamlike sense of nostalgia for better times. By contrast, during the street protest scenes, the color has been drained away, giving them the appearance of news footage. The sound design is very evocative too—a rich soundscape of protest yells, urgent whispers, haunting singing, and tense silence.

Shirin Neshat was herself born a few years after the coup, in 1957. At age seventeen, she was sent to the United States to complete her education. This was just before the Iranian revolution of 1979, which abolished the monarchy in favor of an Islamic state and meant that Neshat was suddenly exiled from her home country. She would be unable to return, even to visit, for almost twenty years.

After attending the University of California at Berkeley, Neshat moved to New York and started making art. In the early 1990s, she gained a following for her photography, which explored the idea of femininity within Islamic fundamentalism. She moved into video later that same decade and created a series of installations focusing on gender politics, religious authority, and identity. Her work was displayed in museums all over the world, and she quickly gained a reputation as a strong female voice in the visual art world.

In 2002, a friend gave Shirin Neshat a Farsi copy of *Women Without Men* by Shahrnush Parsipur. She was instantly drawn to the mix of mysticism and historical events and knew it was the right story for her to tackle. "In my work, I've asked deep, personal, philosophical questions as a person and as a woman," Neshat has said; "I've also engaged with larger issues that are above and beyond me, too." She began to use *Women Without Men* as inspiration to create more art about religion, gender, and politics.

It also made sense to use the book as the basis for her first feature film. But the process proved tricky, with Shirin Neshat and her collaborative partner Shoja Azari forbidden from making a film in Iran. For casting they looked to Europe, searching for actors who spoke Farsi with an Iranian accent. And when filming started, Casablanca in Morocco was used to double for Tehran.

When it was complete, *Women Without Men* was screened at the Venice Film Festival, and Neshat won the Silver Lion for Best Director. The film was banned from being screened in Iran, but that didn't stop it from being distributed. "I had heard that piracy is a big deal in Iran," says Neshat; "I hear about big American films that haven't even been released in theaters but Iranian people are watching [them] in their living rooms. Our film opened in Los Angeles on April 9, but on April 8, the film was already selling in underground stores in Tehran. I got a call from my sister who [had] already bought a few copies of it. I was delighted by the power of piracy that allowed this film to be distributed. Many Iranian people are looking at this film."

Since then, Shirin Neshat has kept working, though she has largely returned to short films. Her second feature came eight years after *Women Without Men*. Called *Looking for Oum Kulthum*, it again explores ideas of gender and the restrictions placed on women, this time through the fictional story of an exiled Iranian filmmaker who wants to make a film about an Egyptian singer.

Though she still lives in exile from Iran, where her work is forbidden to be displayed, Shirin Neshat remains a powerful voice for her people. In 2014 she gave a TED talk about the importance of using art as a form of protest and how optimistic the new movements happening in her country make her feel. "Art is our weapon," Shirin Neshat said; "Culture is a form of resistance."

✸ THE FEMALE GAZE

The four female characters in *Women Without Men* represent the many different ways women have historically been repressed. Though the setting is 1950s Iran, the themes of silencing, controlling, shaming, and abusing women explored here are universal. One particularly visceral scene takes place inside a bathhouse, where most of the women are partially covered up. There is a young boy among the women who finds the character Zarin completely naked, scrubbing her skinny body raw, trying to feel "clean." This is an example of Shirin Neshat's unflinching approach to showing trauma, and it leads the audience to also wonder about the future effects on this young boy. But *Women Without Men* is uplifting, too, showing how each of these women finds freedom, independence, and ultimately, happiness.

≡ FAST FACTS

★ Shirin Neshat was inspired to make art after she took a trip back to Iran in 1993, nineteen years after she left. She decided to document exile and identity through a series of photographs.

★ *Women Without Men* took Neshat six years to make, and she worried the Iranian symbolism would make it hard for western audiences to follow. "We have been censored for so long that the only way we can express ourselves is through the use of metaphors and allegory," she said; "So for a western audience to understand it, they have to read between the lines—the way Iranians express themselves—when they are used to people being very direct."

★ The film's score was composed by Ryûichi Sakamoto, who in addition to being an Oscar-winning composer, is known as the "godfather of techno and hip-hop."

★ There is a dedication at the end of *Women Without Men* to "those who lost their lives fighting for freedom and democracy in Iran, from the constitutional revolution of 1906 to the Green Movement of 2009."

★ Neshat's work has been shown in major museums around the world, winning accolades such as the 2014 Crystal Award by the World Economic Forum. This is given to artists who have made a contribution to improving the state of the world.

Moira Macdonald on *Bright Star* (2009)

"Don't come back," a flame-haired little girl says sternly to a withered leaf; "There is no autumn around here."

Jane Campion's beautiful *Bright Star* is about a relationship that reached autumn far too soon; a story of young love's bright burning and too-quick end. Set in the London suburb of Hampstead and beginning in 1818, it focuses on the poet John Keats (Ben Whishaw), who at twenty-three fell in love with his eighteen-year-old neighbor, Fanny Brawne (Abbie Cornish).

Their relationship had little future: He was poor and in ill health; her mother wished her to make a better match. And yet, as is documented in a remarkable series of surviving love letters, these two found a way to make time stand still. As he wrote in the poem that gave this film its title, she was steadfast and unchangeable; he lived to hear her "tender-taken breath."

They lived in adjoining houses (she with her mother and young siblings, he with a friend) for much of the time until 1820, when Keats, suffering from tuberculosis, traveled to Italy for the warmer air. He and Fanny never met again.

Campion, triumphantly back in the emotional realm of *The Piano*, fills *Bright Star* with poetry (right through the end credits, accompanied not by music but by Whishaw's soulful reading of "Ode to a Nightingale"), both in words and images.

In one paradisaically lovely shot, Fanny's bedroom is transformed into a butterfly garden; in another, she lies on her bed as a wind makes the sheer curtain billow above her, as if she's overcome by the force of something bigger.

And as Fanny, Keats, and his friend Charles Brown (Paul Schneider) walk on Hampstead Heath, the camera pulls back and they become distant figures on the vast brown field, dwarfed by nature.

Cornish and Whishaw, two little-known actors about to become much better known, give ardent performances as the young lovers engulfed in the all-encompassing nature of a first true passion. And while giving us a detailed portrait of early-nineteenth-century life—it's striking how little Fanny has to do, other than stitch and desultorily play with her brother and sister—Campion makes the film remarkably intimate in its dusky candlelight, pulling us into the world Keats and Fanny create.

They change before our eyes (these are, we remember, very young people, with the explosive emotions that come with youth), with Cornish in particular displaying a haunting, quiet seriousness later in the film, as if love is crushing her.

Bright Star is a gentle, quiet film; little happens, but we find immense pleasure in the movements of a cat, the innocence of a small girl (lovely Edie Martin, who plays Fanny's little sister), the resolute path of a needle through an elaborate garment, the way that poetry can briefly transport us to a lovelier place.

"Let's pretend I will return in the spring," says a pale Keats to Fanny, before his departure for Italy; just try not to be moved.

This review originally appeared in The Seattle Times.

Moira Macdonald has been a staff critic at The Seattle Times *since 2001, writing about movies, books, dance, and other things that delight her.*

Fish Tank

ContentFilm/Kasander Film Company, 2009, UK | Color, 123 minutes, Drama

A teenage girl living in a housing estate dreams of being a hip-hop dancer and develops a crush on her mother's new boyfriend.

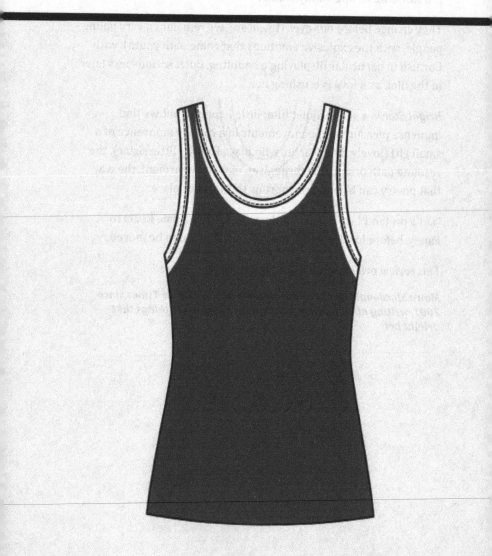

Director: Andrea Arnold

Producers: Kees Kasander, Nick Laws

Cinematography: Robbie Ryan

Screenplay: Andrea Arnold

Starring: Katie Jarvis ("Mia"), Michael Fassbender ("Conor"), Kierston Wareing ("Joanne"), Rebecca Griffiths ("Tyler"), Sarah Bayes ("Keeley")

"When I started Fish Tank, I was aware I was making another smaller film, and some people said I should be making a bigger film with more money, perhaps even a Hollywood film. But I've been lucky to have had a lot of freedom. I'm pretty much making the films I want."

—Andrea Arnold

"I liked the tone of her films. I like the way, as a filmmaker, she's very nonjudgmental of the characters, their actions and decisions in her stories, and that there's no clear right or wrong. It's a mixture of all of those things combined in each of the characters. So I liked the way she described the human condition, how we behave with each other and what we do to each other, and how that affects us."

Michael Fassbender

The British New Wave was a cinematic movement that first took shape in the 1950s and gained popularity throughout the 1960s. In a similar manner to the other New Waves happening around the world, young directors in England began to challenge the mainstream, using their voices to talk about poverty, race, and the widening class divide. They made social realist films called "Kitchen Sink Dramas" which delivered an uncompromising look at everyday life.

From the directors to the protagonists, this was a cinematic movement dominated by men. The filmmakers leading the way were Karel Reisz, Tony Richardson, Lindsay Anderson, and a bit later, Ken Loach and Mike Leigh. Their films typically featured "angry young men" who were disillusioned with society. But in the late 1990s and early 2000s, two women started to make their mark in the social realism genre: Andrea Arnold and Lynne Ramsay. Arnold in particular seemed to take the tropes from the British New Wave and give them a new spin by focusing on female characters.

In *Fish Tank*, the story follows an angry fifteen-year-old girl who lives in a council estate. This is Mia, played by first-time actress Katie Jarvis. The story begins with Mia taunting a group of girls about their dancing, then headbutting one of them and running away from the scene of that crime to create a new one by trying to free a horse tied up in a vacant lot. She's angry with her rarely-sober mother Joanne (Kierston Wareing), her feisty little sister Tyler (Rebecca Griffiths), and her former best friend Keeley (Sarah Bayes).

"In freeing her young star's physicality in *Fish Tank*, Arnold also demonstrates one way a girl might learn to swim up and out."

Lisa Schwarzbaum,
Entertainment Weekly

Mia's one escape is through dance. She loves listening to hip-hop music and watching videos online of dance crews performing and makes up her own routines when nobody is watching. One morning, she is dancing in the kitchen when her mother's new boyfriend Conor (Michael Fassbender) walks in. He is charming and shows her some rare kindness—he lends her a video camera as encouragement to enter a dance contest. It's no surprise that Mia soon develops a crush on Conor, and his response is one the audience may expect but hopes won't actually happen.

The world Andrea Arnold creates around Mia is one of loneliness and isolation. Beneath her hard exterior, Mia craves the kind of love and safety to which all teenagers are entitled. It's thanks to Arnold's writing and Katie Jarvis' strong performance that we can sympathize with this volatile character. Mia is trying to understand herself; she is struggling to control her own emotions, wrestling with them between fury and fear.

This was the first film role for Katie Jarvis, who was discovered by an assistant while Katie was having a loud fight with her boyfriend at a train station. Arnold and her team had already auditioned established actresses, but Jarvis had something the other actresses didn't—authenticity. Having grown up in a housing estate in Essex, Jarvis knew the world that Mia inhabited and brought a raw sense of truth to the character. Immediately after making *Fish Tank*, Jarvis discovered she was pregnant, and she gave birth to her daughter just before walking the red carpet at the Cannes Film Festival.

Michael Fassbender, on the other hand, was already a known commodity by the time *Fish Tank* was released in the USA. He'd caught the eye of critics in Steve McQueen's *Hunger*, playing the Irish militant Bobby Sands. And audiences had noticed him in Quentin Tarantino's *Inglourious Basterds*, where he had a memorable role as a British Army officer. Later, he would go on to star as the villain Magneto in the *X-Men* franchise and be nominated for two Academy Awards—one as the title character in *Steve Jobs* and the other as a cruel slave owner in *12 Years a Slave*. But *Fish Tank* remains one of his best performances to date. With Conor, Fassbender creates an immense amount of unease, playing him with the perfect mix of charisma and menace; too much of either one, and the major turning points of the film would not have rung true.

These well-judged performances were helped by Arnold's careful direction. She filmed the story in sequential order and only gave her actors the pages of the script they would be shooting that day. This was a new way of working for Michael Fassbender, who had signed on without reading the whole script. Initially he was nervous, but he said later that Arnold made him feel safe. "It was very rewarding, that sort of experience, and challenging," Fassbender said; "It's always nice to have a risk element there, something that you don't know whether you're going to fall flat on your face or you're going to pull it off. It's quite exciting."

Arnold's process also helped to take some of the pressure off new star Katie Jarvis. As Arnold explains, "She didn't have to take on the idea of the whole film. A day is possible, whereas if you think about the next six weeks, that could be overwhelming."

The stylistic signatures of Andrea Arnold's work are all present in *Fish Tank*, beginning with the realistic setting. Arnold wanted to show how vibrant estate life could be, without sugar-coating it. There's trash on the sidewalks and graffiti on the walls, and there are tiny little apartments which all look the same. The sense of claustrophobia and tension is enhanced by her use of handheld camera, which grows increasingly unsteady as emotions rise. And finally, as with many of her films, *Fish Tank* is shot in a 4:3 aspect ratio. This square frame, instead of the more traditional rectangle, gives the appearance of being a window into Mia's world. "I think it's a very beautiful frame for one person," Arnold explained in an interview; "It is a portrait frame. My films are generally from the point of view of one person. I think it's a very respectful frame. I keep using the word respect, and I don't know why I keep saying that, but that's what it feels like to me.... It makes them really important. The landscape doesn't take it from them. They're not small in the middle of something. It gives them real respect and importance."

Like her character Mia, Andrea Arnold also grew up on a council estate. She was born in 1961 in Kent, England, to parents who were just teenagers themselves when they had her. From a very young age, Arnold kept notebooks filled with observations about people, events, and places, to turn into stories later on. At eighteen, she left school and moved to London, where she discovered a love of movies watching films such as Francis Ford Coppola's *Apocalypse Now*, *The Elephant Man* by David Lynch, and *Blood Simple* by the Coen brothers.

Career-wise, Arnold seems to have had nine lives. There was a stint in a dance troupe called Zoo, and there were roles as an actress on television and a stint as a host on a children's TV show called *No. 73*. After that, Arnold moved to Los Angeles to study at the American Film Institute. By the time she returned to England, she knew that she wanted to direct.

Her first short film was called *Milk*. Released in 1998, it was an emotional ten-minute movie about a woman who decides not to attend the funeral of her child. A few years later came *Dog*, another short, which focused on a teenage girl whose day with her boyfriend is interrupted by a surprising event. Her third short, *Wasp*, was another gritty film that follows an alcoholic single mother as she neglects her children. This was the movie which put Andrea Arnold firmly on the list of directors to watch—especially after she won the Academy Award for Best Live Action Short in 2005.

Following that success, in 2006 Arnold was invited to join a project created by filmmaker Lars von Trier called *The Advance Party*. The idea was to have three different directors make three separate films about the same characters. Arnold's contribution was the first of the trilogy, called *Red Road*. Her feature film debut, it was about a CCTV operator who obsesses over the man who killed her husband and child. *Red Road* took Arnold to the Cannes Film Festival, where she won the coveted Jury Prize.

Three years later, she returned to the festival, where *Fish Tank* again won her the Jury Prize. In 2011, Arnold directed an adaptation of *Wuthering Heights*, and in 2016, she made yet another appearance at Cannes with *American Honey*. This was her first movie made in the USA, about a young girl who joins a group of teenagers who travel the country making money by selling magazine subscriptions door-to-door. For the third time, Arnold won the Jury Prize. And just as *Fish Tank* had done for Katie Jarvis, *American Honey* again helped to launch the career of a newcomer—this time it was Sasha Lane, whom Arnold had found while sunbathing on a beach.

It would be easy to look at the filmography of Andrea Arnold and see only movies about the grim aspects of life, but that is not entirely true. While each of her stories is unflinchingly real, each also contains moments of great beauty. Her films also stand in contrast to many others of the British New Wave tradition, thanks to the way she takes the time to explore the inner world of young women. And Arnold thinks it's about time we saw more movies made by women. "We've grown up mainly on male stories," she says, "And most of the films have been written and directed by men. That's only half of the human race! We actively have to employ more females, perhaps we need to at this point. There are a lot of capable women out there."

🎬 THE FEMALE GAZE

Andrea Arnold's films tell their stories through the point of view of the main character. In *Fish Tank*, we see the world through the eyes of Mia. This gives the viewers a real sense of intimacy and sometimes, discomfort. Mia is a vulnerable, volatile teenage girl, who is not in any way romanticized or idealized. Her life is shown in raw, real terms. And when we see Conor onscreen, it is through the "gaze" of Mia and is strongly colored by her crush on him. In one scene, Mia picks up the camera, and looks at Conor through the lens, lingering over his shirtless body. The way this relationship is dealt with is delicately done—the audience understands her crush as much as they feel disturbed by how Conor takes advantage of her. No matter how much she desires him, Arnold ensures we never forget that Mia is a minor and he is the adult.

≡ FAST FACTS

★ Andrea Arnold finds inspiration for her films in things she observes in everyday life. Each of her movies start with one image, around which she then shapes the rest of the movie. For *Fish Tank*, Arnold "had an image of a girl pissing on the floor in someone else's house. I thought, 'What is this girl doing?' I start [by] thinking about what that means, who she is, and where she comes from..." From there, Arnold creates a mind map, following each thought until a story forms.

★ Arnold originally wanted a non-actor to play the role of Conor, thinking a bin-collector she had spotted at a park might be the right fit. But she later decided it would be better to put an actor in that role playing opposite Mia as a non-actor, and Michael Fassbender was a perfect fit.

★ On set, Arnold likes to shoot in sequence, but she doesn't like to plan where the camera will be. "I don't really block the scenes," she says; "I want it to be organic, and I like to do it when we're there...I try not to control it too much. I try to keep it alive without squashing it."

★ It helps that Arnold has worked with the same cinematographer, Robbie Ryan, since *Wasp* in 2003. She says she likes how game he is to go anywhere with the camera. "He's like a goat. We shot *Fish Tank* on 35mm, and I remember him just hopping on these rocks next to a cliff with the camera."

★ Arnold is the only filmmaker who has won the Jury Prize in Cannes three times over

★ She is perplexed by the low numbers of female directors, saying in one interview, "I know plenty of women in the industry. I know writers and producers. I even know quite a few directors of photography. But they're not getting to direct. You can be at a festival, and 80 to 90 percent of the films are by men. That's a shame, because women have a different sensibility, and it would be nice if that were reflected."

The Kids Are All Right

Antidote Films/Mandalay Vision, 2010, USA | Color, 106 minutes, Drama/Comedy

A married lesbian couple try to cope when their children seek out their sperm donor father.

Director: Lisa Cholodenko

Producers: Gary Gilbert, Jeffrey Kusama-Hinte, Celine Rattray

Cinematography: Igor Jadue-Lillo

Screenplay: Lisa Cholodenko and Stuart Blumberg

Starring: Julianne Moore ("Jules"), Annette Bening ("Nic"), Mark Ruffalo ("Paul"), Mia Wasikowska ("Joni"), Josh Hutcherson ("Laser")

"I think people have found The Kids Are All Right *incredibly fresh because it's like, finally, somebody doesn't have to die. I feel really cynical about the gay martyr movie. I think we're way past having to be represented like that. You know, I challenge people, if they're going to put gay life or gay characters onscreen, to do it in a much more complex, fresh, and worthy way."*

—Lisa Cholodenko

"Its role in the gay marriage debate may be one of frank acceptance—hardly anyone seems surprised to see two women raising teenagers together, and both kids have turned out pretty great. But with its progressive bent and perfectly crafted character dynamics, *The Kids Are All Right* may be the first great relationship comedy of the decade. If we're lucky, it'll set the tone for what's to come."

Katey Rich, Cinemablend

The inspiration for *The Kids Are All Right* came to writer/director Lisa Cholodenko after she and her partner Wendy decided to have a baby. As they looked at their options, Cholodenko started to think about the possible ramifications for their future child. "We had gone through a lot of conversations of which way to go," said Cholodenko in an interview. "Do we go with a friend? Do we do this with this anonymous person? And what does that mean, and what will it mean for the child in eighteen years? When I sat down to write an original script, I was sort of consumed by this idea."

The idea was further fleshed out when she and Wendy decided to use a sperm donor, and visited a local cryobank. As they searched through the files, Cholodenko couldn't help but think about the men behind the donations. "The donors are anonymous, so you can't get pictures of them as adults," she explains, "but you can get a baby picture, and I remember being really struck by this one." That ended up being the donor they chose, and her script was put on hold while Cholodenko and her partner had their baby in 2006.

Years later, she picked up the script again, joined by her writing collaborator Stuart Blumberg. His perspective as someone who had anonymously donated in the past proved vital to the story. "At first I was being very provocative with him," Cholodenko explains. "I said, 'Well, let's call your university and see if you have any offspring.' And all of the blood drained out of his face, and I could see that that was something he was horribly afraid to discover."

> "From *High Art* to *Laurel Canyon* to her latest *The Kids Are All Right*, Cholodenko has proven herself more like a documentary filmmaker, painstakingly trying to present people onscreen as they really are—complicated and messy, forever defying labels and bouncing out of boxes—as opposed to how we wish them to be or how they present themselves. Which, of course, is a damn hard sell."
>
> Lauren Wissot,
> *Slant* magazine

The experiences of Cholodenko and Blumberg formed the plot of *The Kids Are All Right*, about a married lesbian couple who are shocked when their children seek out their sperm donor. Annette Bening stars as Nic, an obstetrician, the more serious of the pair. Julianne Moore is Jules, the carefree half, who in her forties is just launching a new landscaping business. Their son, the exotically named Laser, is played by Josh Hutcherson. Jules and Nic worry about Laser spending all his time with his best friend, who they see as a bad influence. Mia Wasikowska plays their daughter Joni. She is getting ready to leave the house and go to college, which makes Nic and Jules anxious.

The mothers are also dealing with a mid-marriage crisis of sorts, trying to keep the spark between them alive. All of this is further complicated when Laser and Joni track down their anonymous sperm donor father. He is Paul (Mark Ruffalo), the handsome, laid-back owner of an organic restaurant. He's happy to meet his kids, and even hires Jules to help him landscape his garden. But Jules and Paul spending so much time together ends up having drastic consequences for the family.

> "Witty, urbane and thoroughly entertaining, *The Kids Are All Right* is an ode to the virtues of family, in this case a surprisingly conventional one even with its two moms, two kids and one sperm donor. Whatever your politics, between peerless performances, lyrical direction and an adventurous script, this is the sort of pleasingly grown-up fare [that is] all too rare..."
>
> Betsy Sharkey, *Los Angeles Times*

Despite (or because of) the unique family dynamics, the most revolutionary aspect of *The Kids Are All Right* is how it shows a lesbian couple going through the same marriage and family issues as any heterosexual couple. The ideas here are universal—how challenging it is to keep a relationship strong after many years, concerns about whether one's partner still finds one attractive, the stress of one child leaving home for college, and the worry that the other is hiding something. The character of Paul must also face the very idea of family, which he had never found enticing up to that point. But how do you earn the title of father if you haven't been around to raise your children?

Each character is searching for identity in their own way, and it's a testament to the strong writing of Lisa Cholodenko and Stuart Blumberg that these stories are woven together so seamlessly. The shifts in tone are handled gracefully, moving from comedy to drama and back again in the most subtle of ways. The characters feel lived in, with a real sense of history evident in their relationships with one another. It's also an honest story, featuring both people and places in Los Angeles which feel true to life. And there's a nice bit of metaphor involving Paul's garden as a symbol of fertility.

Apart from the writing, praise is due to the stellar cast, who each bring an ease of experience to their roles. Annette Bening and Julianne Moore are multi-Academy Award nominated actors (with Moore winning in 2015 for *Still Alice*), and they both worked with Cholodenko on the script before filming began. Their mutual talent for adding nuance to a performance is well utilized here, allowing them to convey exactly what their characters are going through without the need to vocalize it. The two veterans are well matched by the dynamic younger cast members, Mia Wasikowska and Josh Hutcherson. And Mark Ruffalo is perfect as the likable Paul, with a real vulnerability visible beneath his veneer of cool.

It's no surprise that *The Kids Are All Right* was warmly received by critics and audiences when it was released in 2010. The film premiered at the Sundance Film Festival in January, and a year later was nominated for four Academy Awards: Best Actress for Annette Bening, Best Actor for Mark Ruffalo, Best Original Screenplay, and Best Picture.

The Kids Are All Right was the third feature film both written and directed by Lisa Cholodenko. She was born in Los Angeles in 1964 and came out as a lesbian at age seventeen—a fact her mother had long suspected. At that time, Cholodenko explains, "The temperature and the culture [were] different. So it was fraught for me in the sense that I was in high school, and there weren't other people who were gay that I knew...I had a great love affair in high school, and let myself have that love affair and tried to keep it to myself. My mother took me aside one day and said, 'Well, it's obvious to me that you're in love with this person. You're struggling to kind of sort it out. So why don't you go get some therapy and feel better about it...it's hard to see you struggling.'"

After high school, Cholodenko attended San Francisco State University, getting her first break in film as an editorial assistant on *Boyz in the Hood* under director John Singleton. This experience spurred her to move to New York to pursue a career in filmmaking by studying at Columbia University School of the Arts. During this time, Cholodenko made the short film *Dinner Party*, which won Best Girl's Short at the Seattle Lesbian and Gay Film Festival. She also started working on her first screenplay, which became her debut feature film in 1998. *High Art* starred Ally Sheedy and Radha Mitchell as two women who fall for each other and begin a tumultuous, drug-filled relationship. The movie was chosen to screen at the Sundance Film Festival, where it won Cholodenko the Screenwriting Award.

For a few years following *High Art*, Lisa Cholodenko worked in television before returning to film in 2002 with her second feature, *Laurel Canyon*, starring Frances McDormand, Christian Bale, and Kate Beckinsale. After that came *Cavedweller*—which she didn't write, but did direct—starring Kyra Sedgwick and Aidan Quinn.

After more work in television including an episode of the hit show *The L Word*, Cholodenko had her biggest success to date with *The Kids Are All Right*. But it has taken another eight years for Cholodenko and Stuart Blumberg to start writing together again. For this upcoming project, the two are adapting the Oscar-nominated German film *Toni Erdmann*, about a different complicated family relationship—this time between a daughter and her eccentric father.

✦ THE FEMALE GAZE

The Kids Are All Right remains a unique film for the way the central family is depicted. Here, the two mothers are dealing with the same problems heterosexual relationships face, the children are well-adjusted, and not much time is devoted to characters remarking on how "unusual" their family make-up is. By treating this family like any other, Lisa Cholodenko makes a powerful statement about marriage rights. Representing all kinds of relationships onscreen goes a long way to normalizing the concept for those who don't have experience with the LGBTQ community. This film was released before same-sex marriages were legally recognized in the United States, at a time when LGBTQ couples were fighting for the same rights as heterosexual couples.

≡ FAST FACTS

★ Julianne Moore sought out Lisa Cholodenko to direct her after watching her 1998 film *High Art*. Moore wondered why she had never been offered a role in that film and actively tracked down Cholodenko, who was already a big fan of hers.

★ *The Kids Are All Right* was made with Moore in mind, and Annette Bening's part was rewritten to suit her style once she had signed on.

★ The film was made for $4 million and was shot in twenty-three days. To date, it has made $34.7 million worldwide.

★ Just before the Sundance Film Festival, Steven Spielberg called Julianne Moore to tell her that he had watched and loved the film. Lisa Cholodenko saw that as a good omen.

★ During the press tour for *The Kids Are All Right*, Lisa Cholodenko admitted she had been asked a variety of insensitive questions, saying, "People are asking me what my leads did to prepare to play gay characters. And I stop and go, 'What did they do? They didn't do anything!' Because that's not what they were playing. They were playing people who are three-dimensional who happen to be gay. I really appreciated that we didn't have those kinds of conversations on set."

We Need to Talk About Kevin

Independent, 2011, UK/USA | Color, 112 minutes, Drama/Thriller

A mother deals with the aftermath of her son's violent crime.

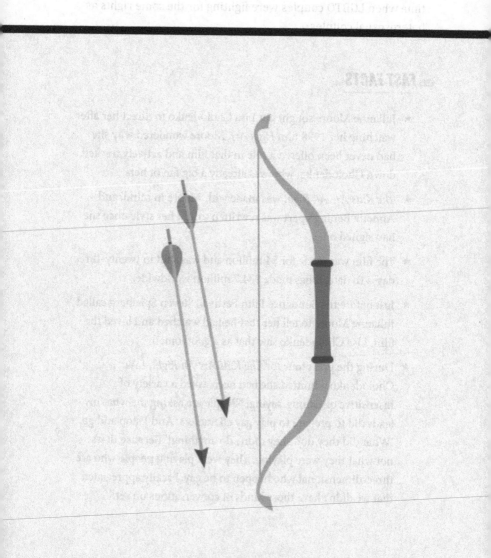

Director: Lynne Ramsay

Producers: Jennifer Fox, Luc Roeg, Robert Salerno

Cinematography: Seamus McGarvey

Screenplay: Lynne Ramsay, Rory Stewart Kinnear, based on the novel by Lionel Shriver

Starring: Tilda Swinton ("Eva"), John C. Reilly ("Franklin"), Ezra Miller ("Kevin"), Jasper Newell ("Kevin" in elementary school)

"You've got to stick up for what you believe in. If you don't do that, you're doing a disservice to the audience, because you're making something really diluted. And if you do that when you're a guy, you're seen as artistic—'difficulty' is seen as a sign of genius. But it's not the same for women. It's a tough industry, and if you're a woman, it's harder, whether you like it or not."

—Lynne Ramsay

The question at the center of *We Need to Talk About Kevin* is a difficult one to answer: is it nature or nurture which led the title character to commit a horrific crime? Viewers will likely change their minds several times throughout the film's almost two-hour run time as they watch Kevin's mother struggle with the question herself. This fear of making mistakes and ruining your child is one many parents feel. But what does it mean to be scared of your own creation?

The mother here is Eva Khatchadourian (Tilda Swinton), a former travel writer who reluctantly moves from New York to a quiet suburban neighborhood at the insistence of her husband Franklin (John C. Reilly). Franklin wants more room for their young son Kevin (played by Rock Duer, Jasper Newell, and Ezra Miller respectively) to grow, oblivious to the struggle his wife is already experiencing. As a baby, Kevin does not stop crying. Eva tries everything, eventually wheeling his stroller to where a set of jackhammers are being operated just to get a moment of some other noise. She is resentful of this new strain on her life. In one scene, while changing his diaper, Eva smiles fakely while telling Kevin in a sing-song voice, "Mommy was happy before Kevin came along. Now she wakes up every morning and wishes she was in France!" He can't understand her, but perhaps on some level he does.

Years later in their sleek new house, Eva pastes travel mementos to the wall of her office. Kevin, aged six, tells her it looks stupid, and promptly destroys her wall art with paint. He also refuses to be toilet-trained and purposely soils his diaper so that Eva has to change him. It's a battle of wills, and Kevin is playing the long game, seemingly determined to break his mother's spirit. But when Franklin comes home, Kevin smiles and greets his father joyfully, playing the perfect son. The birth of their daughter Celia (Ashley Gerasimovich) does nothing to curb his increasingly cruel behavior, and as Kevin grows into a teenager, Eva becomes more and more wary of him.

This all culminates in an incident reminiscent of the 1999 Columbine school shootings and countless others since. In the aftermath, Eva stays on in the same town, enduring abuse from the locals. Her house is splattered in red paint, she gets slapped across the face by another parent, and a male coworker sneers that "nobody would want her now." Yet she goes to visit Kevin in prison every week and sits silently opposite the son who has ruined her life.

There is a video online of Sue Klebold, the mother of one of the Columbine school shooters. In 1999, her son and his friend killed thirteen people and wounded twenty-four before taking their own lives. The video is a recording of her speech at a TED conference in which she speaks frankly about coming to terms with her son's violent end. She acknowledges the years of obsessive thinking over whether she could have stopped the mass shooting. Her own grief is couched in apologies and guilt for feeling terribly sad about losing her own son when he took so many others with him. It's a situation mirrored in the character of Eva, who doesn't move away from either Kevin's prison, or the prison he has created for her from the town. Eva accepts the abuse in the belief that she deserves it and mines her memories looking for the point when she might have been able to stop him.

"She's the real McCoy. Lynne is making films in her head all the time. She is one of those rare directors who creates the kind of films that just would not be there if she didn't make them."

Tilda Swinton

The true genius of director Lynne Ramsay is the way she is able to take the audience inside Eva's mind as she tries to find closure. The story is told in a nonlinear fashion, using flashbacks and the repetition of sounds and images. Slowly the pieces of the story are woven together, taking viewers to a conclusion we know is coming but fear all the same.

Eva's clouded memories reveal both a reluctant mother unable to cope with her son's bad behavior and that Kevin is a sociopath with an inherently cruel streak beyond any trauma his privileged life could have inflicted on him. He is intelligent, cunning, and actively hates everyone. In prison, Eva comments that he doesn't look happy. "Have I ever?" he sneers.

These flashbacks also show Eva's hapless husband Franklin, who has deceived himself into believing his family is normal. This idea of "performing" is one that Lynne Ramsay uses throughout the film. Eva performs her role as a smiling mother, just as Kevin plays the good son for his father. "I actually wanted to call the film *Performance*," said Ramsay in an interview. "That's what it's essentially about—façade and performance. The dad is looking away, the mum is not quite there, and the son is playing them against each other. It's the essential family drama taken to terrible extremes."

This is the kind of film that gets under your skin and stays awhile. It's like a beautiful nightmare, one created through the rich cinematography of Seamus McGarvey, a haunting score by Jonny Greenwood, and Ramsay's evocative sound design. There are several recurring motifs, such as the sound of a water sprinkler—a seemingly benign suburban noise which becomes a symbol of horror. Music is twisted in meaning too, with the upbeat '50s pop song "Everyday" by Buddy Holly transformed during a Halloween scene into something surreal and spooky. Even the clothes the teenaged Kevin wears are more than what they seem. His tight T-shirt features a happy print of a smiling hot dog and mustard bottle giving each other a high five—he is the child who refuses to grow up.

Another strong recurring motif is the use of the color red. The film begins with Eva being bathed in what appears to be blood, but is actually tomatoes at a famous international festival. Later, in the aftermath of the incident, the red of the ambulance's lights flash across Eva's face. At the grocery store, she hides from a victim's mother and is flanked by a red wall of tomato soup. And after she wakes up from a nap, her skin is covered in red—a reflection from the paint splattered maliciously over her windows. Later, when she scrapes the dry paint off, it flakes all over her face and hands, and like Lady Macbeth, no amount of scrubbing can make Eva feel clean.

Kevin and Eva start to resemble one another as we watch him grow up; both are slim, with dark hair and steely gazes. These two are clearly connected—they are each full of resentment and haughty pride. After his mother rants about overweight people eating bad food, Kevin remarks, "You know, you can be kind of harsh sometimes." Eva looks at him and retorts, "You're one to talk." There is little doubt who Kevin belongs to.

These moments reveal how perfectly cast the roles are. Tilda Swinton moves easily between the different stages of Eva's life: the carefree travel writer, the exasperated mother, the fearful mother, and finally, the beaten down woman, stripped of everything she once cared about. The three young actors who play Kevin are wonderful too; they each display an unusual intelligence and a talent for unsettling stares. And John C. Reilly, known for his more comedic roles, is believable as the fun-loving father who cares for his son so much he refuses see what a monster he is.

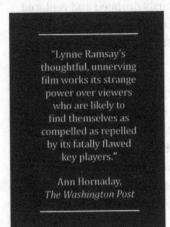

"Lynne Ramsay's thoughtful, unnerving film works its strange power over viewers who are likely to find themselves as compelled as repelled by its fatally flawed key players."

Ann Hornaday,
The Washington Post

Each of these actors were chosen by Ramsay herself, who has a talent for creating films full of atmosphere. Her remarkable craft brings together images and sound in an unforgettable, visceral way. Born in 1969 in Glasgow, Scotland, Ramsay started out by focusing on images—as a photographer. She studied photography at Napier College in Edinburgh before moving into cinematography, going on to attend the National Film and Television School. Ramsay's graduation film was a short called *Small Deaths*, showing three moments in a girl's life. It played at the 1996 Cannes Film Festival, where it won Ramsay the Jury Prize for Best Short Film. Just two years later, she won that same award for her third short, *Gasman*, about a young girl who watches her family during a Christmas party.

Then in 1999, Lynne Ramsay made her feature film debut with *Ratcatcher*. Set in Glasgow during a strike by trash collectors in the 1970s, the plot follows a twelve-year-old boy struggling with guilt over his friend's accidental death. Both this movie and her next feature, *Morvern Callar*, deal with the idea of death and grief, beautifully told through poetic imagery and a layered sound design. *Morvern Callar* was her first adaptation; it was based on a 1995 novel by Alan Warner about a young girl dealing with the aftermath of her boyfriend's suicide.

After those two impressive feature films, she was signed to adapt another novel—Alice Sebold's *The Lovely Bones*. Ramsay had acquired the rights to the book as it was still being written, and she wrote her version of the screenplay before it was released in 2002. But after *The Lovely Bones* became a bestseller, the production company decided to hire a "bigger" name to direct the adaptation. Ramsay was unceremoniously dropped and replaced by Peter Jackson of *Lord of the Rings* fame. Jackson wrote his own script with Fran Walsh and Philippa Boyens, and his version was released in 2009.

"She's a punk rock lady, but also a fastidious perfectionist who's exciting to work with because she's engaged with every aspect of the shoot to an almost hyperactive degree."

Ezra Miller

Lynne Ramsay was gutted, but in 2006, she agreed to adapt another bestseller: *We Need to Talk About Kevin* by Lionel Shriver. The film took her five years to make due to budget and production issues, but was very well received by critics.

Following that success, Lynne Ramsay was given a script for a Western called *Jane Got a Gun*. She became determined to direct it and described the movie as "super dark, gritty, right up my alley." Ramsay managed to secure financing for its production and cast A-list actors Natalie Portman and Jude Law in the lead roles. She even learned how to ride horses in preparation for filming. But on day one of shooting *Jane Got a Gun*, Lynne Ramsay walked away from the movie.

This seemingly sudden move was widely reported in the press, with producers quoted recounting their shock and anger. But to Lynne Ramsay, it had been a long time coming. Months before, she had started to realize her producers were not on the same page as she was. Their demands made her feel that her work was about to be compromised. As she said later, "It was really at the eleventh hour I realized, 'You know what? The guys who are financing this film want a totally different film from this script—a happy ending. No one had any money. The props guy didn't even have a budget—he kept having to use his own credit card.... The bottom line is, it's not a light decision for me to do that, and it wasn't quite how it was reported either."

The producers took her to court, and Ramsay countersued. In the end, the legal battle was dropped, and the film went ahead under director Gavin O'Connor. Lynne Ramsay was devastated and retreated to Santorini in Greece to recuperate. "At first, I was gutted, you know?" she says, "But I pulled myself together.... I guess I'm a bit of a fighter—I'm from Glasgow. It all fueled a kind of spirit, like, 'I will prevail. I'll just put all that energy that I had for the last film into a new one.'"

Ramsay stayed on in Greece and wrote a new script, again based on a book. This time it was a thriller by Jonathan Ames called *You Were Never Really Here*. The story followed an anti-hero—a hitman who ends up saving a young girl from sex slavery. Ramsay returned from Santorini with both a script and a daughter, having fallen in love while there. She soon got financing and secured Joaquin Phoenix for the lead role, and started the filming for *You Were Never Really Here* while looking after her young baby.

In 2017, Lynne Ramsay returned to the Cannes Film Festival for the sixth time to premiere *You Were Never Really Here*. In 2018, the film was released worldwide to rave reviews.

✸ THE FEMALE GAZE

With *We Need to Talk About Kevin*, Lynne Ramsay taps into a primal fear for women about motherhood—that our own child might turn into a monster, and it might be our fault. By using dreamlike imagery and disconnected sound design, Ramsay puts us directly into the mind and memories of a mother having a breakdown. The character of Eva is trying to figure out where she could have stopped her son from committing a crime, and Ramsay does not absolve Eva from any damage she may have caused. We recognize Eva's culpability while at the same time empathizing with her, quite a feat for any movie featuring a mother character resentful of having a child.

≡ FAST FACTS

★ After a long wait to get to the big screen, *We Need to Talk About Kevin* was filmed in just thirty days on a budget of $7 million.

★ This was Lynne Ramsay's first film made in the United States; she made all of her previous movies in the UK.

★ Tilda Swinton signed on early to be one of the executive producers and described the film in an interview as a Greek tragedy: "The play Euripides didn't have the balls to write."

★ Jonny Greenwood was the composer; this was his fourth time working on a film score. He is best known as the lead guitarist and keyboardist for the acclaimed rock band Radiohead.

★ *We Need to Talk About Kevin* was not nominated for any Academy Awards, but it did receive several BAFTA nominations, plus a Best Actress in a Drama nomination for Tilda Swinton at the 2012 Golden Globe Awards. Swinton lost to Meryl Streep in *The Iron Lady*.

★ The author of the book, Lionel Shriver, admitted she picked the name Kevin Khatchadourian "out of the phonebook on an ordinary afternoon."

Wadjda

Razor Film, 2012, Saudi Arabia | Color, 97 minutes, Drama

Wadjda is a ten-year old girl determined to get a bicycle, despite being told she cannot.

Director: Haifaa Al Mansour

Producers: Roman Paul, Gerhard Meixner

Cinematography: Lutz Reitemeier

Screenplay: Haifaa Al Mansour

Starring: Waad Mohammed ("Wadjda"), Reem Abdullah ("Mother"), Abdullrahman Al Gohani ("Abdullah"), Sultan Al Assaf ("Father"), Ahd ("Ms. Hussa")

"I'm so proud to have shot the first full-length feature ever filmed entirely inside the Kingdom. I come from a small town in Saudi Arabia where there are many girls like Wadjda who have big dreams, strong characters, and so much potential. These girls can, and will, reshape and redefine our nation."

—Haifaa Al Mansour

"This charming and deceptively simple film about a rebellious young Saudi girl with a dream that defies the culture in which she lives is a breath of fresh air; the insight into lifestyle and culture [is] fascinating. The debut feature of Saudi's first woman filmmaker Haifaa Al Mansour, *Wadjda* is an exploration of freedom in a country in which there is little."

Louise Keller, *Urban Cinefile*

Simply by virtue of existing, *Wadjda* is a groundbreaking film. It was the first feature shot entirely inside Saudi Arabia, a country with a tiny film industry where going to the cinema was banned from 1983 until 2018. But when you throw in the facts that *Wadjda* was the first film by a female filmmaker in a country where women have little power and that it features a feminist storyline...then it becomes clear how remarkable it is that this film ever got made.

Wadjda is a radical movie with a deceptively simple storyline. The plot follows a ten-year-old girl, the title character Wadjda (Waad Mohammed), who is trying to save enough money to buy a bicycle. She wants to race her friend Abdullah (Abdullrahman Al Gohani), a young boy allowed to own and ride a bike of his own. But the rules are different for Wadjda, who is told by her mother (Reem Abdullah) that bike riding is not a virtuous quality for a young girl. "If you ride a bike, you can't have children," Wadjda is sternly told.

On the cusp of adolescence, Wadjda is only beginning to learn about the expectations placed upon her as a Saudi woman living in a patriarchal culture. She pushes back wherever she can, for instance, by wearing sneakers instead of plain black shoes and by playing outside, something that repeatedly gets her into trouble because men might see and hear her. Her teacher Ms. Hussa (Ahd) scolds Wadjda, saying, "A woman's voice is her nakedness."

When Wadjda learns of a competition at school with a cash prize for whoever can recite the Koran and answer trivia questions, she decides to become a devout student. Her teachers believe she has turned a corner and accepted her fate as a well-behaved young woman. But secretly, Wadjda only wants to win so she can buy that bicycle.

Her mother also struggles with transportation, since by law, she needs a male chauffeur to drive her around town. Up until 2018, women in Saudi Arabia were forbidden from driving themselves, a rule which severely restricted their independence. Here, Wadjda's mother also has the added stress of her husband's (Sultan Al Assaf) search for a second wife. Polygamy is allowed within Saudi Arabia and is sometimes encouraged in the case of a wife not bearing a son. Since the mother in *Wadjda* has only a daughter, she faces the real fear of her husband leaving her for a new wife.

There are many quietly powerful scenes in this film. In one, we see Wadjda inside her apartment, looking at a picture of a tree pinned to the wall, with names written on the branches. "Interested in your father's glorious family tree?" asks her mother, adding, "You aren't included, it only includes men's names." After her mother leaves, Wadjda writes her name on a piece of paper and defiantly pins it under her father's name.

This is a great example of the complex issues hidden within the storyline. *Wadjda* is not an overt criticism of Saudi culture; it simply shows the restrictions women there are placed under and the subtle ways by which they attempt to subvert those restrictions. By doing this, director Haifaa Al Mansour allows the audience to draw their own conclusions, without the director having turned any of the characters into caricatures. "It was important for me that the male characters in the film were not portrayed just as simple stereotypes or villains," Al Mansour explained in an interview; "Both the men and the women in the film are in the same boat, both pressured by the system to act and behave in certain ways and then forced to deal with the system's consequences for whatever action they take."

Though the very real fear of being ostracized is present throughout the film, *Wadjda* is filled with joy. This has a lot to do with the charming personality of its main character—Wadjda is brave, with a ready smile and a curious mind. To the audience, her bicycle becomes an important symbol of freedom. But to Wadjda, it is only about wanting to beat her friend in a race, and she doesn't understand what the big deal is.

Understandably, director Haifaa Al Mansour faced many obstacles in getting this film made. One stumbling block was the casting. As a conservative country with no local film industry, it was difficult to find a girl in Saudi Arabia with both the natural ability to act and a willingness to appear on camera. It was at during a casting session in Riyadh that Al Mansour met young Waad Mohammed. She knew right away that Mohammed was something special. "All the girls that we had seen before her did not have the spirit that was needed;" said Al Mansour. "They were either too sweet or not cheeky enough. And suddenly Waad appeared, with her headphones on her head, wearing jeans and with tattoos on her hands. I was also looking for a girl that has a nice voice to be able to sing with her mother, memorize and chant the Koran, and Waad has a very beautiful and sweet voice." As part of her audition, Waad Mohammed sang a song by Justin Bieber.

The next challenge was the filming itself. As it is forbidden for a woman to work directly with men, Haifaa Al Mansour often had to direct from inside a production van, speaking commands through a walkie-talkie. Often, she would get frustrated and come out to talk in person. But despite filming in several conservative areas, Al Mansour said she didn't receive many complaints. "I knew a woman making a film in Saudi would get attention as a political event," she said in an interview; "But it was most important to me to make a good film. I wasn't trying to clash with people; I was trying to make a film. And I know people, if they see me, they will get offended, or people will come question and try to stop us. I don't want to provoke people. I'm making a film in Saudi Arabia—I'm a woman—about a young girl who wants a bicycle. That's enough. I don't have to push it."

Haifaa Al Mansour wasn't trying to make a bold statement because she knew simply making a film at all was statement enough. Her real intention was to inspire Saudi women to challenge the complex social and political views around them. As she put it, "Although it is hard to deconstruct the deeply rooted traditions that deny women a dignified existence, especially since they are mixed with narrow interpretations of religion, it is a purpose that is worth striving for." And even within the five years since the film's release, things have changed. As of June 2018, women are now allowed to obtain driver's licenses and drive alone, without a male guardian present.

It is obvious that *Wadjda* was made by a woman who genuinely loves her home country. Haifaa Al Mansour was born in a small town near Riyadh, Saudi Arabia, the eighth of twelve children. Her father was a poet who regularly brought home books and movies to share with his family. There was no cinema to visit, but Al Mansour's love of film was stoked during these family movie nights.

Still, Haifaa Al Mansour had no intention of being the first female filmmaker in her country. She decided to study literature at an American university in Cairo, Egypt. When she moved back to Saudi Arabia after graduation, she got a job as an English teacher for an oil company. But she quickly became frustrated by the treatment of women as "invisible," and so decided to follow her heart and study filmmaking. She moved to Australia, where she got a master's degree in Directing and Film Studies at the University of Sydney.

It was during this time that she watched a variety of movies, which changed her perspective on the way the form could be used. "I grew up with mainstream cinema," Haifaa Al Mansour says, "and I didn't start really looking at film as an art form until grad school, where I was exposed to so many amazing films and approaches to the craft. I had always been impressed by Iranian filmmakers,

> "*Wadjda* doesn't leave the audience feeling hopeless. Indeed, Al Mansour suggests quite forthrightly that her home country might be in the throes of some kind of glacial progress—thanks not only to new generations of Wadjdas, but Abdullahs as well. The most radical and cheering message of *Wadjda* is that a change isn't just possible, but inevitable."
>
> Ann Hornaday, *The Washington Post*

especially in the way that they work around the censorship and cultural taboos of their environment."

Her first foray into directing consisted of three short films, *Who?*, *Bereavement of the Fledgling*, and *The Only Way Out*. The first, *Who?*, followed a serial killer disguised as a woman in a burka. Haifaa Al Mansour said she wanted to make a statement about identity and how it is stolen from women who are told to cover up. In 2005, Al Mansour made her first feature film, a documentary called *Women Without Shadows* exploring various taboos facing women in Saudi Arabia. This was met with acclaim for her bravery and much criticism for discussing sensitive issues.

But the backlash didn't discourage Haifaa Al Mansour, whose next movie was *Wadjda*, which put her firmly on the international stage. The film was nominated for a BAFTA award for Best Film Not in the English Language and was screened in theaters around the world. By 2016, Haifaa Al Mansour had been invited to join the Academy of Motion Picture Arts and Sciences as one of only a few representatives from the Middle East. A year later, her first film in the English language was released, a biopic of the author of *Frankenstein* called *Mary Shelley*. She currently has two more feature films lined up—one to be shot in the USA and one back on her home soil.

Not only have Haifaa Al Mansour's films broken through the wall of silence which surrounds women in Saudi Arabia, but they allow her to proudly represent her homeland to the world. "Nobody knows what it is like to be in Saudi," she says, "and for me it is important to create that ownership—even for people in Saudi, when they see the neighborhoods. One day we did a cultural screening of *Wadjda* in Saudi, and we invited a lot of Saudis and young kids. And one of them came to me, and he was really emotional and told me, 'I understand, I feel how Americans feel now when they see an American movie.' And it was amazing. It made me almost like, 'Ah, I'm gonna cry.' "

▶ THE FEMALE GAZE

Wadjda is a quietly feminist movie that shows a young girl who successfully maneuvers around the societal expectations placed on her. The bicycle is a symbol of freedom in a country that has so many restrictions on women's behavior. But Haifaa Al Mansour doesn't make any bold condemnations of these rules. Instead, she simply presents the daily struggles of women in Saudi Arabia. The men aren't vilified, and the women aren't all innocent. This lack of stereotyping allows audiences to connect with the characters and come to their own thoughtful conclusions.

≡ FAST FACTS

* ★ Haifaa Al Mansour didn't follow a typical path to becoming a director. She grew up in a small town with eleven siblings at a particularly conservative time in Saudi Arabia. "A lot of the religion and culture was about excluding women from public life," she has said.

* ★ Al Mansour based the character of Wadjda on her niece, who she describes as "a hustler" with a great sense of humor. Her niece has since been pressured to change her ways and become more conservative, which Al Mansour says is a "great loss of potential."

* ★ It was difficult to find financial backing for *Wadjda*, but eventually Haifaa Al Mansour convinced Rotana Studios, owned by Saudi Prince Al-Waleed bin Talal, to fund it. Bin Talal has long been an advocate for empowering women and growing the film industry in Saudi Arabia.

* ★ Since the release of *Wadjda*, the rules have changed; girls are now allowed to ride bicycles. Though they still need to have male supervision, Haifaa Al Mansour says it is important to celebrate these achievements because, "It changes the way people think and changes the mindset."

The Babadook

Screen Australia/Causeway Films, 2014, Australia | Color, 93 minutes

An exhausted single mother has a hard time coping with her young son, who believes in a monster called The Babadook.

Director: Jennifer Kent

Producers: Jan Chapman, Jeff Harrison, Jonathan Page, Michael Tear

Cinematography: Radek Ładczuk

Screenplay: Jennifer Kent

Starring: Noah Wiseman ("Samuel"), Essie Davis ("Amelia"), Hayley McElhinney ("Claire"), Daniel Henshall ("Robbie"), Barbara West ("Mrs. Roach")

"Women do love watching scary films. It's been proven, and they've done all the tests. The demographics are half men, half women. And we know fear. It's not like we can't explore the subject."

—*Jennifer Kent*

It's difficult to say why this is true, but in the last decade, Australia has become a reliable producer of very scary horror films. And one of the most frightening, for reasons beyond the jump scares, is *The Babadook* by Jennifer Kent. This film is a beautifully designed, handmade nightmare, complete with references to early cinema, a dose of magic, and scares that deal with real issues.

The Babadook is set seven years after a tragic car accident which took place on the way to the hospital where Amelia (Essie Davis) gave birth to Samuel (Noah Wiseman). Amelia is now a single mother dealing with her troubled son without her husband Oskar (Ben Winspear), who died in that accident. The trauma of Oskar's death hangs heavily over their house, with Samuel feeling the need to be his mother's protector and Amelia grieving her lost love. Amelia is a caregiver in a home for the elderly who struggles to manage her son, who makes homemade weapons and has difficulty sleeping, convinced that there are monsters under his bed. Samuel's insistence on sleeping in Amelia's room means she also gets no sleep, and with the added stress of Sam's upcoming seventh birthday—the anniversary of her husband's death— Amelia slowly starts to lose her grip on reality.

This is all compounded by the mysterious arrival of a children's book called *The Babadook*, a creepy pop-up story about a dark monster who knocks on your door and asks to be let inside. Needless to say, if you do, the consequences are terrifying. "If it's in a word, or it's in a look," reads Amelia, "you can't get rid of The Babadook." The book itself also proves hard to get rid of; it turns up on their doorstep after it has been thrown away, this time with new illustrations showing a mother as the monster.

At first glance, *The Babadook* may seem to be a movie filled with horror clichés—there's a monster conjured from a curious object and a shadowy house containing a disturbing child. But director Jennifer Kent aimed to do exactly that. Her film is steeped in cinema history, with references ranging from the work of pioneer French filmmaker George Méliès to 1960's Italian horror master Mario Bava, Stanley Kubrick's *The Shining*, and 1920's German Expressionism, particularly *The Cabinet of Dr. Caligari*. In one scene, a Méliès film from 1900 called *The Magic Book* plays on the television and is watched by the sleep-deprived Samuel and Amelia. And the idea behind *The Babadook* book seems to be inspired by that short film, which shows characters who come to life from a magical book filled with drawings.

The creepy drawings inside *The Babadook* pop-up book were designed by illustrator Alexander Juhasz, with Kent drawing inspiration from the work of Edward Gorey and pioneering shadow-puppet filmmaker Lotte Reiniger. The handmade, analog quality of the book is reflected in the film sets, and when we do see the Babadook monster, it's in stop-motion animation. Everything feels like a twisted version of reality or a dark fairytale. The walls and furniture are in varying shades of gray; their sharp angles and corners are filled with thick shadows. The shadows seem born from the subconscious minds of the characters. As Kent explains, her film was never about, " 'Oh, I wanna scare people.' Not at all. I wanted to talk about the need to face the darkness in ourselves and in our lives. That was the core idea for me, to take a woman who'd really run away from a terrible situation for many years and has to face it. The horror is really just a byproduct."

It's this danger of repressed trauma that ends up being the true horror in *The Babadook*. This is a psychological study of loss and motherhood—it shows both the everyday stresses of a single mother and the brutal force of maternal instincts. All of it is anchored by Essie Davis, an actress who has long been a staple of Australian movies, though usually in supporting roles. Her revelatory lead performance here feels like a master class in acting—going between the extremes of a fragile widow, a demonic woman, and a protective mother. She's also able to convey the guilt of a mother who struggles to love her difficult child, a mother who is fighting with misplaced resentment about that fatal accident. Davis is well matched by young Noah Wiseman, who was just six years old at the time of filming. Jennifer Kent and her crew were careful to protect him from the darker moments of the movie; they brought in an adult stand-in for the scenes where Amelia lets loose at her son. "He drew pictures of himself as Sam," Kent explains, "and pictures of the Babadook, so he was processing it all. We tried to help him understand that the film was really a positive story. It's heading right through the center of hell to get to the light."

"I've never seen a more terrifying film than *The Babadook*. It will scare the hell out of you as it did me."

William Friedkin, director, *The Exorcist*

When Jennifer Kent was Noah Wiseman's age, she enjoyed scary movies. "I was attracted to them more than Disney cartoons," she said in an interview. "I think it was for me a way to integrate the whole of life. Getting scared was a way of developing courage to face the world." Kent was born in Brisbane, Australia, and showed an early love of performing and writing stories. As a child, she would stage her own plays for family, and as a teenager decided she wanted to be an actor.

After high school, Kent studied performing arts at the National Institute of Dramatic Arts (NIDA) in Sydney, whose famous graduates include Cate Blanchett, Judy Davis, and Toni Collette. Essie Davis also attended NIDA, though she was a year ahead of Kent. Davis later described Kent as an "eerily phenomenal actress" and "the best girl at the whole school." Kent graduated from NIDA in 1991 and started acting in TV shows. In 1998 she had a small role in the film *Babe: Pig in the City*.

A few years later, everything changed when she saw *Dancer in the Dark* by Lars von Trier. This came just as Kent was growing disillusioned with acting and had started thinking that she wanted to make her own films instead. In the time it took her to watch *Dancer in the Dark*, Kent decided she wanted to work with Von Trier. "I got his address and wrote him a really heartfelt email about why I wanted to come and learn from him," Kent later explained. "I said I'd rather stick pins in my eyes than go to film school." This tactic worked, with Von Trier hiring Kent as his assistant on *Dogville*, starring fellow Australian Nicole Kidman. This movie, released in 2003, ended up being Kent's film school. "What I think I learned from him was that it's OK to be stubborn. Women are not socialized to be stubborn and to hold on to a vision, yet here I saw someone who had to do that, someone who had a very singular vision and followed it from start to finish. Not without difficulty—there was a lot of difficulty—but he was courageous, so that was a very valuable experience."

In 2005 Jennifer Kent directed her first film, a short called *Monster*. The inspiration for this story came from a friend of Kent's who was having trouble connecting with her son. "He was seeing something he was calling the Monster Man, and the only way she could deal with this really difficult child was to see it as real and talk to it. I had the idea, well, what if it was real?"

That idea was obviously one that Kent found hard to put out of her mind, and in 2009 she took part in the Binger Filmlab in Amsterdam in order to develop it into a feature film script. While writing, Kent watched as many movies as she could, from the silent work of F. W. Murnau and Carl Dreyer to the visceral horror of John Carpenter, Mario Bava, and Dario Argento. To fund her feature directorial debut, Jennifer Kent was given a government grant through Screen Australia, and she also raised $30,000 on the crowdfunding platform Kickstarter.com.

The Babadook was selected to play at the 2014 Sundance Film Festival, where it was quickly bought by IFC Films for distribution in the USA. When it came out in theaters, the film was met with critical acclaim, and to date, it has made its $2 million budget back five times over.

"One of the strongest, most effective horror films of recent years, with awards-quality lead work from Essie Davis, and a brilliantly designed new monster who could well become the breakout spook archetype of the decade."

Kim Newman,
Empire magazine

With this film, Jennifer Kent joins a wave of new Australian directors working in horror, alongside Justin Kurzel (*Snowtown*), Damien Power (*Killing Ground*), Ben Young (*Hounds of Love*), Sean Byrne (*The Loved Ones*), and Cate Shortland (*Berlin Syndrome*). Shortland and Kent are two of the few female filmmakers working in their home country, with a recent study finding that just 16 percent of directors in Australia between 1970 and 2014 have been women.

The success of *The Babadook* opened doors for Jennifer Kent internationally, but she remains determined to work on her own original projects. "I'm going in carefully," she says. "It's a long career that I want to have, and I want to be able to say something with my films." One of the projects she is currently working on is *The Nightingale*, a revenge story set in 1820s Tasmania. As Kent explains, "It's a story of letting go of someone, letting them die. Which doesn't sound like a very cheery subject, but it's a very hopeful film actually...I don't have any desire to be the queen of horror. It's the idea that grabs me."

🎥 THE FEMALE GAZE

Within the horror genre, female characters have regularly been objectified and cast as victims. The "final girl" trope has sometimes allowed women to fight back against the male villains, and on occasion the female is even the villain. But it's rare that the audience of a horror film is allowed into a woman's mind. With *The Babadook*, viewers witness the downward spiral of the character Amelia, who is suffering from both grief at losing her husband and her resulting conflicted feelings toward her son. The idea of a mother resenting her son for simply being born—as if he had somehow taken the place of her husband—is one rarely explored in cinema. Amelia finds it difficult to get along with Samuel, who tests her patience and causes her to lose sleep. But at the same time, she also feels a deep maternal bond and is highly protective of him. *The Babadook* shows the very real and connected struggles of a loss of self, grief at the death of a spouse, and being a single mother.

🎬 FAST FACTS

★ Jennifer Kent wrote five drafts of the script for *The Babadook* before filming began.

★ Cinematographer Radek Ładczuk says the film is split into five different sections, each exploring a particular emotion. It starts with anxiety, then moves to fear, terror, possession, and finally, courage.

★ On the appearance of the Babadook monster, Jennifer Kent wanted it to appear as if it were a creature playing at being human. "There are gloves, but there are no hands. There's a mask. His hair looks like a wig. The top hat. Every part of it is pure disguise."

★ Kent has explained that though it is never made explicit in the film, the intention is to communicate that Amelia wrote the book *The Babadook*. "Amelia used to write children's books, so it makes sense that she used her book-making skills to create the mysterious, haunted object that infiltrates their life," Kent said. "If that's the case, the second book depicting herself as the monster was also made by her, possibly in an insomniac trance."

★ Following the release of the film, demand was high for a real *The Babadook* pop-up book to be created. A crowdfunding project led to the book being released in 2015.

★ There were four copies of the original book made for filming, and only one survived the production. That one now belongs to Jennifer Kent.

Grae Drake on *The Babadook* (2014)

"Knock knock," someone on the other side of the front door of my childhood home would innocently rap.

"Who could that be?" I remember my mom whispering urgently every damn time. "We weren't expecting anyone. Go see who it is. Be quiet. Don't move the curtain. Look through the closed curtain. Be invisible. You know how this works." She would take a beat, barely breathing. "So...who is it?"

You would think with all that intensity we were being hunted down by loan sharks. It was almost always someone looking for the similar-but-wrong address just adjacent to us. While time and emotion have certainly shaped my memory of our abnormal response to a completely normal event, the fear of whatever is on the other side of that door lingers.

This unique but paralyzing fear is one of the many reasons that Jennifer Kent's *The Babadook* resonated with me. The idea of letting something cross your (symbolic or actual) threshold—whatever it is—is terrifying. And that's only one thing in the rich tapestry of this film that leaves the viewer feeling unnerved.

Kent, an Australian filmmaker, is a writer, actress, and director. Her short film version of *The Babadook* was called *Monster* and screened in over fifty film festivals around the world. When she expanded the concept into a feature-length film, I couldn't rip my eyes from it; I experienced that same terror I had felt when I heard a knock on the door, but recognized that what Kent had crafted went much deeper.

Essie Davis plays Amelia, a widow whose husband was killed in a car accident on the way to the hospital as she was giving birth—a painful fact that her imaginative son (Noah Wiseman) feels comfortable sharing with anyone who will listen. Noah's sweet openness makes him the weird kid, and his dear mom is the only one who can really handle his construction of monster slaying machines and constant little kid shenanigans. Sure, he talks an unusual amount about protecting his dear mother from a monster, but she is too exhausted to pay it much mind.

For bedtime, she reads a children's book that mysteriously appears on Noah's shelf. It tells a tale of a funny man dressed in a black trench-coat who tries to play himself off as goofy—but we know better. He calls himself the Babadook, and he just wants to be let in.

With aesthetic nods to German expressionism, using shadow and stark contrast, Kent paints a picture of great conflict and dread. This certainly isn't just a story about a scary monster guy with a fierce manicure popping out of wardrobes. Amelia's challenges as a single mother in the real world are colliding with the pressure cooker of this imaginary world.

Although the complexities of motherhood often prove fertile ground for horror movies (pardon the pun), the aspect of *The Babadook* as a parable involving loss and grief management makes it stand out—and disturb you for far longer than other films in the genre.

It even made me consider opening my front door. That's the twist.

Host, journalist, and media sensationalist Grae Drake is without a doubt one of America's most celebrated personalities in entertainment journalism. With her signature pink hair and devil-may-care attitude, the Senior Editor of Rotten Tomatoes has cemented her place in the hearts and minds of viewers and celebrities alike with her piercing wit matched with her one-of-a-kind expert analysis.

Girlhood
(Bande de Filles)

Hold Up Films/Lilies Films/Arte France Cinéma, 2014, France | Color, 113 minutes, Drama

As a teenage girl tries to find her place in the world, she discovers friendship within a girl gang.

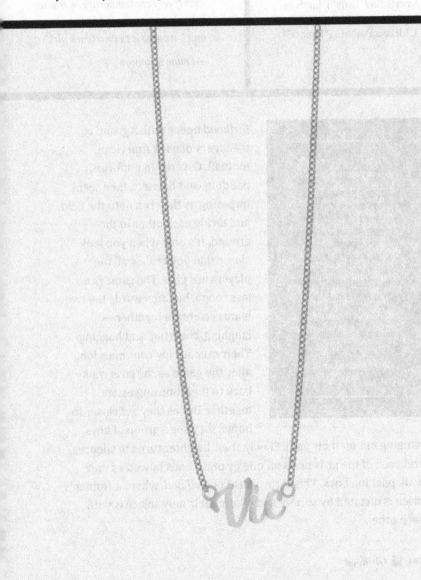

Director: Céline Sciamma

Producers: Rémi Burah, Bénédicte Couvreur, Olivier Père

Cinematography: Crystel Fournier

Screenplay: Céline Sciamma

Starring: Karidja Touré ("Marieme/Vic"), Assa Sylla ("Lady"), Lindsay Karamoh ("Adiatou"), Mariétou Touré ("Fily"), Idrissa Diabaté ("Ismaël")

"I wanted to stick with the rules of the emancipation novel and tell the story of a young girl who wants to live her life and be free, who wants to avoid the destiny set for her. I really wanted to put a stone in that traditional French narrative, but with a very contemporary character never seen onscreen. And I very much wanted it to be a black girl."

—Celine Sciamma

"If there's a teenage girl in your life—of any race, whether sister, cousin, daughter, friend, whomever—you would be wise to show her this film. If there's a black teenage girl in your life? You would be mistaken, you would be borderline negligent, not to show her this film. It's rare that I use the word, but *Girlhood* is an important work of art."

Barry Jenkins, director of *Moonlight*

Girlhood opens with a group of teenagers playing American football. Covered in uniforms, padding, and helmets, they seem imposing as they run onto the field and tackle each other to the ground. It's only when you look closer that you realize all the players are girls. The game is no less rough, but afterwards the two teams celebrate together—laughing, cheering, and hugging. Their raucous joy continues long after the game as the girls walk back to their housing estate together. But as they get closer to home, they see a group of boys hanging out on their path. Slowly, their laughter turns to silence, and each of the girls peels off one by one, heads bowed as they walk past the boys. This is the world of *Girlhood*, where a woman's place is dictated by society and where their only solace is with each other.

At the center of the film is Marieme, played impressively by newcomer Karidja Touré. The story is divided into four chapters, as Marieme tries on different identities in order to survive. In the first section, she's a quiet and reserved school girl—though just beneath the surface lingers a deep anger. Her fury is brought out when she learns her grades aren't good enough to continue on to high school. Instead, her teacher suggests she learn a trade. Stomping out of the classroom, she's called over by a group of girls wearing matching leather jackets. The three teens are Fily (Mariétou Touré), Adiatou (Lindsay Karamoh), and their leader, Lady (Assa Sylla). Lady is intrigued by Marieme's anger and invites her to the mall.

This provides a respite from Marieme's home life, where she is physically abused by her older brother. Her mother spends her days and nights working, so Marieme is left with the responsibility of helping the family and protecting her sister from abuse. She also has a crush on local boy Ismaël (Idrissa Diabaté). And while the feeling is mutual, he is good friends with her brother, which makes the situation impossible.

In the next segment, Marieme has evolved to look just like the other three girls. She's now a leather-jacket wearing member of their girl gang, stealing clothes and bullying students into giving up their lunch money. Lady gives her a new name, "Vic," short for "*victoire*" or "victory." And despite their criminal activity, this group of girls gives Marieme a sense of belonging for the first time. They lift each other up, protect each other, and have a lot of fun in the process.

The most striking scene in *Girlhood* comes when the girls have rented a hotel room in Paris. Trying on their stolen dresses, they dance around the room, lip synching to "Diamonds" by Rihanna. Seeing these four girls singing about shining "bright like a diamond" and dreaming of a better life is a truly joyous moment. This scene was important for director Céline Sciamma, who said it was "definitely the heart of the film. It's the birth of a friendship between them, and it's the birth of the friendship between the audience and them."

Sciamma shot this scene on the understanding that they had paid a fee to the record company for use of the song. It was only during postproduction that she heard she needed to get permission from Rihanna herself. "We sent the scene to her management," Sciamma explained later. "They called and said, 'We saw the scene, we think it's beautiful. We've looked at your previous work, we think it's interesting, so we're going to make an exception for you. Normally, we never give it, or we give it for a tonne of money that you wouldn't imagine.' "

During this segment of the film, we also see the girls participating in violent fights, watched and cheered on by a crowd. It's in stark contrast to a later crowd scene in which several girls dance with each other in a public space, laughing and showing off their moves.

By the third segment, the situation at Marieme's home has become untenable, so now we see her in a blonde wig and a tight red dress, running errands for a local criminal. In between jobs, she wears baggy clothes so as to not attract unwanted attention from the other men.

In the last section, Marieme is seen finally being herself. You can see this in the way she holds herself and in her appearance; now Marieme is wearing her natural hair. And though the ending feels melancholic, there remains the hope that she will be ok.

All of this is told with a tender touch by Céline Sciamma, who manages to show both the violence of gangs and how they can act as substitute families. Marieme and her friends are young women with a lot of potential but without many options available to them. They have to navigate their way through the rules imposed on them by male figures of authority. The only place they can feel free is within their group of friends—yet even here, there is a certain hierarchy at play. The French title of the movie is *Bande de filles*, purposely meant to evoke Jean-Luc Godard's 1964 New Wave film, *Band of Outsiders*. Both films are about a group of outsiders trying to find their way through life. And interestingly, the English title, *Girlhood*, recalls another film released the same year: *Boyhood* by Richard Linklater.

What makes *Girlhood* truly stand out is that it tells the story of a young, black, French woman—the type of character usually relegated to the background of cinema. Because director Céline Sciamma is white, the film caused debate over whether or not she should be allowed to tell this story. In one interview, Sciamma acknowledged the anger, saying that it "speaks to the larger issue of the fact that there are so few black women directors, especially in France. I have the privilege and the power to tell the story the way I want, and they don't.... Obviously, I can't tell the story of what it is to be a black girl, but maybe I can tell something else. *Girlhood* is not about what it's like to be a black girl, it's about what it's like to be a girl."

"Girls are not a monolith, they are not all the same, they are not 'the other,' although you'd never know it considering some of the films out there. It takes an intuitive and devoted filmmaker like Sciamma to go beneath the surface of 'girlhood,' to remove the normal trappings, and to look at all of the different forces and influences in play."

Sheila O'Malley, rogerebert.com

To be able to tell such an emotional story, Sciamma needed a cast who were up to the task. But she particularly wanted to find nonprofessional actors. With the help of her casting agents, the girls were scouted from shopping malls, train stations, and—in Karidja Touré's case—an amusement park. Touré thought it was strange, but took the business card and gave Sciamma a call. That call ended up changing her life. This is an astonishing performance by a nonactor, not only because Touré needed to play different versions of the same character, but because she was in every scene. This role earned Touré a nomination for the Most Promising Actress César Award, equivalent to the French version of an Oscar.

Céline Sciamma was also nominated for a César, for Best Director. This was her third feature film; it continues her theme of how society tries to put teenage girls in boxes. Sciamma was born in 1978 in Pontoise, in the northwest of Paris. Her love of film can be traced to her teenage years, when she would visit her local arthouse cinema three times a week, consuming a wide variety of movies. This led Sciamma to seek out film scripts, reading them alongside biographies of filmmakers.

She studied screenwriting at La Fémis, a film and television school in Paris. Her first job in film was cowriting two short movies with Jean-Baptiste de Laubier, a director and composer who later worked with Sciamma on the score for *Girlhood*. Her breakout film, released in 2007, was called *Water Lillies*. This was Sciamma's first feature film and her directorial debut. The script was based on her thesis screenplay, which looked at the complexities of teenage sexuality, and *Water Lillies* went on to play at the Cannes Film Festival.

Her second feature was *Tomboy* in 2011. This again explored the idea of female sexuality, following the story of a young girl who pretends to be a boy when she moves to a new neighborhood. *Tomboy* was shot in just twenty days with a crew of fifteen people, on a tiny budget.

For *Girlhood*, Sciamma decided to focus on friendship, though again with a sensitivity to the ways in which society pushes an agenda on women. She was particularly interested in how women support each other. "In my first two films," says Sciamma, "the group was important because it was about wanting to belong to a group—that was the characters' goal. But this time I really wanted to talk about the bond between girls and the roles you're often assigned when you're in a group."

Once again Sciamma went to the Cannes Film Festival, where *Girlhood* premiered during the Directors' Fortnight programming. The film went on to be selected for inclusion in the Toronto and London Film Festivals. Now, Céline Sciamma is hard at work on her next film, *Portrait of the Girl on Fire* (*Portrait de la Jeune Fille en Feu*), which will continue her work of telling stories about women and society.

🎥 THE FEMALE GAZE

With *Girlhood*, Céline Sciamma demonstrates the expectations society imposes on teenage girls. Marieme's world is dominated by men, including her own brother, who uses violence to keep her under control. The only way girls can hope to earn respect in their neighborhood is to adopt a similar mentality, which leads to taking part in brutal fistfights with other girls. The winner collects a memento in the form of the loser's bra, which is paraded around and laughed at as a symbol of weak femininity. The film also explores the hierarchies that exist within groups—even though Lady's girl gang likes to think they are living outside the boundaries set by the men in their neighborhoods, each girl has a clearly defined role—with Marieme relegated to the bottom, needing to prove herself in order to gain respect.

≡ FAST FACTS

★ Céline Sciamma sees her three films to date—*Water Lillies*, *Tomboy*, and *Girlhood*—as a "loose trilogy," all based around the theme of teenage girls trying to find their own place in the world.

★ The initial inspiration for *Girlhood* came when Sciamma walked past a group of girls on the street. "They had this strong energy as a group," she said. "I felt I could really connect with them...I thought it was time to put those girls onscreen."

★ The timing of the English title of *Girlhood* with Richard Linklater's *Boyhood* was completely coincidental. Sciamma picked the title a year and a half before either film was released.

★ This was the first film for all four main actors playing the girls: Karidja Touré, Assa Sylla, Lindsay Karamoh, and Mariétou Touré. Despite sharing the same last name, Karidja and Mariétou Touré are not related.

★ Leading actress Karidja Touré says it's rare to see French films featuring all-black casts. "When you look at cinema and the luxury market in France," she says, "you only see white faces—as if that's all there is. It's hard for everyone else, and it's totally inaccurate."

Aline Dolinh on *The Lure* (2015)

The Lure is the best—and likely only—Polish rock opera about cannibalistic mermaids ever made. Set in a fever-dream version of 1980s Poland, director Agnieszka Smoczyńska's debut tells the story of two sisters—Silver (Marta Mazurek) and Gold (Michalina Olszańska)—who leave the sea behind in order to pursue discotheque stardom. Despite its whimsical premise, the film's DNA ultimately owes less to Disney than it does to the most macabre parts of the original Hans Christian Andersen tale. Smoczyńska's mermaids are sharp-toothed sirens hungry for human flesh, and their struggle to adapt to earth-dwelling life inevitably results in tragedy.

The delightfully campy visuals blend a grimy late-Soviet aesthetic with lurid, surreal neon tones, and the wildly ambitious soundtrack by Polish band Ballady i Romanse further blurs genre conventions, incorporating everything from traditional Hollywood dance numbers to synth Euro-disco tunes and even punk rock. One early montage, which shows the sisters discovering the wonders of a human shopping mall, is so discordantly sunny it could be an outtake from the far more sterilized musical *La La Land*.

In this world, the existence of mermaids is not only taken for granted but outright commodified. As they become rising stars in the underground club scene, Silver and Gold are cast in topless, Playboy-esque photo shoots while swathed in fishnets and pearls. The crowd goes wild for the sisters' acts, one of which finds them perched burlesque-style atop a giant martini glass as their gleaming tails writhe in full view. Their unmistakable otherness becomes a source of curiosity and exoticism.

Gold is the more pragmatic and cynical of the two, and she shows few qualms about seducing and devouring humans to satisfy her hunger. She sees their foray into nightclub stardom as a momentary detour from their grander ambitions—which involve ultimately swimming to America. Yet romantic Silver, who

Mazurek plays with the bright yet guileless charm of a young Sissy Spacek, considers trading in her fins for good when she falls for bass player Mietek (Jakub Gierszał). When she decides to literally tear herself in half for love, it's presented as a hyper-stylized, Cronenbergian medical pageant set to a wistful piano ballad.

The film shows Silver and Gold's fraught struggle between humanity and monsterhood as analogous to their own burgeoning sexualities and coming of age, and it makes those comparisons even more palpable through these gory sequences of consumption and transformation. The sisters are frequently depicted as coquettish fetish objects, giggling and stroking their tails for a sleazy nightclub owner (Zygmunt Malanowicz)—the kind of girls you would expect to see as the first victims in any other grindhouse feature. But they just as easily become aggressors, tearing screaming motorists limb from limb and gorging themselves on their victims' organs. Though its pacing becomes faintly sluggish throughout the middle stretch, *The Lure* works because Smoczyńska uses the language of kitsch and B-movie horror to spell out the genuine material anxieties that young women have about their bodies and the sovereignty (or lack thereof) they possess over them.

Aline Dolinh is a writer and undergraduate student at the University of Virginia. In the past, she's served as a poetry reader for The Adroit Journal, *and her pop culture writing can be found online at* Film School Rejects *and* Vinyl Me, Please.

Mustang

CG Cinéma, 2015, Turkey | Color, 94 minutes, Drama

Five orphaned sisters are locked inside their house with their grandmother and uncle, who want them to remain "pure" and marry them off.

Director: Deniz Gamze Ergüven

Producer: Charles Gillibert

Cinematography: David Chizallet and Ersin Gök

Screenplay: Deniz Gamze Ergüven, Alice Winocour

Starring: Güneş Şensoy ("Lale"), Ilayda Akdoğan ("Sonay"), Tuğba Sunguroğlu ("Selma"), Elit Işcan ("Ece"), Doğa Doğuşlu ("Nur"), Nihal Koldaş ("Grandmother"), Ayberk Pekcan ("Uncle Erol")

"If I had the body and the voice of an alpha male, it would be easier. It took nine years from leaving film school until Mustang *was screened at Cannes, and those years were demoralizing. It's difficult not to be affected."*

—Deniz Gamze Ergüven

"*Mustang*, Ergüven's feature debut, stays with you. Gorgeously shot and brilliantly acted by a cast of unknowns, it's a movie about the policing of young women's sexuality that pulses with the same raw, untapped feminine power that's so unsettling to those who would seek to contain it."

Julia Felsenthal, *Vogue*

In the opening scenes of *Mustang*, five vivacious sisters living in a small Turkish village decide to walk home from school. Lale (Güneş Şensoy), Sonay (Ilayda Akdoğan), Selma (Tuğba Sunguroğlu), Ece (Elit Işcan) and Nur (Doğa Doğuşlu) want to soak up the sun, so they skip the bus and go to the beach. There, they wade in the sparkling water while still wearing their school uniforms and laugh as they play a game, splashing each other from the shoulders of some local boys. On their way home, the sisters stop by a garden to pick some apples, but are quickly chased away by the owner.

This "forbidden fruit" metaphor turns out to be a harbinger of things to come. The girls arrive home to find their grandmother (Nihal Koldaş) furious. She has been told that the sisters have been "rubbing their private parts against the necks of boys." Fearing that their purity has been ruined, their uncle Erol (Ayberk Pekcan) whisks them off to the doctor for a virginity test. They pass, but their grandmother and uncle decide that the spirited girls must be contained. Bars are placed over their windows, the doors are heavily locked, and access to the outside world is suddenly cut off. The five sisters are forbidden to leave their house. Anything that may "pervert" them is confiscated. They are made to wear traditional dresses, and are taught how to cook, clean, and impress the prospective teen husbands arranged for them.

"*Mustang* beautifully expresses the girls' unbridled energy, a force that refuses to be locked up, controlled, or repressed. It's a moving portrait of sisterhood, a celebration of a fierce femininity, and a damning indictment of patriarchal systems that seek to destroy and control this spirit."

Katie Walsh, *Los Angeles Times*

All of this is seen through the eyes of the youngest sister, Lale. And while the other girls begin to fall into despair, the spunky Lale remains hopeful—constantly planning a way for herself and her sisters to escape this "wife-factory." Director Deniz Gamze Ergüven has said her inspiration was the 1979 Don Siegel film *Escape from Alcatraz*, and as Lale ponders and plans, there are definite similarities to this classic movie. But *Mustang* is also a fairytale of sorts, featuring as it does five beautiful sisters locked within an impenetrable tower—though in this retelling, the hero is a young girl. Ergüven looked to legends and Greek mythology, weaving them together with the grim social reality many women face within the conservative regions of Turkey.

And the actions of the girls' grandmother and uncle in *Mustang* often seem to reflect what is happening more widely in the country. In one scene, the family eats dinner together while a speech by Turkish politician Bülent Arinç blares from a television in the background. This real speech is all about the way women should behave—lowering their heads when men look at them and not laughing loudly in public. Ergüven fears for women in Turkey under the rule of President Recep Tayyip Erdoğan, who has made public statements about women not being equal to men. "He says you have to be a mother and at home, and that's all," explained Ergüven in an interview. "When you see a man, you should blush and look down. It's like something from the Middle Ages. The subtext is that women are only seen as sexual. That's why they must cover every inch of their skin. This is dangerous because it generates more violence against them. Rapes happen everywhere, but in Turkey, women come out onto the streets to protest because such attacks only seem to echo what the government is saying."

> "The way the girls react to the tightening of the vise around them provides a consistent source of surprise and even hope. Each responds differently, from acquiescence to defiance, but their loyalty to each other and the strength of their sisterly bond remains true.... And the fact that Ergüven chose nonprofessional actors to play these five vibrant young women gives the film an added layer of authenticity."
>
> Christy Lemire, rogerebert.com

In a similar way, the elders in *Mustang* fear young female sexuality. The girls' natural power is deemed dangerous, something to be policed and contained. The irony here is that the girls were innocent before they were made to focus on their "purity." It was the elders who defined them as sexual beings, thus turning their childish beach game into an act with sexual connotations. Their grandmother worries about their virginity, yet marries them off to men they don't know, instructing them to have sex with their new husbands right away. And their uncle sees the girls as sex objects—locking them inside to keep them away from lecherous men, while using them in a horrific way for his own benefit.

It is only in their relationship to each other that the five girls have any identity separate from men. Their vibrant spirit remains when they are together. They give each other strength, share private jokes, and cry when they are torn apart.

Mustang is the feature film debut of Deniz Gamze Ergüven, who was born in Ankara, Turkey, in 1978. At six months old, her family relocated to Paris, France, due to her father's career as a diplomat. They spent nine years living in Paris, and that was where Ergüven found a love of cinema, visiting local theaters as much as she could.

After school, Ergüven went to university in Johannesburg, South Africa, to study for a degree in literature and African studies. But as soon as she heard about a particular film school in Paris, she knew she needed to change track. "It was literally an epiphany," she says. "I was studying literature and African history. There was this film school called La Fémis in France that I was told of. It's very competitive to get in. I thought, 'Oh, this is my spot.' It may feel arrogant, but for me, you can be born an actor, and I think you can also be born a director. I felt really very strongly that that was my language."

The entry exams were difficult, but Ergüven made it through and was accepted; she went on to study at La Fémis for four years. While there, she made as many short films as she could and started to develop a feature set during the LA riots. Following film school, Ergüven moved to Los Angeles for three years to conduct research and continue writing her script. But as a Turkish-French woman, she found it impossible to convince financiers to fund this American story.

To keep her spirits up, she applied for any program she found that offered help to first-time directors. Eventually, Ergüven was accepted into Le Cinéfondation, run by the Cannes Film Festival. She was one of only two young women in the program, where she quickly bonded with French screenwriter and director Alice

Winocour. "She also had a script that was completely crazy for a first feature film," says Ergüven. "When we saw each other, we had the exact same problems in our lives. It was as if we were coming out of the same spaceship."

Winocour became an important force in Ergüven's career and encouraged her in pursuit of her dreams. "Every door was closed," Ergüven says. "It's completely out of character, but I gave up. Alice is the one who put me back on the saddle—literally. I had told her about this treatment of *Mustang* that I had written. All the main scenes were already there. She's the one who was the mastermind of some kind of evil master plan to do *Mustang* first. At some point, she put me in a state where I was literally writing twenty hours a day. I wrote the first script in three years and *Mustang* in just a few weeks. I was in a trance."

Mustang turned out to be Deniz Gamze Ergüven's big break. After being selected to play at the Venice and Toronto film festivals, it was nominated for the Best Foreign Language Film at the Academy Awards, representing France—despite being made in Turkey. The movie was wholly embraced by Ergüven's adopted country of France, where it won four César awards in 2016.

Unfortunately, in Turkey, the reaction was not so unanimous. Though the critical response was largely positive, Ergüven started to receive online threats. "I think I heard it all," she said of the experience; "'You are the enemy of the nation.' 'You're trying to make a bad representation of the country.' 'What kind of religion are you from?' 'You're not one of us.' Some anonymous person wrote down every single place I was: 'At this hour, she's going to be at this TV station.' That really freaked me out. This was a week after the terrorist attacks. Already every inch of my skin was tense. I was scanning the crowd around me. I was super jumpy."

Following the film's release in Turkey, Ergüven was interviewed by the Nobel prize-winning author Orhan Pamuk. No stranger to controversy himself, Pamuk asked Ergüven how she was handling the harsh reception to the film. Ergüven told him about the violent threats she'd received and how upset it made her. His response helped. "First of all, he said that lots of people around him had seen it and liked it. Then he said, 'But you will be attacked.' And he explained why. After all, he knows; he's had plenty of violent criticism himself. 'Don't get depressed,' he told me. What he was saying was: Keep going."

And that is exactly what she did. In 2017, Deniz Gamze Ergüven finally got to see her LA riots movie released—called *Kings*, and starring Halle Berry and Daniel Craig.

🎥 THE FEMALE GAZE

The idea of both looking and being seen is threaded throughout *Mustang*. The girls are watched constantly by their relatives and neighbors, while they simultaneously strain to look out past the bars on their windows. The film is shot through the eyes of young Lale, whose spirit is free though her physical body is not. *Mustang* also explores the complicated feelings toward female sexuality in Turkey and in many other places around the world. Though Lale's grandmother believes she is helping her granddaughters by finding them husbands, the girls see marriage as another way in which they are trapped. They are told to give their husbands their virginity on the first night of their marriages and that they won't like it at first but will "soon get used to it." In one scene, the family of the groom knocks on their bedroom door in order to inspect the sheet to see evidence that the girl has lost her virginity. Their uncle views the girls primarily as sexual beings, and there's a sad irony in the way he installs metal bars to protect them from men just like himself.

★ Deniz Gamze Ergüven looked to several movies for inspiration while writing *Mustang*. She liked the family bond seen in 1960's *Rocco and His Brothers* by Luchino Visconti, the tense story of *Escape from Alcatraz*, and the vibrant soccer-loving girls in *Offside* by Jafar Panahi from 2006.

★ Ergüven chose the title *Mustang* as a way to refer to the wild nature of the five sisters.

★ Of the five girls who star in *Mustang*, only one had acted before. Ergüven discovered the others in various ways—she found Tuğba Sun Guroğlu at the baggage claim of the Charles de Gaulle airport. Getting the right mix of five girls proved difficult; Ergüven's casting director had to see thousands of actresses and place them in various roles until they clicked.

★ Due to the sensitive issues explored in *Mustang*, involving sex, marriage, and death, Ergüven talked to the girls' parents before filming began to reassure them that the girls would be comfortable and protected throughout.

★ The girls grew incredibly close on set and still keep in touch.

★ Ergüven filmed *Mustang* while pregnant with her son, saying he was the unofficial "codirector" of the movie.

★ Despite being filmed on location in Turkey, by a Turkish director, with Turkish actresses speaking entirely in the Turkish language, *Mustang* was eligible as a French entry for the Oscars because of its financing, since the majority of its $1.5 million budget came from French financiers. A producer also pushed for the idea of "liberty" in the film as a core French value. The Oscar committee in Turkey did not object as they had already passed on submitting the film, claiming it didn't reflect the country in a positive light.

Danielle Solzman on *The Edge of Seventeen* (2016)

There are not that many films made today that are made in the spirit of all those 1980s high school classics written by John Hughes. What writer/director Kelly Fremon Craig does with her feature debut *The Edge of Seventeen* is deliver a coming-of-age film worthy of being named alongside the films of that era.

What Kelly Fremon Craig gives is an authentic film about what it's like growing up in the digital age. Can you imagine John Hughes making a movie in which a character accidentally messages somebody about wanting to make out with them? It's hard to imagine him writing something like that, but that's exactly what happens in *The Edge of Seventeen* when Hailee Steinfeld's Nadine sends a text by accident to someone she's crushing on.

Steinfeld delivers a standout performance in the leading role of a teenager who is extremely upset when her best friend Krista (Haley Lu Richardson) makes out with Nadine's older brother, Darian (Blake Jenner). With her brother dating her best friend, Nadine acts out in a way that her own mother (Kyra Sedgwick) can't understand. Then Nadine turns to history teacher Mr. Bruner (Woody Harrelson) for sage words of wisdom. With her dad having died in a car accident, her teacher serves as a father figure.

With comparisons between *The Edge of Seventeen* and the following year's *Lady Bird*, one can only look forward to what the future brings us from writer-director Kelly Fremon Craig.

Danielle Solzman is a transgender film critic based in Chicago and writes for Solzy at the Movies among other outlets. You can follow her on Twitter: @DanielleSATM

Lady Bird

Scott Rudin Productions/Entertainment 360/IAC Films, 2017, USA
Color, 93 minutes, Comedy/Drama

In her final year of high school, Christine yearns for experiences outside her hometown and finds it difficult to get along with her mother.

Director: Greta Gerwig

Producers: Scott Rudin, Eli Bush, Evelyn O'Neill

Cinematography: Sam Levy

Screenplay: Greta Gerwig

Starring: Saoirse Ronan ("Christine Lady Bird McPherson"), Laurie Metcalf ("Marion McPherson"), Tracy Letts ("Larry McPherson"), Beanie Feldstein ("Julie Steffans"), Lucas Hedges ("Danny O'Neill), Timothée Chalamet ("Kyle Scheible")

"It wasn't until I actually started writing Lady Bird *that I thought, 'Where's this movie? Why hasn't this one been made?' John Hughes movies I love; they loom so large for me. But that's not what it felt like, did it? That's not what it is inside. I wanted to show what it was inside."*

—*Greta Gerwig*

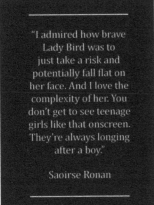

"I admired how brave Lady Bird was to just take a risk and potentially fall flat on her face. And I love the complexity of her. You don't get to see teenage girls like that onscreen. They're always longing after a boy."

Saoirse Ronan

During a high school audition scene in *Lady Bird*, the titular character is asked whether Lady Bird is her given name. Standing on stage, somewhat indignant, she answers yes, because "it was given by myself to myself." And so the name Lady Bird becomes a symbol of this character's search for her own creative identity as well as a rejection of her mother.

Our main character's real name is Christine (Saoirse Ronan), but she insists that everyone call her Lady Bird. It's 2002, and she's in her final year at a Catholic high school in Sacramento, which she dismissively calls the "Midwest of California." Lady Bird dreams of going to college somewhere romantic and culturally exciting like New York. But her mother Marion (Laurie Metcalf) has other ideas. The two bicker constantly over everything, with Lady Bird's patient father Larry (Tracy Letts) often caught in the middle acting as interpreter between mother and daughter.

With Larry about to lose his job, Marion is worried about money. But Lady Bird has other concerns, namely, auditioning for school plays with her best friend Julie (Beanie Feldstein) and harboring crushes on boys. First, there's the sweet theater kid Danny (Lucas Hedges) whose grandmother owns the house Lady Bird wishes she lived in. Later, there's the cool, guitar playing Kyle (Timothée Chalamet), who reads books, recites conspiracy theories, and uses phrases like, "That's hella tight."

> "A finely wrought, deeply felt mash note to Gerwig's hometown of Sacramento, and the rare film about teenage life that puts equal weight on the dark, sad, and tough parts as it does on the joyous, raucous, euphoric moments."
>
> Katie Walsh, *Tribune News Service*

The idea for *Lady Bird* originated in writer/director Greta Gerwig's own experiences growing up in Sacramento. This is not her life story, but the script is infused with the deep authenticity of someone who has lived there. Gerwig knew she wanted to tell a coming-of-age tale about a young woman and worked on the screenplay for years. One day, two lines of dialogue popped into her head. "I wrote at the top of the page—I don't know where it came from—'Why won't you call me Lady Bird? You promised that you would,'" Gerwig said. "And I looked at the sentence and I thought, 'Who is this person?'"

Lady Bird turned out to be a complex teenage girl—the flawed type not often seen onscreen. Coming-of-age stories have long been the domain of young male characters, with films about teenage girls often tiredly centered around getting a boyfriend. Gerwig became determined to create a female equivalent of *The 400 Blows*, *Boyhood*, or any John Hughes movie. "I just don't feel like I've seen very many movies about seventeen-year-old girls where the question is not, 'Will she find the right guy' or 'Will he find her?'" says Gerwig. "The question should be: 'Is she going to occupy her personhood?' Because I think we're very unused to seeing female characters, particularly young female characters, as people."

In many ways, *Lady Bird* is indeed like a John Hughes film or any other standard American teen movie. There's the first sexual experience, the teen rebellion, a big prom, and an airport goodbye. But in the hands of Gerwig, these tropes are given a feminist makeover. (It's worth noting, too, that there is no make-over montage in *Lady Bird*.) The two objects of her affection, Danny and Kyle, are only part of her story. When her relationship with Danny doesn't go where she expected, Lady Bird's self-worth doesn't take a hit. She simply crosses out his name on her wall and replaces it with another. She does lose her virginity, but it's not a big deal. It's unremarkable sex—quick, awkward, and not an experience that changes her at all. "I found when it happened that I really like dry humping more," Lady Bird says to Julie. Instead of being about finding validation through the attention of a man, *Lady Bird* focuses on the richness of female bonds.

In fact, the main relationship in the film is between mother and daughter. It's a credit to Gerwig's strong writing that their dynamic is incredibly nuanced and so particular to a teenage girl and her mother. Marion wants to raise a daughter who has a sense of the hard work it takes to succeed as a woman. And with Lady Bird's natural ambitions and determination to carve out her own place in the world, she's mostly there. It's obvious that they belong to each other, even if they sometimes wish they didn't. They're both headstrong and stubborn and able to turn from laughter to anger in an instant. In one scene, they're shopping for clothes when Marion asks Lady Bird if she is tired, adding, "I just couldn't tell, because you were dragging your feet." Her daughter rolls her eyes, retorting, "Why didn't you just say 'pick up your feet'?" The fight escalates, with Lady Bird accusing her mother of being passive-aggressive. Then suddenly, Marion picks up a dress. "Oh, it's perfect!" Lady Bird says ecstatically. "Do you love it?" Marion asks with a smile.

The other central relationship is between Lady Bird and her best friend Julie. Through their dynamic, Greta Gerwig shows how fulfilling female friendships can be. In one scene, Lady Bird embarks on a big, dramatic run to the one she loves—but here, that person turns out to be her best friend. As Gerwig explained to actress Saoirse Ronan, this was her "boom-box-over-the-head moment," like John Cusack in *Say Anything*. And Ronan could relate to this, saying in an interview that she and her own best friend have had "so many romantic moments together where we just declared for each other. And to see that on the screen...to me, that's the moment where Molly Ringwald goes out to the car, and he's waiting for her."

Gerwig and Ronan became instant friends themselves, and collaborated closely to create the character. Though still only in her twenties, Ronan is already a well-established actress with an impressive filmography and three Oscar nominations. Each of her characters feel lived-in and effortless. That's especially true here as Lady Bird, where the Irish star is a believable American teen—an explosion of emotions careening wildly between extremes. As Gerwig explains, "You feel like you could look straight through Saoirse, like you can see her insides and her brain working. I want an actress to feel like she's in full possession of the character—not like you're lending it to them, but that they own it."

Ronan was nominated for an Academy Award for Best Actress, with Laurie Metcalf nominated for Best Supporting Actress. Metcalf's is a role that might normally have been a caricature of a nagging mother, but in Gerwig's hands, it feels fleshed out and real. The audience understands the reasons why she pokes at her daughter, and she is not devoid of emotion—there's a remarkable scene where the camera stays close on Metcalf's face and does not cut away as she slowly goes from obstinance to despair.

With *Lady Bird*, Greta Gerwig became the fifth woman to be nominated for a Best Director Oscar, eight years after Kathryn Bigelow became the first woman ever to have won. Gerwig was also nominated for Best Original Screenplay and was named Best Director by the National Board of Review. *Lady Bird* was her first solo film as a director, though not by any means her first time behind the lens.

Gerwig was born in Sacramento in 1983 and attended a Catholic high school. But that's where the similarities between herself and her character appear to end. "I was so rule-following and people-pleasing and gold-star-getting. I didn't want to rock the boat," says Gerwig; "I was much more coloring inside the lines. But I think for me, art was always the place where I could go too far."

At first, Gerwig thought she might like to be a ballerina, and she started taking classes as a child. But as she grew up, she literally grew up—and was soon deemed too tall for ballet. So she decided to become a playwright instead; after school, she moved to New York to study English and philosophy at Barnard College. Then her boyfriend at the time introduced Gerwig to filmmaker Joe Swanberg, who told her he was looking for actors for a low-budget film. Gerwig decided to give it a go. "I'd applied to graduate school for playwriting, and I got rejected by every school," she said in an interview with *The Guardian*. "I felt that theater was closed, but when it came to film, the door was very slightly ajar. If I have any virtues, it's that I'm good at walking through doors that are slightly ajar."

That door ended up changing her life. Gerwig began acting in independent movies, joining a group of young creatives. They and their style of filmmaking—handheld cameras, improvised scripts—later became known as "mumblecore." It was less a formal cinematic movement and more a creativity born of necessity. Gerwig played a variety of characters in films such as *Baghead* by Jay and Mark Duplass, Joe Swanberg's *Hannah*

Takes the Stairs, and *Nights and Weekends*, which she codirected with Swanberg.

After gaining notice in indie films, Gerwig was cast in several mainstream studio films, including a remake of *Arthur* opposite Russell Brand and *No Strings Attached* with Natalie Portman. But her most fruitful collaboration came from her role in Noah Baumbach's film *Greenberg*, starring Ben Stiller. While comedy-drama didn't do too well at the box office, it started a friendship between Baumbach and Gerwig, and they ended up writing two films together.

Both became huge indie hits. The first was *Frances Ha* from 2012, which starred Gerwig as an aspiring dancer. And the second was *Mistress America* from 2015, co-starring Lola Kirke, with Gerwig playing an eccentric stepsister. In addition to those, Gerwig had roles in several films with lauded directors: Whit Stillman's *Damsels in Distress*, Todd Solondz's *Wiener-Dog*, Rebecca Miller's *Maggie's Plan*, and *20th Century Women* by Mike Mills.

"Left to her own devices, Gerwig has arrived and solidified her place as one of the most invigorating, observant, and authentic voices in movies today with a director's acumen to match."

Lindsey Bahr,
Associated Press

Throughout it all, Gerwig was writing. She finished her script for *Lady Bird* in 2015, though it took several years to get the financing together. This meant that by the time production started, Gerwig was more than prepared. On set, she was determined to create a welcoming environment. Cell phones were banned to keep everyone in the moment, impromptu dance parties were held, and name tags were worn.

Each day, there was a different question to accompany the name tags, with the answer to be written underneath. In one behind-the-scenes photo, Gerwig can be seen wearing a name tag with "Greta, *Breakfast at Tiffany's*" written on it.

Lady Bird premiered at the 2017 Telluride Film Festival, where it garnered unanimously positive reviews. That trend continued as the film was released later that year; it set a record on the review aggregator Rotten Tomatoes for maintaining a 100 percent score throughout 166 reviews. It was also a hit on the awards circuit as well as with audiences and has earned $78 million worldwide to date.

For now, Greta Gerwig will continue to balance acting, writing, and directing. Her next directorial project will be a new adaptation of Louisa May Alcott's *Little Women*, which sees her reuniting with Saoirse Ronan and Timothée Chalamet, who have signed on to star alongside Emma Stone and multi-Oscar winner Meryl Streep.

🎥 THE FEMALE GAZE

With *Lady Bird*, Greta Gerwig claims a space for female coming-of-age stories, working in the style of John Hughes. What's different about this storyline is that Christine does not need the validation of a boy, and her story is not centered around whether or not she will find a boyfriend. Her main relationships are instead with her mother and her best friend. By twisting the usual tropes of teen comedies, Gerwig celebrates the vibrant inner lives of teenage girls and the bonds between female friends.

☰ FAST FACTS

- ★ Greta Gerwig's first draft of *Lady Bird* was 350 pages long.
- ★ To help her actors get into the mood of their characters, Gerwig asked each of them to make and listen to their own playlist.
- ★ Instead of the silence normally needed while shooting dance scenes, Gerwig played music loud during the prom scene to

get Saoirse Ronan and Beanie Feldstein into the mood. And Gerwig also wore a prom dress that day in solidarity with her actors.

★ To get permission to use their music, Gerwig sent personal letters to Justin Timberlake, Alanis Morrisette, and Dave Matthews. To Morrisette she wrote, "I saw the film *Dogma* because I read that you played God, which seemed totally fitting to me."

★ Lady Bird's audition song was inspired by the late Elaine Stritch, a Broadway star who once performed Stephen Sondheim's "Everybody Says Don't." Ronan liked the way she sounded like "a real dame, a real broad, and I thought 'OK, that's what I'm going to do.'"

★ When asked what she wanted audiences to take away from seeing *Lady Bird*, Gerwig answered, "I want them to call their moms."

Aisha Harris on *Lemon* (2017)

The first time I saw Janicza Bravo's *Lemon*, I was absolutely perplexed. The second time I saw it, I was even more perplexed. Yet both times I was enraptured by how weird, surprising, and unsettling it is: Isaac (Brett Gelman), a thirty-something white guy, becomes unhinged after his blind girlfriend leaves him, threatening and manipulating practically everyone in his path. Michael Cera plays a self-absorbed asshole; the underrated Nia Long is the ingenue. There are moments of disturbing awkwardness, rage, and violence.

When I interviewed Bravo for my podcast *Represent*, she illuminated what she was trying to do, noting that she'd watched many of her peers make "interchangeable" comedies centering thirty-something white guys. "*Lemon* is...having a conversation with this form, this kind of white male who is floundering. And there's just something about those guys in those movies, that everything works out for [them], and everybody's like, 'I don't know, there's something *about* him,' and I'm like, really? Because I'm watching him, and he should *go*."

Now *Lemon* makes sense to me—and I can't help but admire Bravo's sharp visionary take on a well-worn, male-dominated genre. It's not a perfect movie, and some may find it hard to crack. But seeing a woman of color defy expectations of what a film directed by a black woman "should" look like and do it so precisely is a sight to behold.

Aisha Harris covers culture at **The New York Times.** *Prior to that, she covered culture for* **Slate** *and served as the host for the* **Slate** *podcast* **Represent.**

Merritt Mecham on *My Happy Family* (2017)

After a long day, Manana (Ia Shugliashvili) serves herself a slice of cake and sits down at the kitchen table to eat it—but before she can take a bite, her mother scolds her for eating dessert before dinner.

Manana is a grown woman, middle-aged with adult children of her own, yet she cannot escape the demands of her mother, much less her husband and children. While they constantly call her name, she moves through the multigenerational home as if she is invisible. That is, until the day she decides that she's moving out: Manana is leaving her family to live in an apartment across town, alone.

"Happy is the family with a peaceful mother, where she sacrifices herself for her family." These lyrics play in the background while Manana tidies up after her family, providing the titular moment for *My Happy Family*. Written by Georgian filmmaker Nana Ekvtimishvili and directed by Ekvtimishvili and her husband, Simon Groß (more commonly known together as Nana & Simon), the film observes the effects of one woman deciding to break free from her overly dependent family and the demands of patriarchal Georgian culture. The film is patient but energetic, a tender portrait of a woman who feels lonely in crowded rooms and has come to realize the power of making a decision as simple as deciding what and when she'd like to eat.

"Why did you leave?" is the question Manana's friends and family constantly lob at her. Manana refuses to answer, in an effort to be strong in her decision—but maybe she doesn't know. Manana searches through past and future as she attends a class reunion and confronts the fact that she will be soon be a grandmother. "Why did I leave?" gradually conflates with "Who am I?" Perhaps there was never enough space for Manana to figure that out.

The cinematography in scenes with Manana's family is often stifling and claustrophobic, reflecting this need for space. Long shots and teeming frames become overwhelming. The camera follows Manana but struggles to find her, instead getting pulled away as other characters push themselves into the frame or walk in front of Manana and block her from view. The sound design is similarly busy, with lines of dialogue shouted and overlapping while background music and the sounds of the city all drown out Manana's quiet voice.

The one respite in Manana's life is her apartment—a room of her own. And while the film raises more questions than it answers, it's in the scenes in her apartment that the film transcends. For a moment, no one is demanding anything of Manana. Instead, left with space to be herself, she sits in an armchair in front of an open window, listens to classical music and the wind rushing through the trees, and eats a piece of cake.

Merritt Mecham is a writer based in Salt Lake City, UT, and is never happier than when she's watching a film on the big screen.

The Rider

Caviar/Highwayman Films, 2017, USA | Color, 104 minutes, Drama

A rodeo rider has a tragic accident and is told he may never ride again.

Director: Chloé Zhao

Producers: Chloé Zhao, Bert Hamelinck, Mollye Asher, Sacha Ben Harroche

Cinematography: Joshua James Richards

Screenplay: Chloé Zhao

Starring: Brady Jandreau ("Brady Blackburn"), Tim Jandreau ("Wayne Blackburn"), Lilly Jandreau ("Lilly Blackburn"), Lane Scott ("Lane Scott")

"Through Brady's journey, both on and off screen, I hope to explore our culture of masculinity and to offer a more nuanced version of the classic American cowboy. I also want to offer an authentic portrait of the rough, honest, and beautiful American heartland that I deeply love and respect."

—Chloé Zhao

One of the most enduring tropes in American films has to be that of the cowboy. Since almost the beginning of cinema itself, this mythic hero has been appearing onscreen—riding horses, saving frontier towns, and ultimately getting the girl. One hundred years later, it seems impossible that there'd be anything new left to say about the American cowboy. But Chloé Zhao, a filmmaker originally from Beijing, found a way—through realism. Her movie *The Rider* is "docu-fiction," meaning the stars are real people who are essentially playing themselves, though the story they are telling is fictional.

In this story, the central figure—the cowboy—is Brady Blackburn (Brady Jandreau). He is a rising star on the rodeo circuit until a tragic riding accident leaves him horribly injured and in a coma. When he wakes up, he is told he is lucky to be alive. Brady, who now suffers from seizures, cannot ride again without risking his life. He struggles with being sidelined and feeling like he has lost his identity. He tries to continue to work with horses, but constantly fights with his gambling father Tim (Tim Jandreau).

Without his prize money coming in, the family is threatened with losing their home, a move that would disrupt his sister Lilly (Lilly

Jandreau) the most, as she has Asperger's Syndrome. All Brady wants is to be back on a bucking bronco for those eight magical seconds. But his visits to fellow rider Lane (Lane Scott), who was even more grievously injured, show what may happen to him if he continues to ride.

> "I never dreamed of doing anything like this. I never did any drama class or anything like that. But Chloé wasn't scared of horses and cows, so why should I be scared of cameras and lights? I've always been presenting myself in front of people, and at a very young age I kind of gave up on basically worrying about what people thought. I always just tried to be myself the best I could, and as long as I was happy with myself, that was all that really mattered."
>
> Brady Jandreau

The Rider is not Chloé Zhao's first rodeo—either literally or figuratively. Her first feature film was called Songs My Brothers Taught Me and was filmed on the Pine Ridge Indian Reservation in South Dakota. There, Zhao met a group of Oglala Lakota Sioux men—Native Americans who grew up on the Indian reservation but were also bona fide American cowboys. Zhao became fascinated by this seeming contradiction in terms—Indian and cowboy—and cast a few of the men in her movie. A few years later, Zhao returned to the reservation and met Brady Jandreau, a twenty-year-old Lakota cowboy who competes in rodeos and specializes in breaking in wild horses to sell. He invited Zhao to watch him work, and she was transfixed by how this real-life horse whisperer managed to gain the trust of his untamed horses. She wanted to make a movie around him but didn't know what the story might be.

Then, on the first of April in 2016, Brady Jandreau entered a rodeo in North Dakota. He had enjoyed great success up until that point, but on this ride, he was thrown off and the horse crushed his head. Jandreau was rushed to the hospital with internal bleeding in his skull and was in a coma for three days. After waking up, he had a metal plate inserted into his head and was advised by doctors not to ride ever again. But as soon he could walk, Jandreau was back at work breaking in (and riding) wild horses.

When Chloé Zhao visited him, she asked why he continues to risk his life; in his answer, she knew that she had found a story. He explained to her that just a month before his fall, he'd had to shoot one of his horses after its leg was badly cut from barbed wire. "If an animal around here gets hurt like I did," Jandreau said, "they'll get put down. I was only kept alive because I'm human, and that's not enough. I'm useless if I can't do what I was born to do."

Zhao could see the importance of telling a story like Brady's, not only in terms of the devastation of the accident, but in his being told he couldn't do the very thing he felt was the basis of his identity. She wanted to explore the very definition of the "American man," including both the struggles Jandreau and other young men went through in living up to an idealized image of the tough American cowboy and how that cowboy image has evolved to include Native Americans. It's a lot to pack into a film, and after spending time researching her topic, Zhao knew the story would only work if she could convince Jandreau to star in it. Surprisingly, he was game, and she also managed to recruit his family and friends to play versions of themselves.

"Her work burns so bright it burns my eyes."

Ava DuVernay, presenting Chloé Zhao with the Film Independent Bonnie Award

And the brilliance of *The Rider* lies in how Zhao managed to extract natural performances from her cast of untrained actors. While the script was written to include their real experiences, they still had the hard task of guiding the fictional story—recreating some of their own darkest times, and believably selling other events that never happened. This blurred line between narrative and realism is irresistible; it stokes our curiosity about what is real and what is not. It's a quietly beautiful, soulful movie, and the casting lends a deep emotional resonance to the story.

The cast also helped director Chloé Zhao to understand their world, given that she grew up far away from the American West and Indian reservations. Zhao was born in 1983 in Beijing, China, and had no access to Hollywood movies until a decade later, in the 1990s. When western culture came in, she says, "It was like a tsunami because we'd been closed off for so long." Among the movies she devoured were *Pretty Woman*, *Aliens*, *True Lies*, and *Indecent Proposal*.

Later, Zhao moved to London to attend high school and discovered what she had been taught in China wasn't necessarily the truth. "A lot of info I received when I was younger was not true," she explained in one interview, "and I became very rebellious toward my family and my background. I went to England suddenly and relearned my history." This quest for the truth led to studying political science for four years at a college in Massachusetts. To pay the rent, Zhao worked at a bar, and she realized what she actually enjoyed was meeting different people and hearing their stories. After figuring out that film could be the right medium to explore this, she moved to New York to attend NYU's graduate film program.

Three years into her studies, Chloé Zhao read an article in a newspaper about the rates of teen suicide on a Native American reservation. She started traveling out to Pine Ridge to find out more and met and talked to young people there. Zhao was careful to immerse herself completely in this world; she spent three years making visits and writing over thirty drafts of the script to hone the right story. This became *Songs My Brothers Taught Me*, which was filmed with a nonprofessional cast and followed the story of a Lakota Sioux brother and sister living on a reservation. The film premiered at the Sundance Film Festival in 2015 and played at the Cannes Film Festival in the Director's Fortnight section.

Two years later, Zhao was back in Cannes, where *The Rider* had also been selected for the Director's Fortnight. This time around, she won the major prize. The Telluride, Toronto, New York, and Sundance film festivals followed, as did a slew of awards, including nominations for Best Feature and Best Director at the Film Independent Spirit Awards. At that awards show, Chloé Zhao was also honored with the Bonnie Award, established to shine a spotlight on mid-career female filmmakers, to help her continue to make more movies. Zhao says she is inspired by the current conversation around women in film and hopes that it will end up making a difference. "I feel like the industry really wants to support female filmmakers. It feels a lot more open now," says Zhao. "At the same time I'm also very careful, because the people who jump on the bandwagon now will jump off when the next social issue becomes popular. But there's a huge shift. There's some part of it that's going to stick."

🎥 THE FEMALE GAZE

Chloé Zhao has called *The Rider* "my version of a feminine gaze on one of the most masculine images in American culture." Combining the true story of injured cowboy Brady Jandreau with her own fictional script, Zhao has crafted a careful examination of American masculinity and identity. Who is Brady, if he is not the tough cowboy he always thought he was? And does that make him any less of a man? The idea of male bonding and the culture around masculinity is also looked at through the relationships between Brady, his father, and his friends.

★ Finding it difficult to get even the small budget for *The Rider* financed, Chloé Zhao covered the production costs using her own credit cards and those of her cinematographer, Joshua James Richards.

★ Zhao was determined to show Brady Jandreau's sister Lilly in the film and to highlight how her autism is not her sole defining characteristic. "Why can't people just be that way and still be one of the heroes of the film?" explained Zhao. "It doesn't have to be about the issue of their injury or disability. They can still be celebrated."

★ Former bull rider Lane Scott is also featured in the film; Scott is a true friend of Brady Jandreau's, having grown up with him. Scott was paralyzed after a horrific car accident and now is in a wheelchair. Zhao said that working with him was "probably one of the most humbling experiences of my life, because there's just so much spirit in Lane. That kid is not beaten down in any way."

★ Chloé Zhao took cinematic inspiration from Terrence Malick, and decided to film as much as she could using natural lighting at the "magic hour"—the time of day when the sunlight is soft and golden. "We almost never shot before 12 p.m., often shooting between four to eight every day, and it was almost always magic hour."

★ To make sure the cast sounded authentic, Zhao asked them to rewrite their lines of dialogue in the way they would naturally say them. And to elicit the right emotions, Jandreau gave her a list of memory triggers she could use to make him cry on cue.

Carla Renata on *A Wrinkle in Time* (2018)

Anyone who knows me knows that I am a huge child at heart. It's a characteristic handed down from my beautiful, playful mother—a quality that allows me to have an open heart and mind when watching projects meant to tap into one's inner child.

One of my favorite films of all time is *The Wizard of Oz*. I mean, who doesn't love that moment when Dorothy realizes what she had searched for in Oz was inside her all the time? Well, what *The Wizard of Oz* did for me is what *A Wrinkle in Time* will do for this new generation of young people.

Based on the popular novel by Madeline L'Engle, *A Wrinkle in Time* takes us on the journey of Meg (Storm Reid) and her little brother Charles Wallace (Deric McCabe) as they "tesseract" through time to bring back their scientist dad (Chris Pine), who is being held captive by the "it." They are helped by Mrs. Which (Oprah Winfrey), Mrs. Who (Mindy Kaling), and Mrs. Whatsit (Reese Witherspoon), who serve as a more elegant version of the Scarecrow, Tin Man, and Lion as they guide Meg and Charles Wallace through their journey in time.

Gugu M'batha Raw (Mrs. Murry) and Chris Pine (Mr. Murry) are exquisite as the parents of these adventurous young time travelers. For me, this is Chris Pine's finest moment on film to date. A big thumbs-up to Zach Galfianakis (Happy Medium) who brings humor, humanity, and empathy to Meg as she struggles to believe and move forward, as well as to Mindy Kaling, whose character here is a huge departure from her roles in *The Mindy Project* and *The Office*. However, the real stars of *A Wrinkle in Time* are Storm Reid and Deric McCabe. The emotional depths Storm Reid taps into as a first timer on film are stunningly heartfelt; and Deric McCabe is a star...period.

The spot-on direction of Ava DuVernay brings this beautifully crafted story to light. DuVernay tackles and effectively conveys elements like gossip, bullying, and relationships between mother and daughter, daughter and father, brother and sister, and most importantly, expresses how the power of love can overcome hate and prejudice by any means necessary. If you just believe... anything is possible.

The film has some peaks and valleys when it comes to pacing; however, *A Wrinkle in Time* is a beautiful, fantastical message about how being different is what makes one unique. Why walk around trying to be someone else when being you is so much more interesting?

A graduate of Howard University, Carla Renata (a.k.a. "The Curvy Film Critic") is the host/creator of Black Tomatoes at Black Hollywood Live and a proud member of (LAOFCS) Los Angeles Online Film Critics Association, (AAFCA) African American Film Critics Association, and (OAFFC) Online Association of Female Film Critics. Her work has been featured online via Ebony.com, AAFCA.com, and TheCurvyFilmCritic.com.

Acknowledgments

First off, I'd love to send a big thank you to everyone who read my first book, *Backwards and in Heels*! It was a huge undertaking, and I cannot express how happy I felt whenever I saw someone clutching my little pink book. And thank you to all my friends for not disowning me for writing a second book so soon after the first. In particular: Lucy Armstrong, Robin Burke, Chad Byrnes, Jacqueline Coley, Amanda DePover, Amirose Eisenbach, Maude Garrett, Ashlea Mackin-Burke, Sue and Brian Mullis, Nadia Neophytou, Ngoc Nguyen, Hema Patel, and Matthew Perez-Mora. I couldn't have done this (once again) without your encouragement.

Thank you so much to Alexa Foreman, Ríona Judge McCormack, and Jeff Stafford for your expertise, knowledge, and help. Thanks to the team at Mango Publishing for all the support on the first book and being excited for this followup, especially to my kind and patient editor, Hugo Villabona.

And of course, a huge thanks to all the women who contributed essays. I am so grateful and honored to have all of your voices in here: Jamie Broadnax, Monica Castillo, Jacqueline Coley, Roth Cornet, Aline Dolinh, Grae Drake, Marya Gates, Aisha Harris, Jenna Ipcar, Miri Jedeikin, Sumeyye Korkaya, Tomris Laffly, Moira Macdonald, Jessie Maltin, Merritt Mecham, Amy Nicholson, Carla Renata, Piya Sinha-Roy, Farran Smith Nehme, Danielle Solzman, Tiffany Vazquez, Holly Weaver, Clarke Wolfe, April Wolfe, Alana Wulff, and Jen Yamato.

About Alicia Malone

Alicia Malone is a film reporter, author, and self-confessed movie geek. She is a host on Turner Classic Movies, FilmStruck, *The FilmStruck Podcast* and is a film correspondent for Fandango.

Alicia was born in Australia and hosted several movie-centric shows before she moved to the United States in 2011. Since then, she has appeared on CNN, the *Today* show, MSNBC, NPR, and many more as a film expert.

Alicia is passionate about classic films, independent movies, and supporting women in film. In 2015, Alicia gave a TEDx talk about the lack of women working in film and why that needs to change. In 2017, she was invited to give a second TEDx talk, expanding on the subject further. She has spoken about women in film at conferences around America, and in 2016, she was named of one of one hundred #WorthyWomen of the year.

Alicia has traveled the world to cover major film festivals and award shows. She's been on the juries of the Overlook, HollyShorts, and Atlanta Jewish Film Festivals and is a member of the Broadcast Film Critics Association and the Los Angeles Online Critics Association.

Her first book *Backwards and in Heels*, about the history of women in Hollywood, was published in 2017.

Printed in the USA
CPSIA information can be obtained
at www.ICGtesting.com
JSHW031737110923
48263JS00010B/41